Evolving Towards the Internetworked Enterprise

T0189227

Giuseppina Passiante
Editor

Evolving Towards the Internetworked Enterprise

Technological and Organizational Perspectives

Foreword by Ronald Maier

 Springer

Editor
Prof. Giuseppina Passiante
Università del Salento
eBMS S.S. ISUFI
Via per Monteroni
73100 Lecce
Campus Ecotekne
Italy
giuseppina.passiante@ebms.unile.it

ISBN 978-1-4899-8651-1   ISBN 978-1-4419-7279-8 (eBook)
DOI 10.1007/978-1-4419-7279-8
Springer New York Dordrecht Heidelberg London

Springer is part of Springer Science+Business Media (www.springer.com)

Foreword

The hype around Web 2.0 and Web 3.0 has again sparked tremendous interest in connectivity, networks and collaboration which are often praised as solutions to resource disadvantages which single small and medium-sized enterprises (SMEs) otherwise supposedly have. However, still many owners, executives and managers of SMEs are rather reluctant to fully benefit from networking and quickly refer to barriers such as lack of time, low awareness of value and benefit of networking or fear of disclosing or diluting competitive advantages. These and other more individual barriers prevent them from engaging more into opening up towards business partners, networking, knowledge sharing across organizational boundaries, co-creating, co-innovating and jointly deploying complementary competencies together with other companies and organizations. This is particularly true for structured, semantics-based, business rules-, process-oriented as well as information and communication technology (ICT)-supported initiatives towards turning single organizations into networked ones. Although there has been abundant evidence of how to benefit from such approaches within primarily large organizations, information on how to go about deploying these in and all the more between small and medium-sized enterprises in a coordinated manner are scarce. They are simply often viewed as too complex and thus less applicable in this type of environment.

However, as business environments have changed, so have companies and organizations. Many of them need to significantly increase speed of innovation concerning products, services and processes, reduce time-to-proficiency of their employees engaged in business and innovation processes and improve productivity of knowledge work in order to benefit from dynamically changing business opportunities. Knowledge-intensive organizations represent a substantial share of SMEs which are considered the backbone of innovation in the European economy. Knowledge intensity refers to, among other things, a high share of highly skilled and creative employees, operations that aim at providing knowledge-intensive products and services, high importance of experiences and high degree of innovations. In some industry sectors, this results in a high number of patents, central importance of customer knowledge, high need for communication and a high degree of information needs. However, compared to more traditional, predominantly manual, data- or service-oriented work, the unstructured, creative and expertise-driven knowledge work cannot be designed with standardized management approaches and cannot be easily supported by information and communication technologies, e.g., workflows or single application systems. This is all the more true for SMEs with their considerably limited knowledge resources. This increasingly renders networking and collaboration with companies and organizations providing complementary competencies into a necessity.

During the last twenty years, businesses have faced four distinctive phases of organizing knowledge work. In a first phase termed human-oriented, organizations realized the value of their people and bundled a number of instruments aiming at the individual knowledge workers and their productivity. The next phase could be called technology-oriented and was backed by tremendously increased opportunities offered by ICTs, particularly networked artificial intelligence- and semantics-based approaches, more recently also termed Web 3.0. Organizations were eagerly experimenting with new ICTs in attempts to benefit from the promised changes that would come about by implementing ICT-based tools and systems. A third phase was primarily fueled by the emphasis on business processes and knowledge work was designed with the same language as was used in organizational design and ICT support of business activities in general, the language of business processes. After human-oriented, technology-oriented and process-oriented phases, recently a fourth phase that could be circumscribed as collaborative has reached businesses. While many large organizations have been engaged in all four phases subsequently and knowledge workers are busy trying out new alternatives for networking and collaborating within and across organizational units such as subsidiaries, factories, departments, work groups, projects or communities-of-interest, questions arise how these activities can be coordinated or guided so that they are in line with organizational goals. What is already a considerably complex and rarely fully embraced initiative within a single organization becomes even more demanding when one targets networks of organizations.

These are the challenges that this book starts out to address. The book lays out the theoretical framework of the so-called internetworked enterprise. Setting the focus both, on the individual enterprise as well as on the network is as much a competitive edge of this book over related approaches as is the integration of semantics-, process-, model- and IT-based approaches towards organizing such complex networks. Moreover, the book does not shy away from the challenges of deploying such initiatives in real-world organizations and provides in-depth lessons learned from a number of carefully selected cases. The book thus aims to help managers providing organizational and technological infrastructures for connecting people, processes and organizations in order to raise the levels of innovation, productivity and ultimately competitiveness of networked organizations.

Ronald Maier   Innsbruck, 31st of May 2010

Contents

Chapter 1 - Towards an Internetworked Enterprise: some issues to be discussed

Giuseppina Passiante

eBMS S.S. ISUFI – University of Salento

Abstract - Recent studies have outlined the rise of a new organization: the Internetworked Enterprise (IE), placing network structure, a focus on communities of individuals and the rejection of a centralized mindset at the core of the new frame of reference. A flatter hierarchy and team-based work organization characterizes this new enterprise, enabling it to respond more quickly to changes in the business environment and to customer demands. As a result of its capacity to use ICTs, the IE takes advantage of the resources of its partners to generate distinctive value for its end-user customer, for whom the value proposition has to be relevant. The use of digital networks allows IEs to co-operate and compete with other e-business community partners by exchanging knowledge and information across transnational borders. A strategy fitting this complex context needs to be formalized, evaluated and, in order to be effective, rapidly and effectively implemented on an operational level. To this end, a "Business Model" becomes a critical driver of strategic decisions allowing identifying new business opportunities, increasing or creating new value, evaluating the effectiveness of the chosen value model and formalizing requirements for operational decisions [1][2]. Indeed, ICTs play a key role in IE model implementation, but their application requires new managerial and behavioral approaches, capable of integrating strategy, organization and technology both flexibly and holistically. This preliminary chapter, introducing the research themes of the book, aims to explain the relevance of the Business Model conceptualization and to integrate it with the "Enterprise Model", representing the most effective solution to support IE design, implementation and management.

1.1 IE theoretical background

Recent changes in the competitive environment have had a profound effect on the way organizations compete and cooperate today. Whereas vertically integrated firms are reconfiguring their value chain and focusing on added value activities, small firms aggregated into industrial districts are growing globally, creating loosely coupled networks of firms. Alternative coordination mechanisms that transcend the traditional dichotomous market and hierarchy can be arrayed in a continuum-like fashion, with discrete market transactions located at one end and highly centralized firms at the other. In the middle, various intermediate or hybrid forms

G. Passiante (ed.), *Evolving Towards the Internetworked Enterprise: Technological and Organizational Perspectives*, DOI 10.1007/978-1-4419-7279-8_1,
© Springer Science+Business Media, LLC 2010

of organizations can be found, ranging from market poles, simply repeated trading relationships, quasi-firm forms, subcontracting arrangements, franchising, joint ventures and decentralized profit centers. Powell [3] and Castells [46] argue that networks are a distinctive form of economic activity coordination where it makes sense to classify as a business network any organizational structure adopting a coordination mechanism in this grey area.

1.1.1 From vertical corporation to network organization

The circumstances in which the organizational functions are performed within or outside of the firm have been studied since Williamson [4][5], who concluded that the related decision is driven by economic transaction costs since companies tend to choose solutions that most efficiently manage these costs. Generally, a hierarchical organization is preferred when production is characterized by high uncertainty in the outcome, high frequency of repetition and huge difficulties in the transfer of objects within the activities. A market choice is preferred when no repetition is required and the transaction investment is performed only once.

The network form arises as a third governance mechanism when there is the need to create integration among actors and to better manage uncertainty [3]. The term "network of companies" generally refers to a broad set of inter-organizational relations that could assume the form of technical assistance, buyback agreements, patent licensing, franchising, know-how licensing, non-equity cooperative agreements, equity joint ventures, cooperative buyer-supplier relationship and strategic networks [6][7][8][9]. Some scholars and practitioners conceive networks as entities where lateral ties substitute vertical ties, creating horizontal and informal structures. Other scholars define the network by stressing the replacement of command relationships with quasi-market mechanisms. Although quasi-market relationships lie at the core of the network's organization, it is possible to observe that bureaucracy does not disappear and hierarchy remains the dominant mode of organization. A network is able to combine the advantages of bureaucratic organizations with an innovation support structure.
The first example of this way of conceiving firms embedded in networks is the Japanese Keiretsu system: a horizontally integrated group of allied firms operating across many industries [10]. However, different types of emerging phenomena guiding network organizations can be found: flexible specialization [11], dynamic flexibility [12], Toyotism with its stable and complementary relationships among producer and suppliers [13], multiple relationship networks among SMEs and large firms [14], franchising models inspired by the "Benetton Model"[15], strategic alliances developed by large firms in specific competitive industrial sectors[16][17]

These networks become critical mainly in contexts where efficient and reliable information is required as well as know-how exchange, where technology capabilities, production styles and other commodities are not easily specifiable.

Following Powell [3], a network of enterprises is characteristic and recurrent in specific industries such as the construction industry [18], the book industry [19], the film and recording industry [20]; strategic alliances and partnerships are typical of the aerospace industry [21] or technology intensive industries [22][6]; business networks related to the vertical disaggregation of large firms are recurrent in the textile industry [23] and the automotive industry [24].

Powell et al. [25] highlight how network collaborations can distribute relevant knowledge produced outside the firms' boundaries or during a market transaction, and explain the growth of biotechnology firms as dependent on the connected network. In his study on collaboration among firms in the textile industry in South Africa, [47] points out how firms targeted in the survey attributed their improvements in the new product development process to external collaborations [47].

The nodes of a network represent all the entities that contribute to optimizing the inter-organizational value chain; accordingly, the management and communication culture of partners has to be improved. Each actor is linked to the other with an exchange and each is reciprocally influenced [26].

Inter-organizational linkages establish a safety net and encourage long-term investment and risk-taking. Firms with a cooperative mentality can reach a higher level of innovation with respect to firms with a purely competitive perspective [27]. Complex relations are generated by simultaneously competitive and cooperative mechanisms [28].

The dynamics guiding the creation and working of a network, can determine two consequences [28]:

1. *Lock-in/lock-out effects*: the creation of a relationship with a new actor can generate constraints in the relationships with other actors, related mainly to resource constraints (time and goods) and trust expectation, including the exclusion of other partners.
2. *Learning races*: in a network there are sets of dyadic relations generated to compete and to cooperate; an actor may decide to participate in an alliance only to learn the higher quantity of information, planning to suddenly exit thereafter.

Furthermore, Simard and West [29] developed a taxonomy of networks split between wide and deep, and formal and informal.

Generally, wide networks are useful to explore new technologies and markets; instead, deep networks are used to capitalize existing knowledge and resources. Companies have to combine deep and wide networks to profit from their external relations [30].

While formal networks start with a defined agreement, new networks can be determined based on informal features. By looking at these types of networks, it is possible to analyze how different networks exist to support innovation management [29].

All economic actions are embedded in a structure of social relations that need to be evaluated for strategic decisions. Behavior and institutions are very constrained by their social relations and are not independent [31].

Firms are connected by networks of social relations on each level on which a transaction takes place [48]. The relational view theory, focusing on firms working in a network, attributes high relevance to resources and capabilities developed in inter-organizational relationships. Competitive advantage is attained not only from within companies but also from exploiting inter-organizational relationships within the network [24].

The critical resources of an organization cannot be considered only in terms of the organizational boundaries, but in the larger landscape including interfirm resources and routines [24]. Collaborative relationships require knowledge-sharing and openness, with trust being the main issue that managers should nurture, developing the ability to obtain and maintain it among the partners [32]. Social relationships help reduce the uncertainty in transactions and support the creation of trust among actors; trust-based relationships improve cohesion among the actors of a network [33].

Markets and industries are economic networks composed of several types of networks of trade, career, finance, partnership and inter-firm contracts. In Padget and Powell's [49] theory of multiple networks, different networks are interconnected, not only on an economic but also on social and political levels; feedback between networks is essential for the growth and evolution of the existing economic markets and for the development of organizational novelty. Social and political networks trace the path and define the space in which economic networks evolve [50]. A feedback mechanism links the multiple domains of a network and also impacts on the multiple levels of network analysis. The dynamics of switching from one domain to another have a high potential to reorganize and affect the scenario; what happens in one domain impacts on the other. Dynamic multiple networks provide an intellectual framework to analyze the common *emergence of relations, products and actors into a coherent architecture of inter-related dynamic models* [50].

The strengths of networks have recently increased primarily through digital technologies that connect and relate dispersed organizational nodes to each other. These nodes can be simultaneously independent or dependent on the network organization, and can be part of several other networks [46]. The networked enterprise takes advantage of the diffusion of new digital information technologies related to the internet and the increasing number of computers connected to the network [34][35].

1.1.2 From industrial cluster to virtual networks

In the last decades, the business environment has changed with unprecedented speed. Firms structured along tight hierarchies first started to cooperate in firmly-coupled strategic networks with stable inter-organizational ties [51], then moved into more loosely-coupled configurations of legally independent firms in order to create competitive advantage [36]. The networked enterprise emerged to represent a suitable organizational form better able to manage unpredictable environments and conditions of uncertainty [46].

Another phenomenon characterizing this economic landscape is the emerging shift from traditional industrial clusters to virtual cluster, driven by digital innovation. The industrial clusters that are emerging in the Web-based business world highlight a new interrelationship between economic and spatial organizations; a new competitive space where "how you do business" is more relevant than "where you do business".

A traditional industrial cluster is a form of network within a specific geographical location where independent and informally linked firms and institutions act as a robust organizational form in the continuum between markets and hierarchies. It can also be described as a set of independent enterprises that work towards a common goal with the aim of increasing flexibility, spreading risk, sharing investment cost (e.g. brought about by the introduction of new technologies), and leveraging mutual capabilities [2]. According to Porter [52], the power of clusters lies in intra-cluster competition, which forces firms to innovate in order to create competitive advantage. Researchers have emphasized the role of social networks and geographic nearness as a mid-point for interactions and exchanges of localized and mainly tacit knowledge.

The emerging global networked environment, enabled by information and communication technologies (ICTs), is creating a new cognitive space that allows the exchange of mainly explicit knowledge and the creation of new sources of clustering phenomena that influence how firms develop products and services. Evidence of this can easily be found in the aerospace supply chain and in exploring in detail the structure of SMEs and large firm networks [37][38]. SMEs use adequate ICT systems and continuously reinforce their technological infrastructure to respond to external turbulence at the right time and to consequently reduce the time to market.

However, technology alone is not able to guarantee the firm's chances of survival and for this reason SMEs require new network strategies that embrace all the actors, specially those involved in the new product development (NPD) process, positioned at each level of the supply chain and leading to whole system innovation [37].

Today the evermore challenging competitive environment, characterized by increasing risks and uncertainty, forces companies to look to new strategies; accordingly, geographical industrial clusters are evolving towards new industrial agglomerations, grasping the opportunities deriving from digital technologies [39].

A co-evolution process is emerging within clusters, positioned between networks of localized knowledge and trans-local knowledge networks [40], and based on the digital exchange of information.

These inter-organizational structures, defined as Virtual Clusters (VC), are characterized by collaborations and complementarities, and by the exchange of mostly digital knowledge. Firms constitute new VCs with the support of ICTs and with the involvement of suppliers, distributors, service providers and clients. *In a VC, each firm contributes with its value to the value of the network supporting this process with the exchange of digital knowledge* [39]. A VC emerges when the business environment is characterized by unpredictable and discontinuous changes, forcing organizations to adopt adaptive business platforms to face the competitive scenario [39]. The structure of a VC is similar to a *"hub and spoke"* configuration with many nodes interconnected through a web of linkages. As Passiante and Adriani [41] point out *"each node is an "Internetworked Enterprise (IE)" that is internally connected via the Intranet, with suppliers and customers via business-to-business networks and with other organizations, business homes and consumers via the public Internet"* [41]. Each link could be a transaction with suppliers, distributors and clients or a transaction with competitors or other industries.

In an IE, an intellectual endeavor needs to exist in order to truly collaborate and share meaning, processes and commitments. In this context, the innovation process is driven by two different forces impacting on the learning process: market-related and alliance-based.

Collaboration across relationships is the first source of value in an IE. The digital infrastructure of an IE can be modeled in terms of an internet-based platform, middleware applications, as well as IE-specific applications [39]. The relationship space enabled by Internet platforms, based on instantaneous shared communications, supports the knowledge conversion process among individuals [39]. The IE form, representing the configuration of each node of a virtual cluster, suggests eliminating the geographic space of analysis and concentrating more on the investigation of the link space [42].

The continuous technological and organizational integration required by firms involved in the development of complex and innovative products, can only be achieved through the increasing integration of firms with distinctive skills [37] only by supporting and integrating skills available in different firms is it possible to design a network of integrated complementarities. Different networks of relations co-exist [50] and play a different role in supporting specific activities.

Looking at the SME cluster in the aerospace industry, innovative activities can be seen as the result of a central position in the R&D network, facilitating the adoption or diffusion of ICT tools [38]. ICTs are widely used and are considered important tools to support the innovative processes, their diffusion is also stimulated by customers through imitation dynamics, according to the needs of the sector [43]. Indeed, the focus has changed from physical goods and services to those that are non-physical and knowledge-based. A shift has taken place from the scarcity of resources to the abundance of knowledge; it thus becomes possible to have much better value at a much lower price and a reduction of transactions costs. Thanks to internetworking, transaction costs have been reduced, even to the zero point; Coase's Law has strongly affected this perspective, (i.e. *"a firm will tend to expand until the costs of organizing an extra transaction within the firm become equal to the costs of carrying out the same transaction on the open market"*). The redefinition of a new value proposition could perhaps require the disaggregation of the actual firm boundaries and relationships, and the re-aggregation into new shapes and linkages. The new value proposition has to be based on a radical transformation with networked digital technologies facilitating the right new forms of value. A new business model has emerged by using internetworking to cut transaction costs [44].

"Internetworking" means the use of computers and the Internet to connect different actors of the network, providing interesting opportunities for companies working in the global market [54]. Organizations can develop an IE by implementing internetworking technologies and new internal and external practices [55], whereby internetworking technologies are intended as hardware and software architecture based on TCP/IP protocols [53]. Therefore, network technologies allow supporting work between organizations and establishing new organizational forms [54].

In VCs, internetworked contributions come together to create value for customers and wealth for their shareholders. A VC is a system of suppliers, distributors, commerce service providers, infrastructure providers and customers using the Internet for their primary business communications and transactions.

The three structures that constitute the VC universe are: 1. internetworked firms, teams, individuals; 2. VCs themselves; 3. the industry environment, which is the distinct space where several VCs compete. Two key dimensions for the design of a VC are the internet infrastructure and the availability of knowledge among participants. The digital fusion between business entities has to be realized through disaggregation and re-aggregation [44].

Some differences emerge from the use of digital applications instead of physical business world practices. They are related to [44]:

- a change in the competition base;
- new competitive advantages based on business model innovation;
- the increase of alliances in order to reinforce and drive changes.

1.2 IE from theory to practice

Considering both firm and market perspectives, the main organizational problem that firms face today to create added value products and services is no longer related to an alignment between the objectives of different departments but to the coordination of the entire network of knowledge-owner firms.

External relations play an important role in organizations working in complex product development where the skills and expertise of several types of organizations are needed. In a study conducted in the aerospace industry [37], relationships among firms, customers and partners emerge as most important in the creation of new products, followed by the those with suppliers and other actors such as universities and research centers. Accordingly, the role of strategic variables in strategic decision-making is key to defining an appropriate business model in relation to each innovation activity [37].

The "business model" concept has been rather intensively discussed in academic literature since the mid 1990s [45]. Here the "model" concept is considered as something more than a simplified representation of a fact and is intended to be an implicit guide for actions. The outcome of such a representation, when transferred to a business environment, should be a structure-preserving or at least homomorphous mapping of a business activity [2].

In a prescriptive sense, the business model refers to how a particular area of commercial endeavors is to be exploited. Some authors identify the core components of the business model, basing their studies on relationship perspectives and proposing the concept of customer driven activity [56]; Others suggest that the business model ultimately expresses the core principles on which the organizational ability to grow and survive is based.

In the last few years, a number of business models have emerged thanks to the Internet revolution. These models demonstrate a remarkable flexibility among organizations, information and ICTs to quickly respond to changing circumstances [45]. In other words, there is an increasing need for business and organizational agility and ability to change. These imperatives are extremely relevant to successfully translate strategic choices into complex adaptive socio-technical systems.

The development of a socio-technical system, as well as any other system, always involves two different perspectives: the functional and the constructional. The functional perspective concerns the question of *what* the system is required to deliver in terms of the system's behavior, performance and interface characteristics, as well as the system's operational conditions, such as reliability, availability, resilience, effectiveness and efficiency.

The constructional perspective, on the other hand, concerns the question of *how* the system must be designed and built and how knowledge on the system's internal operation is managed.

Indeed, business and organization management and governance concern the functional perspective, while the constructional perspective concerns the Business

Model and Enterprise Architecture, which play a fundamental role in supporting the implementation of a strategic perspective in organization and technological systems.

According to Osterwalder [1], the relation between strategy, organization and technology is identified as the "business triangle" that is constantly subjected to external pressures, such as competitive forces, social change, technological change, customer opinion and the legal environment.

Strategy describes the objectives to be achieved, the type of products and services that offer increased value to customers, the sources of competitive advantage to be leveraged to achieve superior business performance [57]. Thus, a strategy is successful if it is consistent with the objectives and values, with the external environment, the resources and capabilities, and in general with the organization and technological system.

Chandler [58] states that structure follows strategy. From the strategy it is possible to determine all the criteria to choose from among alternative forms of organization [57]. If we consider the strategy as a set of activities, it becomes easy to identify its influence on the structure and on organizational processes. Thus, according to Woodward's analysis, a strong relationship exists between organizational structure and technology, which can also be mutually adapted to support a specific business strategy [59][60].

In accordance with the aforementioned considerations, a methodology is required to give a systemic view of all the different dimensions of the enterprise. Indeed, the integration of the various aspects is crucial, whereby the enterprise architecture acts as an integrating force.

This chapter aims to describe a methodology that enables the integration of strategy, organization and technology through the extensive use of the Business Model and Enterprise Architecture. The methodology is articulated in three steps.

In the first step, the Business Model is defined as a constructional strategy representation. In the second step, the Enterprise Architecture concept is introduced as a socio-technical design mechanism supporting a Business Model. In the third step, the Business Model and Enterprise Architecture are linked to create a strong connection between strategy definition and socio-technical system design. This last step is conceived to lend coherence during the design phase, focusing on the agility and ability to change thanks to a clear understanding of the socio-technical implication of the strategic choice.

1.2.1 From the strategy to the Business Model

The first step of our methodological approach concerns the relationship between the business model and the strategy.

Authors debating this issue differ widely in their opinion about the difference between strategy and business models. Some people use the terms "strategy" and "business model" interchangeably [61]; others consider the business model as an enabler of competitive advantage [62]. However, the difference between strategy and business models that has not been discussed in detail concerns the point that strategy includes execution and implementation, while the business model is related to the description of how a business works as a system. Business model implementation or execution is a widely neglected issue.

More in general, the business model is built on the value chain concept [52] and the extended notions of value systems and strategic positioning [63]. Since the business model encompasses competitive advantage, it also draws on the resource-based theory. In terms of the firm's fit within the larger value creation network, the model is related to strategic network theory [7] and cooperative strategies [24]. Moreover, the model involves choices (e.g., competitive strategy, vertical integration) on firm boundaries and relates to transaction cost economics [5]. Many perspectives on business models include the firm's offerings and the activities undertaken to produce them. Here management must consider the firm's value proposition, must choose the activities it will undertake within the firm, and determine how the firm fits into the value creation network. Many authors have written about successful business models, but a business model cannot be successful per se: it can be comparatively sound and consistent, but it cannot be judged until its implementation. Thus, the business model encourages manager and entrepreneur to (a) conceptualize the venture as an interrelated set of strategic choices; (b) seek complementary relationships between several elements through unique combinations; (c) develop activity sets around a logic framework; and (d) ensure consistency between elements of strategy, economics, architecture and growth. Strategic choices that characterize a venture are made both intentionally and by default. The business model makes the choices explicit and acts as a focusing device for entrepreneurs and employees, especially when supported by a set of rules or guidelines that derive from decisions made at the management level. Rules provide a clearer sense of the firm's value proposition and are a source of guidance on actions that might compromise the value equation.

1.2.2 The "Business Model" enabling Architecture: a strategic tool to design effective socio-technical systems

The second step of our methodological approach concerns the Enterprise Architecture concept. Enterprise Architecture is a framework that facilitates describing the way the organization achieves current and future business objectives. It examines the key business, application, information and technology strategies and their impact on business functions. Each of these strategies represents a separate architectural discipline and the Enterprise Architecture is the glue that integrates each of these disciplines into a cohesive framework.

We can conceive the Business Model and the Enterprise Architecture as two different but complementary sides of the same coin: the Enterprise. The former helps managers translate the high level and abstract mid to long-term strategies in concrete terms through a simple representation of the main business components. The latter summarizes the technological and organizational view through a unique conceptual framework. Thus, the enterprise architecture supports the business model giving concrete information pertaining to the operational level. The business model receives this information, connects it to the strategy and gives, as output, the solutions to implement an innovative techno-organizational change. The Enterprise Architecture tries to put integrated human and technology system operations into practice while safeguarding and enabling this change.

Moreover, change efforts are only successful according to the consistency and coherence of the concepts used, which in turn are reflected by coherent and consistent design principles. Architecture avoids "structural conflict" that would otherwise be manifested in conflicting concepts.

According to the "congruence theorem", the higher the degree of fit, or congruence between the various components, the more effective the enterprise [64]. It seems evident that enterprise integration has more facets than mere technology and this is why many technology introductions and related systems fail [65[66].

The notion of formal design has become operative in the principal distinction between the functional and constructional perspective through the concept of architecture.

The concept of technological and organizational change basically concerns the ability to execute various strategic initiatives. For example "the creation of an e-business design is inextricably linked to the management of change" [56]. Implementation of e-business initiatives is complex and requires a profound focus on programs and processes to ensure enterprise-wide alignment.

Finally, as indicated above, the introduction of technology should match the organizational context in which the technology will operate. It thus entails business and organizational change, but in itself does not automatically bring about change: technology alone is not enough to improve organizational performance. A crucial aspect of enterprise architecture is therefore that its competence is not so much based on the ability to foresee the future, but to enable it. Enterprise architecture should hence aid executing planned as well as emerging change.

1.2.3 Linking the Business Model with the Enterprise Architecture

Although conceptually close, Enterprise Architecture and Business Model concepts are quite different. Business models essentially focus on value creation and customers.

Enterprise Architecture includes the organizational model, the process model and the information model. Its main role within a firm is to improve efficiency. In contrast, the main role of the business model is to find and design a promising business concept.

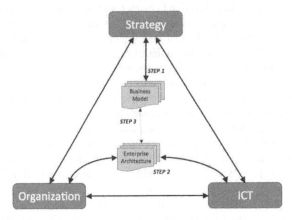

Fig. 1.1 - The integrated methodology: the Business Model and the Enterprise Architecture within the Business Triangle Framework

Designing an Enterprise Architecture helps to clarify the relationship between the organization's strategy and the way it is organized in terms of business processes, domains and functions. The business architecture provides a far sturdier framework to design the organization than individual strategic statements that lack structure, coherence and balance.

This book proposes a new approach to reengineering and monitoring the Enterprise Architecture in an IE, based on the results of a three-year research project (TEKNE - Towards Evolving Knowledge-based interNetworked Enterprise), aimed at realizing an analytic and operative "knowledge based architecture" consisting in:

- a methodology for the definition and design of an IE digital process;
- a platform for the realization of the IE digital process that is efficient, secure and safeguards privacy;
- a system of "a priori", "in itinere" and "ex-post" measures for the "real time" monitoring of the feasibility and efficiency of the digitalization of the single organizational processes.

This architecture has been obtained by integrating organizational, managerial and technological approaches.

The rest of the book is organized as follows: chapter 2 presents the TEKNE project Methodology of change that guides business networks towards the IE techno-organizational paradigm by means of a modular and flexible approach, taking into account the competitive environment of the network and how this environment influences its strategic, organizational and technological levels. Chapter 3 discusses the main results of the TEKNE project in terms of software components that enable enterprises to configure, store, search and share models of any aspects of their business while leveraging standard and business-oriented technologies and languages to bridge the gap between the world of business people and IT experts and to foster effective business-to-business collaborations. Chapter 4 provides models and methods for the design and execution of service-based processes able to exploit all the services offered in an IEs registry. Chapter 5 defines the technological architecture of a modular and multi-layer Peer-to-Peer infrastructure for SOA-based applications intended to sustain Internetworked Enterprise configurations. Chapter 6 introduces the TEKNE Metrics Framework that performs services to monitor business processes. Finally, chapters 7 to 12 highlight some case studies that provide insight on real world scenarios where concepts and results described in the previous chapters are applied and/or verified.

1.3 Conclusion

The profound crisis affecting the world economy in recent years is forcing enterprises, both SMEs and industrial giants, to re-think their *modus operandi*. Competitiveness, promptness and a penchant for change are today becoming the keywords managers need to focus on in order to face the increasing uncertainty of the economic environment, which makes business decisions complex and difficult.

In such a competitive and complex scenario, change management becomes the instrument to better react to and manage the environmental factors that constantly undermine the regular flow of activities by creating distortions both within the single enterprise as well as in the relationships between business network partners. The need for *Change* has to be supported by means conceived as an end-to-end approach, integrating strategic, organizational and technological perspectives. The Business Model and the Enterprise Architecture can support managers in a complementary way, providing a clear representation of the *As-Is domain* and leading towards the desired future status and configuration of the enterprise, namely, the *To-Be domain.* This book proposes a new approach to reengineering and monitoring the Enterprise Architecture of an IE, based on the results of a three-year research project (TEKNE - Towards Evolving Knowledge-based interNetworked Enterprise).

References

[1] Osterwalder, A., Pigneur, Y. and Tucci, C.L. ,(2005). Clarifying Business Models: Origins, Present and Future of the Concept. Communications of the Association for Information Systems, 16.

[2] Conte, T, (2008). A Framework for Business Models in Business Value Networks. Available at http://digbib.ubka.uni-karlsruhe.de/volltexte/1000009399;

[3] Powell W. W., (1990), Neither Market nor Hirarchy: Network forms of organization, Research in Organizational Behaviour, Vol. 12, pp. 295-336

[4] Williamson, O.E., (1975), Market and Hierarchies: Analysis and Antitrust Implications, Free Press,

[5] Williamson, O.E., (1985), The Economic Institutions of Capitalism, The Free Press

[6] Contractor, F.J., Lorange, P., (1988), Cooperative Strategies in Business Markets, Lexington Books

[7] Jarillo, J.C., (1988), On strategic networks, Strategic Management Journal, Vol. 9, pp. 31-41.

[8] Hines, P.,(1994), Creating World Class Suppliers – Unlocking Mutual Competitive Advantage,

[9] Nishiguchi, T., (1994), Strategic Industrial Sourcing, Oxford University Press

[10] Gilson, R. and M. Roe, (1993), 'Understanding the Japanese keiretsu: overlaps between corporate governance and industrial organization', Yale Law Journal, 102, 871–884.

[11] Piore, M.J. and C.F. Sabel, (1984), The Second Industrial Divide: Possibilities for Prosperity, New York: Basic Book.

[12] Coriat, B. 1990, L'Atelier et le Robot, Paris: Bourgois.

[13] Friedman, M. (1988), The Misunderstood Miracle, Ithaca, NY: Cornell University Press.

[14] Ybarra, J.A., (1989), 'Informationalization in the Valencian economy: a method for underdevelopment', in A. Porter, M. Castells and L. Benton (eds), The Informal Economy, Baltimore, MD: Johns Hopkins University Press, p. 224.

[15] Harrison, B. (1994), Lean and Mean: The Changing Landscape of Corporale Power in the Age of Flexibility, New York: Basic Books.

[16] Gerlac, M.L. (1992), Alliance Capitalism: The Social Organization of JapaneseBusiness, Berkeley, CA: University of California Press.

[17] Dunning, J. (1993), Multinational Enterprise and Global Economy, Reading, PA: Addison Wesley.

[18] Eccles, R. (1981), 'The quasi-firm in the construction industry', Journal of Economic Behaviour and Organization, 2, 335–357.

[19] Coser, L., C. Kadushin and W.W. Powell (1982), The Culture and Commerce of Publishing, New York: Basic Books Inc.

[20] Faulkner, R.R. and A. Anderson (1987), 'Short term projects and emergent careers: evidence from Hollywood', American Journal of Sociology, 92 (4), 879–909.

[21] Mowery, D.C. (1987), Alliance, Politics and Economics, Cambridge, MA: Ballinger.

[22] Martini, P. and R.H. Smiley (1983), 'Co-operative agreements and the organizational industry', Journal of Industry Economics, 31 (4), 437–451.

[23] Mariotti, S. and G.C. Cainarca (1986), 'The evolution of transaction governance in the textile-clothing industry', Journal of Economic Behaviour and Organization, 7 (4), 351–374.

[24] Dyer J. H., Singh H., (1998), The Relational View: Cooperative Strategy and Sources of Interorganizational Competitive Advantage, The Academy of Management Review, Vol. 23, No. 4, pp. 660-679

[25] Powell, W. W., Koput, K. W., Smith - Doerr, L., (1996), Interorganizational collaboration and the locus of innovation: Networks of learning in biotechnology, Administrative Science Quarterly, 41, 116-145.

[26] Müller, G., Eggs, H., Englert, J., (1997), Restructuring of co-operation for small and medium enterprises by electronic networks, Symposium Rebuilding of Economic Structure toward 21st Century

[27] Stearns, T.M., Hoffman, A.N., Heide, J.B., (1987), Performance of Commercial Television Stations as an Outcome of Interorganizational Linkages and Environmental Conditions, Academy of Management Journal, 30, 71-90

[28] Gulati R., Nohria N., Zaheer A., (2000), Strategic Networks, Strategic Management Journal, Vol. 21, No. 3, Special Issue: Strategic Networks, pp. 203-215

[29] Simard, C., West, J., (2008), Knowledge networks and the geographic locus of innovation, in Chesbrough, H., Vanhaverbeke, W., West, J., 2008, Open Innovation: Researching a New Paradigm, Oxford University Press

[30] Uzzi, B., Gillespie, J., (1999), Corporate social capital and the cost of financial capital: an embeddedness approach. In Leenders, R., Gabbay, S., Corporate social capital and liability, Kluwer Academic Publisher

[31] Granovetter, M., (1985), Economic Action and Social Structure: The Problem of Webster, Frederick, and Yoram Wind. 1972. Organizational Buying Behavior. Englewood Cliffs, N. J.: Prentice-Hall.

[32] Hollis, M., (1998), Trust Within Reason, Cambridge University Press

[33] Gulati, R.,(1995), Social Structure and Alliance Formation Patterns: A Longitudinal Analysis, Administrative Science Quarterly, 40

[34] Castells, M., (2000)a, The rise of the network society, Wiley-Blackwell

[35] Castells, M., (2000)b, Materials for an exploratory theory of the network society, Article for the Special Millennium Issue of the British Journal of Sociology

[36] Teece, D. J., (1987), Profiting from technological innovation: Implications for integration, collaboration, licensing and public policy, in Teece D. J., The competitive challenge: Strategies for industrial innovation and renewal, MA: Ballinger

[37] Corallo A., Lazoi M., (2010)b, "Value Network Collaborations for Innovations in an Aerospace Company", 16th International Conference on Concurrent Enterprise Collaborative Environments for Sustainable Innovation, Lugano, Switzerland.

[38] Lazoi M., Ceci F., Corallo A., Secundo G., (forthcoming 2010), "Collaboration in an aerospace SMEs cluster: Innovation and ICT dynamics", International Journal of Innovation and Technology Management.

[39] Passiante G., (2003), Industrial Clusters in the Net-Economy: Empirical Evidence and some theoretical approaches, in Passiante, G., Elia, V., Massari, T., 2003, Digital Innovation, Imperial College Press

[40] Doz, Y., J. Santos and P. Williamson (2001), From Global to Metanational: How Firms Win in the Knowledge Economy, Boston, MA: Harvard Business School Press.

[41] Passiante, G., Andriani, P., (2000), Modelling the learning environment of the virtual knowledge networks: some empirical evidence, International Journal of Innovation Management, 4, 1-31

[42] Romano, A., Passiante, G., Elia, V., (2001), New sources of clustering in the digital economy, Journal of Small Business & Enterprise Development, 8

[43] Ceci F., Iubatti D., (2010). The Role of Personal Relationships in SME Networks, Academy of Management Conference, Montreal, Canada, August 2010

[44] Tapscott, D., Ticoll, D., Lowy, A., (2000), Digital Capital: harnessing the power of business webs, Nicholas Brealey Publishing

[45] Timmers, P. (1999), Electronic Commerce. John Wiley & Sons, Inc., New York.

[46] Castells M. (1996). The Rise of the Network Society. Blackwell. Oxford.

[47] Parker, H., (2000), Interfirm collaboration and the new product development process, Industrial Management and Data Systems, 100/6, 255-260

[48] Webster, Frederick, and Yoram Wind. (1972). Organizational Buying Behavior. Englewood Cliffs, N. J.: Prentice-Hall.

[49] Powell, W. W., Koput, K. W., Smith - Doerr, L., (1996), Interorganizational collaboration and the locus of innovation: Networks of learning in biotechnology, Administrative Science Quarterly, 41, 116-145.

[50] Padgett, J., Powell, W., (2003), Market Emergence, available on http://home.uchicago.edu/%7Ejpadgett/papers/sfi/intro.chap. Pdf

[51] Amit, R. and C. Zott (2001). "Value creation in e-business." Strategic Management Journal 22(6-7): 493-520.

[52] Porter, M.E., (1990), The competitive advantage of Nations, Macmillan

[53] Passiante G, Elia V (1999) "A re-thinking of the agglomeration economies in the digital economy" RSA International Conference, Bilbao 18-21 September,.

[54] Orlikowski, W. J; (1992); The duality of technology: Rethinking the concept of technology in organizations. Organization Science, Vol. 3, No. 3, pp. 398-427.

[55] Orlikowski, W.J; (1999); The Truth is Not Out There: An Enacted View of the "Digital Economy", in Understanding the Digital Economy: Data, Tools, and Research, E. Brynjolfsson, B. Kahin, The MIT Press.

[56] Kalakota R., Robinson M., (1999), e-business, Addison Wesley Longman, Inc.

[57] Galbraith J. R., (1995), "Designing organizations, An Executive Briefing on Strategy, structure, and Process", Jossy-Bass

[58] Chandler A.; (1962); "Strategy and Structure: Chapters in the history of industrial enterprise", Doubleday, New York.

[59] Woodward J.; (1958); "Industrial Organization: Theory and Practice"; London: Oxford University Press

[60] Woodward J.; (1965); "Management and Technology"; London: Her Majesty's Stationery Office

[61] Magretta, J. (2002). "Why Business Models Matter." Harvard Business Review 80(5): 86-92.

[62] Stähler, P. (2002). Business Models as a Unit of Analysis for Strategizing. International Workshop on Business Models, Lausanne, Switzerland

[63] Porter M.; (1996); "What is Strategy?"; Harvard Business Review (Nov-Dec. 1996)

Bernes P, Nemes L.Aframework to define a generic enterprise reference architecture and methodology. Computer Integrated Manufacturing Systems 1996; 9(3):179–191.

[64] Nadler, D. A. & Tushman, M. L. (1997). Competing by design: The power of organizational architecture. New York: Oxford University Press

[65] Scott-Morton M. (ed) 1991. The Corporation of the 1990s: Information Technology and Organizational Transformation. Oxford University Press.

[66] Galliers, RD and WRJ Baets (1998) 'Information technology and organisational transformation: the holy grail of IT?', Information Technology and Organisational Transformation: innovation for the 21st century organisation (Galliers, RD and WRJ Baets, eds), Wiley, Chichester, pp 1-16

Chapter 2: A methodology aimed at fostering and sustaining the development processes of an IE-based industry

Angelo Corallo[1], Fabrizio Errico[1], Marco De Maggio[1], Enza Giangreco[2]

[1] eBMS S.S. ISUFI – University of Salento

[2] Engineering Ingegneria Informatica S.p.A.

Abstract – In the current competitive scenario, where business relationships are fundamental in building successful business models and inter/intra organizational business processes are progressively digitalized, an end-to-end methodology is required that is capable of guiding business networks through the Internetworked Enterprise (IE) paradigm: a new and innovative organizational model able to leverage Internet technologies to perform real-time coordination of intra and inter-firm activities, to create value by offering innovative and personalized products/services and reduce transaction costs. This chapter presents the TEKNE project Methodology of change that guides business networks, by means of a modular and flexible approach, towards the IE techno-organizational paradigm, taking into account the competitive environment of the network and how this environment influences its strategic, organizational and technological levels. Contingency, the business model, enterprise architecture and performance metrics are the key concepts that form the cornerstone of this methodological framework.

2.1 The TEKNE project Methodology of change

In the current competitive scenario, the Internetworked Enterprise (IE) is emerging as an organizational model able to leverage Internet technologies to perform real-time coordination of intra and inter-firm activities, to create value by offering innovative and personalized products/services and reduce transaction costs [1][2][3][4]. The transition towards the Internetworked Enterprise model calls for a comprehensive framework in which people with different competences and backgrounds can collaborate to *design, implement* and *measure* the numerous processes required by the IE configuration. The main components of this framework can be grouped into:

- *Design Environment*, able to guide companies during their adoption of the IE paradigm, which includes tools and methodologies for the definition and design of digital processes and related service-based IT solutions

G. Passiante (ed.), *Evolving Towards the Internetworked Enterprise: Technological and Organizational Perspectives*, DOI 10.1007/978-1-4419-7279-8_2,

- *Technological Platform* enabling the inter-organizational execution of efficient and secure digital processes
- *Business Intelligence System* for ex-ante and ex-post measures, for real time monitoring of the feasibility and efficiency of the digitalization of each single organizational process
- *Methodology of Change,* representing the backbone of the framework, containing a detailed description of all the phases and activities necessary to support the firm's transition towards the Internetworked Enterprise.

The last component, the Methodology of Change, is the most influencing element in the successful definition of the framework, since this is the pillar granting a holistic meaning to the overall model. Furthermore, this pillar represents the interdisciplinary collector of the specific perspectives and requirements related to every other component.

This chapter aims to present the TEKNE project Methodology of Change, conceived as an end-to-end approach, integrating organizational, managerial and technological perspectives. The Methodology of Change is designed to provide managerial and operational actors with theoretical and practical tools that enable organizations to face new challenges: to work in partnerships, to offer joint value propositions, to build multi-channel and multi-owned distribution networks and to profit from diversified and shared revenue streams. The Methodology of Change is articulated in a set of phases, related to each other and supported by both existing and ad hoc developed methodologies and tools. Every phase of the methodology is iteratively related to every other. Many of these phases have been widely discussed by scholars and practitioners both from organizational and technological perspectives. The challenging core of the Methodology of Changes is the development of a bridge between two different perspectives: strategic and managerial on one hand, and technological and computer science on the other. Reconciling these two perspectives requires introducing two theoretical models: the *Business Model* and the *Enterprise Architecture*.

The *Business Model* is the executive representation of the strategic perspective. When a company's business becomes more complex and harder to understand and communicate, the relatively new concept of the *Business Model* becomes a means to provide rather simple management concepts that can be used to improve the management of a business in a rapidly moving, complex and uncertain business environment [5] [6]. The Business model can be considered the translation of a company's strategy into a blueprint of the company's money earning logic. Strategy, business models and process models together address similar problems on different business layers. Strategy, on a planning level, provides the vision and long-term objectives, the business model specifies the specific business logic that the organization adopts to reach these objectives; processes represent the actual real-world implementation of the business model [7].

Enterprise Architecture is a comprehensive set of related models describing, on different levels of abstraction and with different perspectives, the techno-organizational model the company should aim at. It defines a logical construct to identify and classify in a structured way the essential type of models to represent an enterprise and its information system [8] [9].

Enterprise Architecture is usually focused within the boundaries of an enterprise, providing business managers a means to control its complexity through an integrated and synthetic set of representations related to both organizational and IT aspects, and defining methodologies and mechanisms that relate information system components to the operative organizational models.

The challenge of creating a bridge between *Business Models* and *Enterprise Architecture* is finding a way to identify the contribution each process adds to the value offered to the end customer. From an IE perspective, this approach requires the Enterprise Architecture to expand its view outside the boundaries of the organization, taking into account the interdependencies with other value-network actors and re-defining its essential concepts from a service-oriented perspective.

Typical abstractions related to what an enterprise produces, how it delivers it and who plays what role in the organization must be re-interpreted with respect to a new unit of analysis: the *service unit*, an atomic organizational element that provides specific capabilities through self-contained resources and end-to-end processes, contributing to one or more value-networks via service composition mechanisms.

2.2 Overview on the adopted approach

Each business unit should be totally focused on its objectives, translating strategies defined by the top management into effective business processes and value-driven services that, in turn, should be directly coupled to real human and/or automatic activities and operations. The methodology aims to define a way to maintain relationships among the strategic, organizational and technological levels of an enterprise consistent and clear, thus granting their alignment and allowing the top management's vision to always be "connected" to day-to-day activities. This approach is very close to that proposed by the OMG[1]'s Model Driven Architecture (MDA). The MDA defines a way to create a system's models on different levels. From abstract and automation-independent models to technology-oriented models and to the actual software code. The model-stack defined by MDA has the following levels:

---

[1] Object Management Group - http://www.omg.org/

- *CIM (Computational Independent Model):* described through languages that are familiar to end users (i.e. business managers), allowing them to easily express their requirements
- *PIM (Platform Independent Model):* on this level, the system is described with the aim of highlighting its architectural characteristics in terms of the Information System's components and behaviors. UML (Unified Modeling Language) models are typical examples of platform independent models since concepts such as "class" or "association" are common to many object oriented platforms (e.g. Java, .Net, C++)
- *PSM (Platform Specific Model):* models belonging to this level describe the system in terms of the specific platform's characteristics and concepts. For example, UML profiles can be used to represent UML models on a PSM level

These models represent the same system through different perspectives. They are connected by specific mappings and transformation algorithms that allow deriving a model through manual, automatic or semi-automatic procedures. Currently, software engineering is the mostly influencing discipline, but new interpretations of the MDA approach are to come. The OMG, in fact, is attempting to generalize the MDA Foundation Model by re-interpreting its concepts with respect to other domains such as Realtime Systems, Process Control Systems and Enterprise Architecture. The TEKNE project methodology of change proposes an original interpretation of the MDA model-stack with respect to the Enterprise Architecture domain, thus enabling a multilevel analysis of business systems in terms of their strategy, organization and technologies.

The main assumption of the methodology, following a new direction taken by the OMG, considers the CIM level as a wider concept of the *Environment* and includes PIM and PSM levels under a single hat called the *System*.

- Environment (CIM Level): the concept of environment is described here, in accordance with business literature, in terms of the competitive and macro environment. The competitive environment is conceived as the arena in which different enterprises cooperate and/or compete. Typical aspects of the competitive environment that affect enterprises are: degree of trust, technological degree, social relationships and network positioning. The macro environment is conceived as a set of external and uncontrollable factors indirectly influencing a business network's decision-making and affecting performances and strategies [10][11][12]. These factors include the economic, demographic, legal, political, and social conditions, the technological evolution and natural forces. This concept of the Environment implies abstractly describing the main endogenous and exogenous elements affecting network dynamics [13] [14]. It is thus fundamental for managers to recognize the variables that directly or indirectly affect their business performances in order to adopt the right countermeasures and solutions as and when required.

- The *System* domain (PIM-PSM), in our specific analysis, is a representation of the enterprise through three main perspectives: *the strategic, organizational, and technological models.* In particular, on the PIM level, the methodology takes into account the models of business objectives, formal and informal organizational structures and roles, intra and inter-organizational business processes, business rules and in general, any model that is necessary to provide a formal description of the structure and behaviors of the enterprise. It is important to underline that these characteristics can be represented at varying levels of detail, depending on the model's purpose. Therefore, a business process model, if used for business analysis, will represent only the core activities and fundamental business rules, while if used to design the technological infrastructure, it will be enriched with system activities and technological details. On the PSM level, the models are actualized with real-world information on people and facts that must be specified to allow deploying and executing the processes and enacting the business tactics.

This new interpretation of the MDA approach provides the means to represent the *as-is* of a networked organization and to highlight the relationships between the environment and the current status of the business system. Following an accurate analysis of the actual strengths and weaknesses of the enterprise and its business network, in order to support the *to-be* conception (i.e. the desired future status and configuration of the enterprise), the methodology adopts the Business Model concept as a logical framework for the definition of the enterprise's key strategic, organizational and technological innovation. The last stage of the methodology, following the representation of the current status (as-is) and the definition of the to-be status, is the definition of a *deployment strategy*, which is a guide for the adoption of the new business model and the new strategic, organizational and technological configuration.

The three methodological stages (as-is, to-be, deployment strategy) are completed by a transverse component that defines metrics and measures that support the quantitative and qualitative evaluation of the change management and innovation process. A vertical integration between financial and business process measures allows managers to align the strategy with the techno-organizational layer [15], whereas a horizontal integration through *ex-ante, in-itinere* and *ex-post* measures assures continuous monitoring of the change evolution between as-is and to-be.

2.3 The Methodology of change step by step

Prior to starting the detailed analysis of each phase of the methodology, some assumptions need to be made:

1. The methodology is conceived as being independent from specific business domains, thus resulting in an approach that can be applied to a wide range of cases
2. Depending on the characteristics and the complexity of the scenario that the methodology is applied to, some phases could be simplified or skipped
3. The methodology is primarily conceived for business analysts and consultants

2.3.1 Environment analysis

The first step of the methodology is the analysis of the environment of the enterprise and its business network. The adopted approach considers endogenous and exogenous *contingency variables*, which represent the set of factors and elements that could directly or indirectly affect network dynamics.

Exogenous variables are those factors related to the macro environment that indirectly affect each node of the network. The identification and analysis of these factors can be executed through various instruments, for example, PEST analysis defines four main groups including Political, Economical, Social and Technological factors:

- Political factors: national/international laws, regulations and government policies that may influence or limit companies and organizations in the market. Institutions define limits and regulations for the good of society and to ensure the freedom and fairness of markets. Often, changes in the normative environment determine the definition of a new business configuration and the adoption of new business models. For example, the introduction of new privacy laws had a huge impact on those companies that extensively relied on customer information without the customer's explicit consent. Taxes on gas or SUVs may shift consumer demand to new and innovative vehicles such as hybrids or even solar energy cars. This may even lead to an increase in the use of the public transportation system. Anti-spamming laws may wipeout business models based on sending out large trunks of unsolicited emails. Regulating advertisement over mobile phones may limit the range of possible business models in m-commerce. New taxes may make a company's value proposition too costly and thus uninteresting to the customer. In general, the legal environment largely influences business models [16]
- Economic factors: economic factors have always influenced consumer purchasing. From the "Great Depression" to September 11th, America has seen how drastically the economy can be affected. It is important for companies to watch trends in the economy to prevent losses in profits and to remain at the top of the market. These include interest rates, taxation changes, economic growth, inflation and exchange rates. For example: higher interest rates may deter invest-

ments because loans are more expensive; a strong currency may make exporting more difficult because it can raise the price in terms of foreign currency; inflation may provoke higher wage demands from employees and raise costs; higher national income growth may boost demand for a firm's products

- Social factors: sometimes a business can be influenced by the social environment and social mood determining a greater or lower inclination to invest or to acquire. This kind of strain is particularly studied in stakeholder theory [17]. For example, if a company's strategy is based on low cost production in developing countries it might draw the attention of militant non-governmental organizations that could mobilize public opinion against the firm. This happened to Nike concerning the ethics of its operations in Vietnam [18]. Besides ethics, changes in the social environment will also indirectly influence customer demand. This is the case in technology adoption where the use and social acceptance of a specific technology by a broad majority completely opens up new markets and customer demand [19].

- Technological factors: new *technologies* create new markets and new opportunities for businesses. It is important for businesses, young and old, to stay on top of new technology. Companies that do not keep up to date will soon find their products and services outdated. They will miss all of the great opportunities and markets that technology brings. Technology (e.g. ICT) and its application in business is rapidly changing and since technology is increasingly applied to every aspect of business, technological change pressures managers into reflecting on how technology can be adopted to improve the firm's business logic. With the rise of the Internet, companies started adopting new web-based channels. Some even tried to figure out how their products could be entirely digitized or at least "digitally enhanced". In addition, falling communication and coordination costs due to cheaper technology have forced companies to become more efficient. They have started to outsource all non-essential business and progressively rely on partnerships. It is no understatement to say that technological change is a major force in changing the business model. In some cases, technological change may even challenge the mere existence of a particular business model [16]. For example, retailing has been transformed by the web. Established retailers such as Walmart and Tesco, having adding a new distribution channel to their traditional business model, now count among the most successful Internet companies. The music industry is most cited as having been turned up side down by the digitalization of sound and images, since its players are incapable of finding new sustainable Internet-era business models.

Networks are triggered not only by macro environment forces, but also by factors that are specific and endogenous to the reference domain. Indeed, depending on the industry analyzed, different patterns can be identified: trends to outsource activities or to form vertical partnerships with suppliers (e.g. the automotive industry), horizontal partnerships with competitors (e.g. the airline industry), or cross-sectional partnerships with technology companies (e.g. consumer electronics –

SonyEricsson). The second group of contingencies is thus about the endogenous variables that characterize the competitive environment.

Endogenous variables are those factors that are directly referable to the analyzed network such as *the degree of trust* between partners of the same project, *social relationships* among actors of a production pyramid, *degree of technology adoption* in customer-supplier interactions.

- Outsourcing level: in many industries, companies increasingly understand the need to focus on their core competencies and collaborate with other firms to fulfill the remaining activities necessary for the delivery of their product. For this reason, companies started to re-evaluate their processes, focusing on value adding activities and outsourcing peripheral activities to companies with superior expertise in those areas. This practice gradually led to networks of companies collaborating closely for the delivery of specific products. This trend is quite evident in the advanced mechanical industry where the complexity of the task demands close collaboration between a variety of companies that cannot undertake the project by themselves. Close collaboration during the design and development phases forges trust-based relationships and leads to more or less stable collaboration schemes. For example, in the aerospace industry, which is particularly complex in terms of products and processes, the prime or the small prime contractor tends to retain core activities (generally highly technological and strategic) and take advantage of different levels of outsourcing of standardized activities.
- Standardization initiatives: in various industrial sectors, initiatives that aim to establish standard procedures for collaboration between industry actors become the precursor of industry-wide networking activity. These initiatives do not explicitly intend to form inter-organizational networks but rather focus on the standardization of common activities that are performed on a frequent basis. In the retail industry, for example the ECR[2] (Efficient Consumer Response) movement aimed to bring about the close collaboration between retailers and suppliers for the alignment of the entire value chain. This initiative led to the creation of worldwide supply chain hubs around the major retailers.
- Co-opetition degree: the outsourcing of firm-specific activities and the close cooperation with other firms to accomplish common goals paved the road for more audacious collaborations. Co-opetition describes cooperation among competitors. It is often linked to the metaphor of a business ecosystem, which emphasizes the coexistence of competition and collaboration as a prerequisite for a dynamic and innovative industry. An example is the biotechnology industry. The need for constant innovation in combination with the small size of many of the biotechnology companies led to collaboration between competitors for the benefit of risk sharing and achieving a "virtual size".

---

[2] http://en.wikipedia.org/wiki/Efficient_Consumer_Response

- Existing social network: another prime factor that affects network creation is the way partners are selected. Not all collaboration opportunities are taken up since firms need sufficient information on their prospective partners in order to avoid opportunistic behaviors. More specifically, they need to know the true capabilities, needs and performance of potential partners to minimize decision risk and guarantee future performance. Existing social networks and trust-based relationships in the marketplace might thus be the trigger for certain partner constellations. An existing social relationship between two management executives may also be the key enabling factor for collaboration ideas leading to the discovery or creation of joint business opportunities and thus the formation of a network.

In conclusion, the analysis of the main contingency variables is crucial to better understand which forces directly/indirectly influence a business network. This phase of the methodology of change has to describe and analyze the contingency variables (with a distinction made between macro and micro environment variables) and thereafter extrapolate the key variable that are used to analyze in detail the main effects of the environment on the entire business organization.

> *In brief:*
> ➢ *PEST analysis to identify the exogenous variables affecting the business*
> ➢ *Identification of the major endogenous variables that characterize the business network*
> ➢ *Analysis of the main effects of the key variables on the business network*

2.3.2 Business Network Analysis

The essence of the contingency theory is that organizational effectiveness results from fitting the characteristics of the business organization to external contingencies that reflect the macro environment and the competitive arena [20] [21]. Since the fit of organizational characteristics to contingencies leads to high performance, organizations must continuously adapt their characteristics and strategies to the changing environment. Following the evaluation of macro and micro environmental variables, this phase of the methodology of change addresses the analysis of the as-is of the networked enterprise through the analysis of its strategy and through an organizational and technological assessment.

Strategy. For any kind of organization, this is the prime factor of value creation. It concerns three main aspects: network mission, market positioning and network resources.

The *network mission* is the explicit representation of its purpose and, more specifically, its goals. A mission statement is the most strategic document of a business network and must contain [22] the set of objectives that the management wants to achieve, differentiating a business network from other competitors, defining the arena in which the business network will compete, stimulating and guiding managers and employees to higher levels of performance, helping to balance competing and often conflicting interests of the various network stakeholders.

Positioning is the second crucial aspect of the strategic analysis. The market-based view (MBV) on strategy assumes that economic success is determined by both the structure of the market in which a business network operates and by its behavior in relation to the five market forces [23]. Competitive advantage thus derives from the strategic fit between a network's behavior and its environment and is hence determined by unique market positioning.

Finally, the network has to work out its core *competencies and resources* ensuring the delivery of unique value to the market in terms of products and services. This requires planning and monitoring the network's tangible and intangible resources and developing products and services based on these resources.

In brief:
> Define the business network mission through long-term goals, values, distinctive competences and policies
> Define the market positioning of the business network
> configure the network resource portfolio through accurate planning and monitoring to satisfy product/service development

The Organizational assessment is the second layer of the business network analysis. Considering that a business network can be seen as a specific set of linkages among a defined set of actors, the structural and behavioral dimensions become complementary tools for a full depiction of a business entity [24]. This consideration implies not only a structural but also a behavioral understanding of the network, defining network organization by the relations between a set of autonomous, yet interdependent, organizations (the network structure) and their interactions within that structure (the network behavior). In addition, network policies and governance mechanisms are necessary to govern the network operations within the network structures.

The *formal structure* is here defined as the set of characteristics that are usually considered in classical BPM (Business Process Management) and Enterprise Architecture projects, including structured processes, roles and responsibilities over activities and formal relationships between actors. Graphical notations are of primary importance in the modeling of the formal structure hence, for example, organizational charts and flow charts should be used to depict and share the actual representation of roles and processes within a business network.

The *informal behavior* comprises coordinating (informal) interactions, which take place within the formal organizational structure of the network in terms of people, social ties, exchange actions, transactions and inter-personal interactions. *The So-*

cial Network Analysis views social relationships, analyzing nodes and their ties. Nodes are the individual actors (organizations) within the network and ties are the relationships between the actors.

Network policies and governance comprise formal rules and regulations as well as informal aspects such as culture and identity. Institutional arrangements and governance structures are needed to deal with the complexity of network relationships and to ensure the implementation of strategies [25].

In brief:
➤ Formal structure representation through flow charts and organizational charts
➤ Informal behavior depiction through SNA in term of people, social ties, exchange actions, transactions and inter-personal interactions
➤ Definition of business rules and regulations

The technological assessment is the third layer of the business network analysis. Network management calls for the coordination of activities and resource sharing between network participants [26]. The role of ICT as an enabler of inter-organizational relationships creates a link between information management and network management.

Regional and international organizations across different sectors utilize ITC capabilities to more efficiently organize their supply chains. Organizations operating with many suppliers introduced collaborating platforms to monitor activities, to restructure existing relationships and to enable information flows [27]. The goal of a technological assessment is to ensure – by managing information infrastructures, systems and resources – that information can be efficiently and effectively deployed throughout the network. This encompasses the management of intellectual property rights throughout the network. In sum, a technological assessment addresses the network's (structural, institutional and human) capabilities to process information [28] [29], i.e., information metabolism [30].

In brief:
➤ Information resource management: identify the core information resources and network information flows
➤ Information system management: ensuring the appropriate use of information and communication technology (ICT) for the completion of inter-organizational tasks and for the enactment of inter-organizational information flows
➤ Information infrastructure management: define standards, IT networks, hardware, devices, etc.

This phase of the methodology concludes the as-is description of the business network by making a brief and schematic summary of the major findings through a SWOT analysis. This analysis highlights the strengths and weaknesses that characterize the business network and outlines the opportunities and threats that are determined by its environment and competitive scenario.

2.3.3 Business Model analysis

The first two steps of the methodology lead to a detailed description of the different aspects of a business network and its environment. They provide a snapshot of the current status (as-is) and give a brief view of the threats and opportunities that the network nodes must affront and take into account to maintain and improve their competitive advantage. The third step of the methodology takes the as-is as input and formulates a structured and clear view of the business model that should be implemented in the business network. The business model is here seen as a means of representing an integrated view of the way the business is organized and to translate the strategic objectives into concrete tactics involving any stakeholder who may play a valuable role in the value creation process. The business model is hence a way to guide an end-to-end redefinition of how a business works and how its building blocks should interact to reinforce its strengths, and identify and minimize its weaknesses in the market arena, leveraging new opportunities and managing risks. The majority of the literature that deals with the notion of business models tries to create taxonomies or conceptual models of existing approaches. Taxonomies enumerate a finite number of business model types (e.g. e-shops, malls, auctions) [31][32][33], while conceptualizations describe meta-models or reference models, allowing to describe an infinite number of concrete cases [16] [33][34][35][36][37][38][39][40]. The methodology of change leverages two existing and widely recognized ontologies to create a shared, formal and explicit conceptualization of a business model [41]: the *Business Model Ontology (BMO)* [16] and the e^3value ontology [42].

2.3.3.1 The Business Model Ontology

The first step is to represent business model components through the BMO. The BMO is a structured synthesis of previous scientific and industrial findings in the field of business models and is particularly influenced by the Balanced Scorecard approach [43] and more generally by business management literature [44]. The BMO is based on four pillars: product, customer interface, infrastructure management, financial aspects. These pillars are divided into nine interrelated business model building blocks: value proposition, target customer, distribution channel, relationship, value configuration, capability, partnership, cost structure and revenue model.

The "product" pillar covers all aspects of what a firm offers its customers. This comprises not only the company's bundles of products and services but also the way in which it differentiates itself from its competitors. Product is described through the "value proposition" element, which can be decomposed into several elementary offerings. The **value proposition** is the first of the nine elements of the business model ontology and can be understood as the statements of benefits that are delivered by the firm to its external constituencies [45] or the way items of value, such as products and services as well as complementary value-added services, are packaged and offered to fulfill customer needs [46] (Kambil, Ginsberg et al. 1997).

The "customer interface" pillar covers all customer related aspects. This comprises the choice of a firm's target customers, the channels through which it gets in touch with them and the kind of relationships the company wants to establish with its customers. The customer interface describes how and to whom it delivers its value proposition, namely, the firm's bundle of products and services. A **target customer** segment defines the type of customers a company wants to address. The most general distinction of target customers exists between business and/or individual customers, commonly referred to as business-to-business (B2B) and business-to-consumer (B2C). **Distribution channels** describe how a company *delivers* a value proposition to a target customer segment. A distribution channel allows a company to deliver value to its customers, either directly, for example through a sales force or over a Website, or indirectly through intermediaries, such as resellers, brokers or cybermediaries. The **relationship** element describes the relationship a company establishes with a target customer segment. A relationship is based on customer equity and can be decomposed into several relationship mechanisms.

The "infrastructure management" pillar is about *how* a company creates value. It describes what abilities are necessary to provide its value propositions and maintain its customer interface. A **capability** describes the ability to execute a repeatable pattern of actions. A firm has to have a number of capabilities at its disposal to be able to offer its value proposition. Capabilities are based on a set of resources of either the firm or its partners. The **value configuration** of a firm describes the arrangement of one or several activities in order to provide a value proposition. A **partnership** is a voluntarily initiated cooperative agreement formed between two or more independent companies to jointly carry out a project or specific activity by coordinating the necessary capabilities, resources and activities.

The "financial aspects" pillar is transversal because all other pillars influence it. This block is the outcome of the rest of the business model's configuration. Financial aspects are composed of the company's revenue model and its cost structure. Together they determine the firm's profit- or loss-making logic and therefore its ability to survive in competition. The **revenue model** describes the way a company makes money. It can be composed of one or several revenue streams and pricing elements. The **cost structure** measures all the costs the firm incurs in order to create, market and deliver value to its customers. It sets a price tag on all the resources, assets, activities and partner network relationships and exchanges that cost the company money.

2.3.3.2 The value flow

If on one hand, the BMO allows a structured and formal description of a business model's core characteristics, then on the other, the e^3value ontology [47] provides a formal way to represent value flows among the nodes of a business network through a simple and intuitive graphical notation. The e^3value ontology focuses on enterprise networks; the business model is seen as a constellation of enterprises, and final customers that jointly create, distribute, and consume products/services of economic value. The ontology identifies some core elements. **Actors** represent the economically and legally independent entities that participate in a value exchange scenario, including end-consumers. The **value object** represent physical or intangible (e.g. service, information) objects that are exchanged among actors and that have economic value for these actors. An actor uses a **value port** to notify to the rest of the value network its willingness to provide or request value objects. Value ports are abstractions of how value objects are requested or provided and hide internal processes and mechanisms from external actors. Value ports are grouped into **value interfaces**, which represent bundled offerings or requests of value objects. A **value transfer** is a connection between the two value ports of two actors, meaning that these actors want to transfer value objects. A **value activity** is an operational activity that is performed by an actor, yields a profit or increases economic value for the actor. The flow of value objects through actors of a value network begins with a **start stimulus**, which represents an end-consumer's demand and concludes with an **end stimulus**, which identifies the offering that satisfies this demand.

The approach proposed by the two ontologies is slightly different since the BMO centers around the design of a firm's business model, whereas e^3value concentrates on the design of a value constellation's business model. However, the combined use of the BMO and the e^3value ontology could allow business managers to analyze and re-design the business model of the single enterprises and of the entire value network through the structured description of the nine business model building blocks and by depicting in a clear and intuitive way how value is issued and consumed by the different network parties.

> **In brief:**
> ➢ Describe the main building blocks of the business model through the BMO approach
> ➢ Describe the value flow between the nodes of the business network through the e^3value ontology

2.3.4 Requirements analysis and architecture design

The definition of the target configuration of the business network in terms of its strategy, organization and technological infrastructure requires business managers and knowledge/process owners to share their vision and to collaborate toward the definition of a clear to-be. After the business model predisposition, it is necessary to deepen the analysis of how the network must enact core activities and processes, specifying any relevant detail such as roles, competencies, objectives, tools, rules and reference standards. Moreover, requirements analysis must be supported by a clear idea of where value should be produced and delivered within the organization through concrete business and technological services. The methodology defines an innovative approach to requirements analysis and some steps to translate the value produced by organizational functions into services.

2.3.4.1 Collaborative Storytelling

The innovative approach to requirements analysis aims to alleviate those problems that have led several change management projects to fail due to scarce understanding of real needs and poor information sharing among process stakeholders. The approach, called *Collaborative Storytelling*, has its foundations in the *dynamic requirements* and *collaboration* concepts. Domain experts and key referents are encouraged to describe the success and failure of current and past business processes and systems through a collective knowledge creation process based on an informal and story-oriented style. The description of stories is supported by the use of shared business vocabularies and business rules and is progressively translated into structured requirements representations, culminating in the definition of storyboards. A story can be defined as *"a narration of a chain of events expressed in spoken or written natural language"*. Storytelling is a technique that was initially developed in marketing and communication areas, but has recently been used in other disciplines such as software engineering for requirements elicitation. Describing and sharing stories is an effective way to make the visions and objectives of the organization explicit, which is a fundamental step to be able to develop the right techno-organizational solutions. A crucial component of this approach is the creation of a knowledge management environment supporting the acquisition and exchange of information during the requirements elicitation phase. In this environment, users should describe their activities and the main difficulties encountered, their needs and the organizational environment they work in. The collaboration enabled by this environment allows the construction of a more complex and detailed knowledge base resulting from a collective effort. The proposed approach is composed of three steps: group storytelling, scenario, storyboard.

Group Storytelling: through the narration of stories in natural language, stakeholders can simply and directly externalize their knowledge. Some reference elements are provided that should always be clearly described in a story. The **domain** represents the area that interests the analysis and specifies the boundaries with respect to other business areas, the **activities** of the business processes, including their objectives, start events, expected results and possible alternatives in case of anomalies, the control and information flow between the activities and the **competencies** that are required to execute the activities.

The objective of collaborative storytelling is to make the way stakeholders interact in business activities through work coordination, social relationships and information flows explicit, and to identify the key resources that enable the execution of these activities.

Scenarios: the second step aims to give a structure to the stories, organizing them into scenarios and enriching the description with the sample user interfaces of a supporting information system. This allows better understanding among end users and business analysts. Scenarios must include information such as: the decomposition of activities in a formal WBS (Work Breakdown Structure), the definition of temporal and/or data dependencies among scenarios, the roles involved in the activities, the information and expected results, the procedures that could be automatically executed by the system, the possible alternatives for the execution of the activities.

Storyboard: the third step transforms the scenarios into storyboards, which are a combination of textual descriptions and sample graphical user interfaces organized in workflows that reflect the time and data dependencies identified in the scenarios. Since storyboards leverage HCI (Human-Computer Interaction) and GUI (Graphical User Interface) principles, they result in easier and faster interaction with end users, leading to more robust and precise requirement specifications with respect to traditional UML Use Cases.

The three steps of the Collaborative Storytelling approach have a common semantic foundation since each textual description must be related to a shared business vocabulary and a set of business rules that allows minimizing the ambiguity of terms used and avoiding the definition of incomplete and inconsistent requirements.

2.3.4.2 Definition of a value-driven architecture

The identification and analysis of the main business requirements and the scenarios that the business network aims to achieve is an iterative process that must be orchestrated and integrated with the definition of the functional architecture that will enable the actual delivery of value to customers. The methodology identifies three steps to define value-driven business services that derive directly from the business units of the organization, thus binding organizational functions to actual value delivery.

The first step aims to identify the contribution of each business function to the value creation process. The methodology defines a matrix in which business model components are combined with functional areas. Each cell identifies a precise "business model component – functional area" couple and contains the description of how the latter contributes to the creation of value through that specific business model component. Through this structured view of the business, it is possible for managers to make a clear assessment of the company in terms of the main value enablers that characterize each functional area, thus assessing the strategic importance of their contribution to the business goals.

The second step transforms the cells of the previously defined matrix into business components, following the Component Business Model (CBM) approach, a framework developed by IBM [48] to model and analyze an enterprise through a logical representation or map of business components or "building blocks". Each business component is like a sub-organization with its own objectives, resources, and activities and provides/consumes specific business services. Components can be internal or external to the organization and are organized according to competency and accountability. Competencies are different in each enterprise and represent a high-level view of components according to the type of business value provided. They are typically aggregated under macro-families such as "manage", "design", "buy", "make" and "sell". Accountability is defined on three levels, i.e. *direct*, for components providing strategic guidance and policy; *control*, bridging the gap between the other two levels by monitoring performance and handling anomalies; and *execute*, providing actual activities and services that drive value creation. The map defined in this step provides the identification of high level and business oriented services.

The third and final step translates the previously defined business services into a full Service Oriented Architecture (SOA). The core services are identified and specified in detail with information on their interfaces and their KPI (Key Performance Indicator). The most important output of this step is a service model of the business network that leverages IT services to support and enable business services and business processes.

In brief:
➢ Analyze business requirements through the Collaborative Storytelling approach
➢ Define the service-oriented and value-driven architecture of the business network

2.3.5 Deployment Strategy

This phase aims to identify a strategy for the techno-organizational deployment of the newly designed configuration of the business network. This phase starts immediately following the design and development of the new solutions and must guide the entire business network towards the adoption of the new solutions, ensuring their effective application to the existing technical and organizational infrastructures. The deployment strategy is composed of eight main stages, each characterized by inputs (information, data and resources), outputs (results), roles (key responsibilities) and tools (technologies and methodologies to facilitate the execution of the phase).

The *first stage* aims to define plans for the techno-organizational deployment considering the results of the previous phases (techno-organizational assessment, design, development). Key roles partaking in this stage are the "boundary spanner" and the "relationship promoter", who have to align the strategy and its implementation across the network nodes.

The *second stage* aims to prepare and promote the change process through communication activities that must be fully supported and sponsored by the top management and by key referents of the organizations in order to spread the vision and the common culture to the entire business network. Mechanisms of social integration are a fundamental aspect of fostering trust-based relationships across the network.

The *third stage* has to support the transition towards the new techno-organizational configuration, guaranteeing that the right resources (tangible and intangible) are always available at the right time. This is achieved through communication tools and logistic/transportation systems that allow the efficient and effective coordination of geographically distributed enterprises.

The *fourth stage* aims to reduce the knowledge gap between users, implementing training plans. Linguistic barriers, cultural/social differences and different learning styles must be taken into account by means of advanced e-learning tools and user-friendly knowledge management systems.

The *fifth stage* is piloting the deployment to a limited part of the network or to a sub-set of the core business processes. The pilot test has the objective of identifying any criticalities that may lead to unsuccessful deployment to the entire business network.

In the *sixth stage,* the technological infrastructure and the software platform are distributed and installed. The most important aspect that must be taken into consideration is the adoption of common standards to guarantee the interoperability across the network nodes and throughout the inter-organizational business processes.

The *seventh stage* aims to strengthen the effectiveness of the new techno-organizational solutions through group and individual coaching sessions that are useful to transmit tacit and procedural knowledge to end users. Coaching activities are supported by e-learning systems, groupware and knowledge management systems. At this stage, it is fundamental to adopt specific best practices to manage the resistance to change that is frequently encountered during change management processes.

The *eight* and last stage aims to evaluate the effectiveness and efficiency of the deployment process, emphasizing successful results and promoting virtuous circles of continuous learning and best practice acquisition.

In brief:
> Plan the deployment process and promote its objectives through the top management's sponsorship
> Roll-out of the techno-organizational solution through software/hardware installation and human resources training and coaching
> Evaluate the progression of the deployment process and emphasize successful results

2.3.6 Measurement of the change impact

A crucial aspect of the methodology of change is evaluating, through *ad hoc* measures, the network performance level to describe present and future scenarios. This means considering not only financial or process measures but also re-evaluating the *concept of value* to better weigh each component of the business network (strategic, organizational, technological layer). This wider perspective grants the possibility to analyze tangible and intangible value exchanges, including knowledge exchanges across all domains of value [49].

Starting from the three levels of analysis previously described (strategic, organizational and technological) it is possible to elaborate a taxonomy of measures that consider both the specific node and the network as a whole. In particular, four main **value domains** are identified and for each different measure, the following are analyzed:

- **Business Relationships**: alliance and business relationship with customers, strategic partners, suppliers, investors, regulatory bodies and government groups;
- **Internal structure**: systems and work processes that leverage competitiveness, including IT and communication technologies;
- **Human competence**: the individual capabilities, knowledge, skills, experience and problem-solving abilities that reside in people;
- **Corporate identity/strategy**: the value of one's vision, purpose, values, ethical stance and leadership as it contributes to brand equity and economic success in business and employee relationships;

Based on the work of influential practitioners and in particular on Verna Allee [50] five groups of measures have been identified (Growth asset development, Efficiency of value conversion, Utilization, Stability, Renewal), with a few examples reported in the next table.

	Business relationships	Internal structure	Human competence	Corporate identity/strategy
Growth asset development	Growth of alliances	Number of core business services Growth of the knowledge base	Percentage with higher education Number of education/training initiatives	Leadership Training Succession planning
Efficiency of value conversion	Contacts to contracts ratio Programs to Partners ratio	Process cycle times Product/service development costs Contracts per employee	ROI from improvement ideas Number of patents per employee	Speed of decision making Number of valuable job applicants Brand recognition
Utilization	Frequency of customer contact	Utilization rate of software licenses, human resources, physical assets.	Knowledge reuse Diffusion of best practices Employee satisfaction	Levels of conformance to values Retention of valued employees
Stability	Turnover/loyalty	Codification of knowledge/processes Maturity level of core business processes	Employee Satisfaction Percentage of contingent work-ers Novice to expert ratio	Consistency of value alignment over time Level of employee awareness Conformance to value and standards Diffusion of ethics and values
Renewal	Number of new partners in the last year Number of new customers in the last year	Number of new business services in the last year Speed of change	Time in training Number of new competence domains in the last year	Frequency of revisiting values by leadership Employee involvement

Table 2.1- Examples of performance measures for business networks.

This type of classification can guide the entire change management process by supporting the identification of the proper key performance indicators and the cor-rect metrics to analyze and monitor the performance of the organizations and the business network as a whole. The approach does not exclude other widespread systems and frameworks. Balanced models consider both financial indicators and non-financial indicators. The most important models are: *Performance Measure-ment Matrix* [51], *Tableau de Bord, Balanced Scorecard* [52] and *Performance Prism* [53]. Quality Models are frameworks focusing on quality measures. The most important is the *European Foundation for Quality Management Excellence Model* (EFQM-Model). Questionnaire-Based Models are frameworks based on issuing questionnaire. The most important is the *Performance Measurement Questionnaire* [54]. Supply Chain Oriented Models are models developed to evaluate a supply chain context. The most important models are: *Lambert & Pohlen* [55], the *Beamon model*, the *Supply Chain Operations Reference Model* (SCOR), the *Hieber framework*.

In brief:
> Define and measure performance metrics to monitor the effectiveness of the change process across the different levels of the business

2.4 Conclusion

The main purpose of the methodology of change described in this chapter is to guide firms towards the Internetworked Enterprise (IE) paradigm. The concept of business organization is not conceived as a secluded entity, but as part of a wider business context in which clients, suppliers, partners and competitors interact and collaborate through ICTs and value-driven activities. The methodology leverages approaches and ideas from diverse disciplines with particular reference to Business Modeling and Enterprise Architecture, bridging the gap between the world of business managers and IT experts. For these reason, the methodology introduces the concept of innovation through three different business layers (strategic, organizational and technological) and takes into account the way the competitive environment and contingency variables influence each business organization in the definition of its strategic objectives, its organizational structure and behavior, and its technological infrastructure. The methodology is a domain-independent, modular and flexible guide for managers and business analysts facing a change management initiative towards the IE paradigm and who want to follow a structured set of guidelines to achieve the best techno-organizational configuration for their business network.

References

[1] O'Brien J. A., 2000 "Introduction to Information Systems: Essentials for the Internetworked Enterprise" McGraw-Hill Education;

[2] Tapscott D., 1996 "The digital economy" McGraw-Hill;

[3] Harreld J. B., (1998) "Building smarter, faster Organizations", in Blueprint to the digital economy (ed. by Tapscott D., Lowy A. and Ticoll D.), New York, McGraw Hill

[4] Ticoll D., Lowy A. and Kalakota R., (1998), "Joined at the bit: the emergence of the e-business community", in Blueprint to the digital economy (ed. by Tapscott D., Lowy A. and Ticoll D.), New York, McGraw Hill;

[5] Chesbrough, H. and R. S. Rosenbloom (2000). The Role of the Business Model in capturing value from Innovation: Evidence from XEROX Corporation's Technology Spinoff Companies. Boston, Massachusetts, Harvard Business School.

[6] Afuah, A., (2004), Business Models, McGrowHill

[7] Osterwalder A., et al., (2005), Clarifying Business Models: Origins, Present, and Future of the Concept, Communication of AIS, Vol. 15.

[8] Zachman J.A. (1987) "A framework for information system architecture" in IBM Systems Journal, vol 26, No. 3

[9] Sowa J.F., Zachman J.A. (1992). Extending and formalizing the framework for information systems architecture. In IBM Systems Journal vol 31, No. 3

[10] Duncan, R. 1972. *Characteristics of organizational environments and perceived environmental uncertainty.* Administrative Science Quarterly: 313 - 327.

[11] Drazin, R. & Van De Ven, A. 1985. Alternative forms of fit in contingency theory. Administrative Science Quarterly, 30: 514 – 539.

[12] Venkatraman, N. 1989. The concept of fit in strategy research: Toward verbal and statistical correspondence. Academy of Management Review, 14(3): 432 – 444.

[13] Achrol, R.S., Reve, T. & Stern, L. W. The environment of marketing channel dyads: A framework for comparative analysis, Journal of Marketing, 47 Fall, pp.55-67; 1983.

[14] Ford, David, Gadde, Lars-Erik, Hakansson, Hakan & Snehota, Ivan (2002) Managing networks, IMP annual conference, Perth Australia, 2002.

[15] Kaplan, R. S. and Norton, D. P., "*The Balanced Scorecard – Measures that Drive Performance*", Harvard Business Review, Vol. 70, No. 1, 1992, pp. 71-79.

[16] Osterwalder, A. (2004). "Understanding ICT-Based Business Models in Developing Countries." International Journal of Innovation and Technology and Management IJITM.

[17] Friedman A. L., Miles (2002). Developing Stakeholder Theory. Journal of Management Studies, Vol. 39, pp. 1-21, 2002

[18] Kahle, L. R., D. M. Boush, et al. (2000). Good Morning, Vietnam: An Ethical Analysis of Nike Activities in Southeast Asia. Sport Marketing Quarterly 9(1): 43-52.

[19] Moore, G. A. (1999). Crossing the chasm: marketing and selling high-tech products to mainstream customers. New York, HarperBusiness.

[20] Burns, T. & Stalker, G. M. (1961) *The Management of Innovation.* Tavistock, London.

[21] Woodward, J. 1965. Industrial organization: Theory and practise. London: Oxford University Press.

[22] Ackoff R. (1986), Management in Small Doses, Wiley, New York.

[23] Porter, M.E. (1985) Competitive Advantage, Free Press, New York, 1985

[24] Mitchell, J. Clyde (1969), Social Networks in Urban Situations. Manchester.

[25] Sabel, C.F. (1993), "Constitutional Ordering in Historical Context," in Games in Hierarchies and Networks, F.W. Scharpf, Ed. Frankfurt/M.: Campus.

[26] Konsynski, B.R. (1993). Strategic control in the extended enterprise. IBM Systems Journal Vol. 32 No. 1, pp. 111–142.

[27] Korczynski, 1994. M. Korczynski, Low trust and opportunism in action: evidence on inter-firm relations from the British engineering construction industry. *Journal of Industry Studies* 1 2 (1994), pp. 43–63.

[28] Teubner, R. A. (2003), "Grundlegung Informationsmanagement," in Working Paper Series of the Department of Information Systems, University of Munster, Working Paper No. 91. Munster.

[29] Wigand, R. T., A. Picot, and R. Reichwald (1997), Information, organization and management: Expanding markets and corporate boundaries. New York: John Wiley.

[30] Brynjolfsson, E. (2003), "The IT Productivity Gap," Optimize, 21.

[31] Timmers, P. (1998). "Business Models for Electronic Markets." Journal on Electronic Markets 8(2): 3-8

[32] Rappa, M. (2001). Managing the digital enterprise - Business models on the Web, North Carolina State University. 2002.

[33] Weill, P. and M. R. Vitale (2001). Place to space: Migrating to eBusiness Models. Boston, Harvard Business School Press.

[34] Chesbrough, H. and R. S. Rosenbloom (2000). The Role of the Business Model in capturing value from Innovation: Evidence from XEROX Corporation's Technology Spinoff Companies. Boston, Massachusetts, Harvard Business School.

[35] Hamel, G. (2000). Leading the revolution. Boston, Harvard Business School Press.

[36] Linder, J. and S. Cantrell (2000). Changing Business Models: Surveying the Landscape, Accenture Institute for Strategic Change.

[37] Amit, R. and C. Zott (2001). "Value creation in e-business." Strategic Management Journal 22(6- 7): 493-520.

[38] Applegate, L. M. (2001). E-business Models: Making sense of the Internet business landscape. Information Technology and the Future Enterprise: New Models for Managers. G. Dickson, W. Gary and G. DeSanctis. Upper Saddle River, N.J., Prentice Hall.

[39] Gordijn, J. (2002). Value-based Requirements Engineering - Exploring Innovative e-Commerce Ideas. Amsterdam, NL, Vrije Universiteit.

[40] Afuah, A. and C. Tucci (2003). Internet Business Models and Strategies. Boston, McGraw Hill

[41] Borst, P. (1997). "Construction of engineering Ontologies for Knowledge Sharing and Reuse. Enschede, NL, Universiteit Twente.

[42] Akkermans, J.M.,Z. Baida, et al. (2004). "Value Webs: Using ontologies to Bundle Real-World Services." IEEE Intelligent Systems 19(4): 57-66.

[43] Kaplan, R. S. and D. P. Norton (1992). The balanced scorecard--measures that drive performance. Harvard Business Review 70(1).

[44] Markides C. (1999). All the Right Moves. Boston, Harvard Business School Press.

[45] Bagchi, S. and B. Tulskie (2000). e-business Models: Integrating Learning from Strategy Development Experiences and Empirical Research. 20th Annual International Conference of the Strategic Management Society, Vancouver.

[46] Kambil, A., A. Ginsberg, et al. (1997). Rethinking Value Propositions. New York, NYU Center for Research on Information Systems.

[47] Gordijn J and Akkermans H (2003). Value based requirements engineering: Exploring innovative e-commerce idea". vol. 8(2):114-134, 200," In Requirements Engineering Journal, vol. 8, pp. 114–134.

[48] IBM Business Consulting Services (2005). Component Business Model. http://www-935.ibm.com/services/us/imc/pdf/g510-6163-component-business-models.pdf

[49] Allee V. (2000). The Value evolution. Addressing larger implications of an intellectual capital and intangibles perspective. Journal of Intellectual Capital, Vol 1 No 1,2000, pp 17-32.

[50] Allee V. (1999). The art and practice of being a revolutionary. Journal of Knowledge Management.

[51] Keegan, D.P., Eiler, R.G. and Jones, C.R. (1989), ``Are your performance measures obsolete?'', Management Accounting, June, pp. 45-50.

[52] R.S. Kaplan, D.P. Norton, "The Balanced Scorecard: translating strategy into action", Harvard Business School Press, Boston, 1996.

[53] C.Adams, A.Neely, M.Kennerly, (2000) .Performance Prism: The Scorecard for Measuring and Managing Stakeholder Relationships, Prentice Hall, Financial Time.

[54] Dixon, J.R., Nanni, A.J. and Vollmann, T.E. (1990), The New Performance Challenge - Measuring Operations for World-class Competition, Dow Jones-Irwin, Homewood, IL.

[55] D. M. Lambert, T. L. Pohlen, "Supply Chain Metrics", The International Journal of Logistics Management, Vol. 12, No. 1, pp. 1-19, 2001.

Chapter 3 - A network-oriented business modeling environment

Cristian Bisconti[1], Davide Storelli[1], Salvatore Totaro[1], Francesco Arigliano[2], Vincenzo Savarino[2], Claudia Vicari[2]

[1] eBMS S.S. ISUFI – University of Salento

[2] Engineering Ingegneria Informatica S.p.A.

Abstract - The development of formal models related to the organizational aspects of an enterprise is fundamental when these aspects must be re-engineered and digitalized, especially when the enterprise is involved in the dynamics and value flows of a business network. Business modeling provides an opportunity to synthesize and make business processes, business rules and the structural aspects of an organization explicit, allowing business managers to control their complexity and guide an enterprise through effective decisional and strategic activities. This chapter discusses the main results of the TEKNE project in terms of software components that enable enterprises to configure, store, search and share models of any aspects of their business while leveraging standard and business-oriented technologies and languages to bridge the gap between the world of business people and IT experts and to foster effective business-to-business collaborations.

3.1 Introduction

The growing importance of the Internet and ICTs in organizations is leading to the creation and definition of new organizational models with increasingly blurred boundaries. New concepts such as Cybermediary [1] [2] [3], imaginary organization [4] and virtual organization [5] [6] have emerged. In particular, technology has become a fundamental enabler in supporting enterprises in the adoption of the *Internetworked Enterprise* organizational paradigm, defined by Tapscott [7] as:

"The basic functional unit of an industry environment. It relies on internetworked, knowledge-based systems to enhance its capacity to learn, be agile, and respond quickly to customer requirements. It collaborates and competes (emphasis added) in industry environments and e-business communities often in several EBCs at once. It embraces digital strategies for developing products and services and for renewing relationships with customers and suppliers".

G. Passiante (ed.), *Evolving Towards the Internetworked Enterprise: Technological and Organizational Perspectives*, DOI 10.1007/978-1-4419-7279-8_3,

The essential element that enables "Internetworked" enterprises to operate effectively is the possibility to collaborate without constraints and in real-time through the Internet and the World Wide Web [8]. The transition process towards an Internet-based infrastructure and thus towards an Internetworked Enterprise organizational paradigm clearly requires considerable effort and strong commitment by the top management, focused on clear and shared strategic objectives. In this perspective, the TEKNE project defined a methodology that guides enterprises through the transition process towards the IE model, taking into account strategic, operative and technological issues (see Chapter 2).

In this chapter we focus on the fact that enterprises, in order to digitalize their businesses, have to invest resources on activities related to modeling business processes (both inter and intra organizational) and to reconfiguring their value-network based on their specializations and on the network needs. New skills and competencies are required on both a technological and managerial level and new technologies must be introduced to enable and foster collaborations with other strategic network partners. The development of models related to the organizational aspects of an enterprise is fundamental when these aspects must be re-engineered and digitalized, especially if the enterprise is involved in the dynamics and value flows of a business network. Business modeling provides an opportunity to synthesize and make business processes, business rules and the structural aspects of an organization explicit, allowing business managers to control their complexity and guide an enterprise through effective decisional and strategic activities. Modeling languages play a fundamental role in helping to understand and share ideas and concepts across different organizations and between people with different cultural and professional backgrounds. Modeling languages should be designed to be easily used and understood and standard languages should be adopted in order to take full advantage of their outcome in terms of interoperability, accuracy and shared understanding among stakeholders.

3.2 Business Modeling

Business Modeling can be defined as the art of representing the enterprise in terms of its strategy, organization and operations (e.g. objectives, processes, behavior, activities, information, object and material flows, resources and organization units, system infrastructure and architectures), making the facts and the knowledge that add value to the enterprise explicit. Given the diversity and heterogeneous nature of these aspects, defining a unique and omni-comprehensive representation of a business is impossible; however, several models are available to show the different perspectives and levels of detail of the organization. These models have been systematized [9] in a conceptual framework defining 30 categories and organized as a matrix. The six columns represent *abstractions*, namely, 6 different aspects that can be modeled in answer to the following questions: What are the essential elements of the organization? How does the organization works? Where are the organization's plants located? Who does what in the organization? When do relevant events happen in the organization? Why are decisions taken with respect to the organization? The five rows of the matrix represent *perspectives*, namely, points of view on the abstractions. Thus, the perspective of a business analyst is different from that of a business manager and the perspective of a software engineer is different from that of a developer. Similarly, the OMG defined in the MDA[1] (Model Driven Architecture) approach not only divides the different models into levels of abstraction but also provides mechanisms for model-to-model (M2M) transformation across levels, allowing the (semi)automatic production of software systems whose functionalities can be easily traced back to business requirements. The key purpose of business modeling is not only in terms of improved enterprise integration but also to support the analysis of an enterprise, and more specifically, to represent and understand how the enterprise works, to capitalize on the acquired knowledge and know-how for subsequent reuse, to design and redesign a part of the enterprise, to simulate the behavior of the enterprise, to make better decisions or to control, coordinate and monitor some parts of the enterprise. Business Modeling techniques and associated languages are very important and useful to support new approaches to enterprise business transformation and improvement, developing smart and new networked organizations.

In terms of business modeling, the aim of the TEKNE project is to develop a set of software components that enable enterprises to configure, store, search and share models of any aspects of their business, leveraging standard and business-oriented technologies and languages in order to bridge the gap between the world of business people and IT experts and to foster effective business-to-business collaborations. The TEKNE project adopts and contributes to the definition of international standard modeling languages, with particular reference to those specified by the OMG and by its Business Modeling & Integration DTF. Moreover, the project, in the absence of standards, identifies the most interesting approaches that have been proposed in scientific and industrial literature. According to the MDA approach adopted by the "Methodology of Change" (see Chapter 2), companies are modeled on different levels of abstractions, progressively spanning from strategies and business objectives to enabling technological services.

The CIM (Computation Independent Model) level defines the conceptual elements that underpin an organization's business environment (stakeholders, resources, etc.) and provides a business-oriented representation of an organization's business model. At this level, SBVR (Semantic of Business Vocabulary and Business Rules), e3-value models and high-level BPMN models are used. The PIM (Platform Independent Model) level describes the business processes and the organizational structure/behaviors of the enterprise through detailed BPMN (Business Process Modeling Notation) diagrams. The PSM (Platform Specific Model)

---

[1] OMG: MDA Guide V1.0.1 - http://www.omg.org/cgi-bin/doc?omg/03-06-01

level leverages XPDL (XML Process Definition Language) models to define the technological services and their orchestration/choreography.

In this context, the primary aim of TEKNE is to define and develop a framework to allow modeling the business on a CIM level, focusing on SBVR and on the specification of a collaborative approach to the composition of business vocabularies and business rules. Indeed, vocabularies and business rules are the cornerstone any other model of the business since they provide the semantic base that must be shared amongst them.

3.3 SBVR Modeling Tool

The ever growing need of communication and information sharing within distributed enterprises and in the context of any value network demands an effective means of sharing a common understanding of the terms and expressions used. This is especially true in those industrial sectors that involve hundreds of actors in the implementation of the final product (aerospace, automotive, etc.) who speak different languages and belong to different cultural contexts. In particular, the complexity of the requirements, constraints and interdependencies that guide the highly dynamic configuration of a value network must be clearly understood and interpreted by all parties in order to achieve effective collaborations. In every type of organization, enterprise information systems are responsible for managing data in order to sustain day-to-day activities and decisions. All documents, processes, rules, etc. (common explicit knowledge) and the experience that people acquire through participation in business activities (personal tacit knowledge) constitute the organization's knowledge base. Information systems should reflect and operate according to this knowledge since it represents the actual structure and behaviors of the enterprise [10]. In particular, business vocabularies [11] and business rules [12] [13] [14] are key features enabling the formal definition of fundamental information on the organization and its core characteristics. Global competitiveness and the rapid changes of business requirements and business models characterize current scenarios and future trends. Consequently, information systems should support these unpredictable dynamics through a flexible and business-oriented approach that allows the organization to be increasingly modified according to sudden needs through an integrated and dynamic reconfiguration of business rules, processes and services. The major difficulties of this approach derive from two types of issues.

The first concerns business knowledge gathering and management in the current knowledge-based economy [15] [16] [10]. This knowledge is usually distributed (sometimes scattered) redundantly and inconsistently across a variety of information systems in the form of documents, executable codes or, in the worst case, people's built-in tacit knowledge [17]. Externalization and sharing of this knowledge is fundamental to ensure and maintain competitive advantage, especially when human resources leave [18]. Business vocabularies enable capturing and sharing many aspects of tacit knowledge, classifying and defining what the organization collectively knows pertains to its business. Vocabularies can be leveraged, for example, to facilitate communication with partners and stakeholders, to identify and make concepts for an academic class clear, to give semantic foundations to the requirement specifications of an Information System, to share a common understanding of the enterprise's guiding principle within an organization, etc. However, vocabularies are not the solution to every problem related to knowledge sharing. Indeed, it is a fact that two people spontaneously choose the same word to designate the same concept with a probability of less than a 20% [19]. This strongly limits the effectiveness of vocabulary-driven interactions, especially when vocabularies are defined, chosen or composed by a limited number of people and when these people do not represent the end users. Moreover, the proliferation of many specialized and heterogeneous (based on different metamodels) vocabularies is a primary source of difficulty for vocabulary developers who must be able to reconcile this conceptual complexity through error prone and long-term work.

The second issue concerns the availability of ICT solutions that enable the implementation of highly configurable and quickly modifiable services and processes to allow their direct coupling with actual business requirements. In this context, the emerging trend focuses on the logical separation of process and business rules, while allowing their modular and dynamic composition [20]. XBeaver is a web-based tool that supports knowledge capturing and management in the form of business vocabularies and business rules, with particular regard to the idea that a top-down and collaborative approach is necessary both to explicitly clarify knowledge and to develop a software architecture capable of overcoming the vocabulary issue outlined above. A highly collaborative and concept-centric (not word-centric) approach would lead to faster and more robust vocabulary and guidance development and thus to better inter/intra enterprise knowledge sharing and interactions.

3.3.1 Overview of SBVR

The use of a semantic metamodel based on a widely accepted standard is a primary requirement for coherently handling the proliferation of vocabularies that currently characterize any organization at any level. SBVR is a publicly available OMG (Object Management Group) specification released in January 2008 that formalizes a metamodel for business vocabularies and business rule modeling. It is the most important and innovative endeavor thus far addressing these issues and has obtained great consensus from both the scientific and industrial communities. Indeed, SBVR has been synthesized from four disciplines: Natural-language and Terminology Science, Fact-oriented Modeling in Formal Logic, Linguistics, Business Consultancy [21]. Its key and distinctive characteristics make it an appropriate solution for the issues outlined in the previous section. Among these characteristics, it is worth recalling that SBVR identifies the concept of community as the basis for any business vocabulary. In particular, the concept of *semantic community* is distinguished from that of *speech community*, where the former is defined as a "community whose unifying characteristic is a shared understanding (perception) of the things that they have to deal with", and the latter as a "subcommunity of a given semantic community whose unifying characteristic is the vocabulary and language that it uses"[2]. Examples of communities that are of fundamental importance from a business perspective are enterprises, industries in which enterprises operate, partner enterprises, standard groups, regulatory authorities, etc. The set of guiding concepts and elements endowed with shared understanding in a given semantic community is called *body of shared meaning*. SBVR separates the body of shared meaning from the signifiers used to represent (exchange, discuss and validate) its elements, allowing different speech communities to share the same semantics, while preserving their own way of representing it using vocabularies expressed in their natural language, in artificial languages such as UML, or in subsets of natural languages such as those used in healthcare or finance.

3.3.2 The conceptual architecture of the SBVR modeling tool

The proposed architecture is a three-tier solution that enables collaboration in business vocabulary and business rule development with the aim of formalizing and externalizing business knowledge. The architecture has a web interface to share a common knowledge base and to collaboratively edit business vocabularies and rule sets according to the SBVR metamodel and mark-up rules.

The following are the main elements of the architecture:

- a centralized repository (knowledge base) that maintains shared vocabularies and rule sets;
- a server-side web application for collaborative knowledge base development and maintenance;
- a light client-side application based on an AJAX (Asynchronous JavaScript and XML) framework.

Repository: the centralized repository is a key element in our approach to satisfy a double meaning of the concept "knowledge sharing": (*i*) allow people involved in a specific business domain to access knowledge, (*ii*) generally accept knowledge and make a community converge towards a unique and shared interpretation of that knowledge. The repository maintains dictionaries and rule sets through a rela-

---

[2] OMG, "Semantic of Business Vocabularies and Rules" http://www.omg.org/spec/SBVR/ , 2008.

tional data base management system and allows their exporting by means of other standard interchange formats (e.g. XMI, OWL).

Server-side: the server-side of the architecture provides core functionalities to fulfill collaboration requirements, providing the basic vocabulary and management of rule sets. In particular, this architecture level provides the following modules:

- an AJAX engine to enable asynchronous interaction with the client-side;
- a collaboration toolkit to provide the collaboration and communication functionalities that fulfill the requirements listed above;
- an SBVR compliant model to support in-memory representation of vocabularies and rule sets;
- a text analyzer for the recognition of the text introduced by the users. This module leverages the user's input and a transformation algorithm in order to populate SBVR models;
- an exchange module to manage the import and export of vocabularies and rules sets translating them into standard interchange formats such as XMI and allowing interoperability with external tools.

Client-side: the client-side of the system is based on a web interface that adopts the AJAX approach. This choice is of fundamental importance since it enables users to collaborate in a ubiquitous, cooperative and concurrent way. Moreover, the asynchronous communication enabled by an AJAX infrastructure between the server and the client side, guarantees the feasibility of an effective and user-friendly interface through special features such as dynamic support for vocabulary and rule definition based on information already existing in the knowledge base.

3.4 Distributed model repository

The management of any kind of electronic artifact requires the availability of a logical place to store, classify, search and retrieve its instances. This place, given the Internetworked Enterprise approach, should not be closed and isolated, allowing the disclosure of some sections of its contents to a sub-set of the business network, thus enabling partners and legitimately interested stakeholders to access and leverage these artifacts. This section describes the repository defined in the TEKNE project to allow value-network enterprises to manage their models and, when necessary, access models published by other enterprises.

General Purpose
The management and modeling of different organizational aspects entails the possibility of handling the conceptual elements that these aspects are based on in a transparent and integrated way. Hence, the necessity to design a general-purpose repository, able to maintain any kind of metamodel considered useful for the management of an organization from an IE perspective. The management of models related to business processes, business rules, organizational structures and any-

thing related to these aspects and of interest to business managers, requires the definition of a conceptual and technological framework that supports the fundamental elements and the essential relationships amongst them in a flexible way.

Distributed
A repository for the management of business models in the context of value-networks must necessarily entail the possibility to share information and models on the enterprises of a business network and on the interactions they are capable of. From this perspective, the nature of the IE paradigm must be reflected by the repository in terms of mechanisms and model management systems that are abstracted from their physical location and that allow network actors to interact in a transparent and cooperation-driven way.

Secure
The need to share information on processes and business rules must not entail security and privacy risks for the organizations nor in terms of their competitive advantage. Publication of information must be limited to those aspects that are essential and sufficient for effective interaction with specific partners and stakeholders.

The reference requirements for the development of the repository architecture take into account some factors directly derived from the project goals and others resulting from the opportunity to adopt standard approaches to guarantee the highest interoperability with third party development environments. Given the open and blurred nature of the boundaries of the Internetworked Enterprise and the need to share models and concepts that characterize the processes of each organization in a controlled way, requires the repository to be distributed. This means that any enterprise in a business network, if supported by the repository, has the possibility to publish its models and access those of partners and stakeholders. These requirements are addressed by adopting a standard approach (MOF) to business modeling and its organizational aspect by defining a conceptual architecture of the repository that supports this approach, and lastly, by developing a search/retrieval system to create a network of repositories.

3.4.1 MOF foundation of the repository

In the context of the TEKNE project, it is important to choose business-modeling languages that are as diffused and acknowledged as possible. This requirement leads to the adoption of standard languages that can represent the different aspects that characterize the enterprises in a clear, unambiguous and simple way. Standard languages defined by the OMG are actually the best choice for three main reasons:

- this set of standards will soon entirely cover the modeling needs of the Enterprise Architecture;
- OMG is composed of the main software vendors in the world, and these enterprises are very interested in the actual diffusion and use of OMG's standards;
- The conceptual infrastructure of OMG's standards are built upon the most advanced, widespread and supported framework available for business modeling.

In particular, the business modeling languages defined by the OMG are built on a common metamodel: the Meta Object Facility (MOF). More precisely, MOF is considered a meta-metamodel since it provides the concepts and facilities necessary to define abstract syntaxes (metamodels). These abstract syntaxes are instantiated in order to represent models of certain aspect of the real world. For clarification of the model and metamodel concepts please refer to Table 3.1, which provides a description of the four architectural levels of metamodels.

Level	Description	Example
M0	Data/instances	A record in a database table, instances of Java classes ("abc" i san instance of class java.lang.String)
M1	Metadata/Models	Tables and columns in a database, concrete classes, methods and attributes, (java.lang.String is an instance of Class, intended as an element of Java language)
M2	Meta-metadata/ meta-models/ languages	The description of the concept "database" (definition of Table, Schema, Column, etc.), description of language constructs (definition of the concept "Class" and its elements)
M3	Meta-metamodel	MOF

Table 3.1 - Architectural levels of a MOF-based modeling framework.

MOF is the semantic and syntactic foundation of all modeling languages adopted in the TEKNE project. Hence, the development of a distributed repository for effective life-cycle management of any kind of model (e.g. BPMN, SBVR) must consider MOF and that developed in terms of MOF-based modeling. The repository is originally placed at level M3 because it provides generic MOF implementation, but in order to be actually used, the repository has to be initialized through specific metamodels, thus shifting to level M2. This initialization procedure is called *Repository Initialization* and is based on standard features of MOF-based frameworks. In particular, the repository will enable the import of MOF-based metamodels specified in standard XMI format, automatically generating the corresponding classes and automatically providing a supporting infrastructure for their management. After a metamodel has been defined and imported in the repository, it is possible for users to create models based on its elements, thus shifting the repository from level M2 to level M1. The repository provides a set of APIs and facilities that enable web-based modeling tools to instantiate and manage the classes of this metamodel and graphically represent their meaning. The creation of new models can be thought of as the *population phase* of the repository.

3.4.2 The conceptual architecture of the model repository

The conceptual architecture proposed by the TEKNE project for the model repository defines a modeling ecosystem that is composed of three fundamental parts: model repositories at the centre of the ecosystem and organized as a network (each repository belongs to an organization), MOF-based modeling tools that enable users to create, edit and manage models stored in the repositories, and an authentication and authorization system that controls and manages access levels to models.

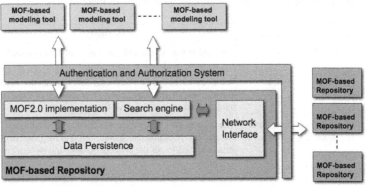

Fig. 3.1 - Conceptual architecture of the model repository

In synthesis, the repository can be divided into four different components, each characterized by specific functionalities.

- **MOF2 Implementation**: amongst the facilities defined by the MOF2 specification, this component provides those considered essential for the distributed model repository. Firstly, the MOF2 implementation must allow importing/exporting models and metamodels in the XML format. Versioning is another important feature that this component must support in close conjunction with managing the models' lifecycle states. In order to enable generic modeling tools to access the system, it is hoped that the model classes are reflective, namely, that they expose their metadata in a MOF compliant way. Another desirable functionality is the support of a language that is compliant with the QVT (Query/View/Transformation) specification.

- **Data Persistence**: the data persistence component is responsible for the persistent storing of models and metamodels. Here different storage system technologies can be used, from the RDBMS (Relational Data Base Management System) to the XML Database, from the file system to the object-oriented database.

- **Search engine**: the search engine enables users to search the local repository and/or the networked repository system with respect to semantic and metadata-based criteria. The search engine interacts with the Data Persistence component for local searches and with the Network Interface component for searches that span the entire network of model repositories.
- **Network Interface**: this component provides access to the networked repositories, allowing transparent interchange of data between them to enable network-wide model searches.

3.4.3 Query/View/Transformation

The possibility to specify and execute queries, views and transformations on models is a key feature of MOF environments and of the MDA approach. Given a network of enterprises, it is usual that they adopt different modeling languages for the same problem (e.g. XPDL, Bpel, jBPM, UML, for representing processes). The proposed model repository is designed to support any type of MOF-based metamodel in order to satisfy the needs of the different enterprises that make-up a network. The co-existence of models referring to different metamodels requires a way to translate these models to make them interoperable. Model-to-model transformation allows not only moving from one MDA level to another, but also enables users to translate models from one specific language to another, subsequent to the definition of ad-hoc mappings. For example, direct transformations between the various process metamodels (XPDL, BPEL, jBPL, UML Activity Diagram, etc.) can be defined to allow organizations to preserve their modeling assets (tools, existing models, competencies) and simultaneously interact with the rest of the business network. The easiest and most effective way to transform models from one language to another is to choose a language and define bi-directional transformations from all the other languages. In the business process modeling field, for example, we propose BPDM as the central language. Every other language that defines a bi-directional transformation to BPDM will automatically be part of a translation system that requires at most two steps to move from one representation to any other (supported by the system).

3.5 Search and retrieval system

An Information Retrieval System (IRS) is a system capable of storing, retrieving and maintaining information. In this context, information can be composed of text (including numeric and date data), images, audio, video and other multi-media objects. An IRS usually consists of a software program that facilitates finding the information the user needs. The system can use standard computer hardware or specialized hardware to support the search function. The success of an IRS depends on how well it can minimize the user's effort in finding the information required. From the user's point of view, the effort is the time required to find the information needed, excluding the time to actually read the relevant data. Minimizing the user's effort to locate the information needed is the main goal of an IRS. This effort can be expressed by the time a user spends in all the steps leading up to reading an item containing the information needed (e.g. query generation, query execution, scanning results of query to select items to read, reading non-relevant items). The success of an IRS is very subjective. Under certain circumstances, the information needed can be defined as all the information in the system that relates to a user's needs. In other cases, it can be defined as sufficient information in the system to complete a task, allowing for missed data. For example, a financial advisor recommending the billion-dollar purchase of another company needs to be sure that all the relevant and significant information on the target company has been located and reviewed when writing the recommendation. On the other hand, a student may only require sufficient references for a research paper to satisfy the teacher's expectations, which are never all-inclusive. The two key measures usually associated with IRS are precision and recall. When a user decides to issue a search looking for information on a topic, the total database is logically divided into four segments: relevant retrieved, relevant not retrieved, non-relevant retrieved, not-relevant not retrieved. The relevant items are those documents that contain information that help the searcher to answer his question. Non-relevant items are those items that do not provide any directly useful information. Precision and Recall are defined as:

Precision = (Number of Retrieved Relevant items)/(Number of Total Retrieved items)

Recall = (Number of Retrieved Relevant items)/(Number of Possible Retrieved items)

Precision measures an aspect of information retrieval overhead for a user associated with a particular search. If a search has 55% precision, then 45% of the user effort is overhead reviewing non-relevant items. Recall measures how well a system processing a particular query is able to retrieve the relevant items that the user is interested in. The main goal of an IRS is to support user search generation. The ambiguities inherent in languages often limit the user's ability to express what information is needed and the differences between the user's vocabulary corpus and that of the authors of the item in the database. Natural languages suffer from word ambiguities such as homographs and the use of acronyms that allow the same word to have multiple meanings. Many users have difficulties in generating a good search statement. The typical user does not have significant experience to formulate Boolean logic statements, typically used in databases. Today it is usual to use an natural language based query, but the completeness of the user specification is limited by the user's willingness to construct long natural language queries. Moreover, the user is often not an expert in the area being searched and lacks the domain specific vocabulary unique to that particular subject area. The limited knowledge of the vocabulary associated with a particular area leads to using inaccurate and, in some cases, misleading search terms. If a user is an expert in the area being searched, the ability to select the proper search terms is constrained by lack of knowledge of the author's vocabulary. Thus, an IRS must provide tools to help overcome the search specification problems discussed above.

Latent Semantic Indexing (LSI)

Information is typically retrieved by literally matching the terms in documents with those in a query. However, lexical matching methods can be inaccurate when used to match a user's query. As there are usually many ways to express a given concept (synonymy), the literal terms in a user's query may not match those of a relevant document. In addition, since most words have multiple meanings (polysemy) the terms in a user's query will literally match terms in non-relevant documents. A better approach would be to allow users to retrieve information based on a conceptual topic or meaning of a document. Latent Semantic Indexing (LSI) (Deerwester et Al. 1990) tries to overcome the problems of lexical matching by using statistically derived conceptual indices instead of individual words for retrieval. LSI assumes that there is some underlying or latent structure in word usage that is partially obscured by the variability in word selection. A truncated singular value decomposition (SVD) is used to estimate the structure in word usage across documents. Retrieval is then performed using the database of singular values and vectors obtained from the truncated SVD. Performance data shows that these statistically derived vectors are more robust indicators of meaning than individual terms.

Advantages and disadvantages of using LSI

The assumption in LSI is that these new dimensions are a better representation of documents and queries. The metaphor underlying the term "latent" is that these new dimensions are the true representation. This true representation was then obscured by a generation process that expressed a particular dimension with one set of words in some documents and a different set of words in another document. LSI analysis recovers the original semantic structure of the space and its original dimensions. The principal advantages of using LSI are related to the synonymy, polysemy and term dependence problems. Synonymy refers to the fact that the same underlying concept can be described with different terms. Traditional retrieval strategies have trouble discovering documents on the same topic that use a different vocabulary. In LSI, the concept in question, as well as all documents related to it, is likely to be represented by a similar weighted combination of indexing variables. Polysemy describes words that have more than one meaning, which is a common property of language. Large numbers of polysemous words in the query can significantly reduce the precision of a search. By using a reduced representation in LSI, one hopes to remove some noise from the data, which could be described as the rare and less important use of certain terms. The traditional vector space model assumes term independence and terms serve as the orthogonal basis vectors of the vector space. Since there are strong associations between terms in language, this assumption is never satisfied. While term independence represents the most reasonable first-order approximation, it should be possible to obtain improved performance by using term associations in the retrieval process. Adding common phrases as search items is a simple application of this approach. On the other hand, the LSI factors are orthogonal by definition, and terms are positioned in the reduced space in a way that reflects correlations in their use across documents. The disadvantages are related to storage and efficiency problems. One could also argue that the SVD representation is more compact. Many documents have more than 150 unique terms. Thus, the sparse vector representation will take up more storage space than the compact SVD representation if we reduce it to 150 dimensions. In reality, the opposite is actually true. For example, the document by term matrix for the Cranfield collection used in Hull's experiments had 90,441 non-zero entries (after stemming and stop word removal). Retaining only 100 of the possible 1399 LSI vectors requires storing 139,900 values for the documents alone. The term vectors require the storage of roughly 400,000 additional values. In addition, the LSI values are real numbers while the original term frequencies are integers, adding to the storage costs. In using LSI vectors, we can no longer take advantage of the fact that each term occurs in a limited number of documents, which accounts for the sparse nature of the term by document matrix. With recent advances in electronic storage media, the storage requirements of LSI are not a critical problem, but the loss of sparseness has other, more serious implications. One of the most important speed-ups in vector space search comes from using an inverted index. As a consequence, only documents that have some terms in common with the query must be examined during the search. With LSI, however, the query must be compared to every document in the collection. However, several factors can reduce or eliminate this drawback. If the query has more terms than its representation in the LSI vector space, then inner product similarity scores will take more time to compute in term space. For example, if relevance feedback is conducted using the full text of the relevant documents, the number of terms in the query is likely to grow to many times the number of LSI vectors, leading to a corresponding increase in search time. In addition, using a data structure such as the k-d tree in conjunction with LSI would greatly speed the search for the nearest neighbors, provided only a partial ordering of the documents is required. Most of the additional costs come about in the pre-processing stage when the SVD and the k-d tree are computed, and actual search time should not be significantly degraded.

Extending SQL for LSI

The level of maturity of Latent Semantic Analysis (LSA) algorithms and the extent to which they can be useful, support the opportunity to implement them in a Database Management System (DBMS) by using the SQL syntax. This paper presents the implementation of a framework that enables the use of the LSA technique in an Open-Source Relational Database Manipulation System as PostgreSQL. The issues related to Information Retrieval tools and Relational Database integration have long been debated within the scientific community due to the very large number of application fields. Accordingly, many different approaches have been proposed to deal with these issues. The huge amount of available unstructured documents brought researchers to investigate tools and develop methodologies to improve efficiency and to automate information retrieval systems.

Nearly all existing DBMS's have a full-text search system, but sometimes lexical matching methods can be inaccurate when they are used to match a user's query. The existence of synonymies or polysemous words in the documents makes it possible for terms in a user's query to literally match terms within non-relevant documents. Naturally, it would be better for users to retrieve information based on a conceptual topic or meaning of a document. The LSA technique (Furnas et al. 1988) tries to overcome these problems by using statistical indexing of documents. The authors present the early results of this integration, specifically the attempt to integrate in PostgreSQL the functionalities of LSA extending SQL language. This kind of integration focuses the LSA technique application's opportunity as an additional autonomous means of information retrieval through simple SQL commands. Whilst we already have the availability of full-text search functionality in PostgreSQL DBMS, with this test we can use both together. The framework introduced was developed on PostgreSQL DBMS, chosen for its level of diffusion in a scientific and enterprise context due to its support of several programming languages such as C. The integration of the LSA technique in the SQL language standard requires the construction of a new data type, differing from primitive data already present in PostgreSQL. This data type is tailored to store all the information related to the document. In particular, for each document, we need to know the number of lexemes, their position within the document and their length. In the case presented, this information is embedded in a structure written in C language. We store the lexemes in a memory block that is contiguous to its structure. The new data type is called LSAVector, where we can store all the information related to a document belonging to a specific Knowledge Base (KB). An LSAVector is basically an ordered map that associates a value, namely the occurrence of a specific word in a specific document, with a key, namely, the word that we are considering. For example, if d1 is a document in which there are only the terms alfa, beta, gamma and delta, the s1 LSAVector associated with d1 is a map with alfa, beta, gamma, delta keys and s1[gamma] = 3 indicating that in d1 the term gamma appears three times.

Application example

As an example, consider using this framework to index and search, via a natural language process, the same kind of document whose source could be a web site, ftp server, file system or samba server. We assume that a crawler takes .doc, .ppt, .pdf, .html files from these sources, strips documents by structure information and places their terms within a simple text field database. Moreover, we assume a simple table, as shown in Table 3.2, which has the following fields:

- ID: is a numeric value used as a primary key
- corpus: is the result of the crawler's strip of the information structure during document capture
- fileName: stores the document's name and path
- fileType: stores the type of document captured by the crawler
- sourceName: stores the name of the source where the crawler captured the document.

This simple table suggests that there are several ways to perform a search on this document. Naturally, we can perform a full-text search on the corpus field or on fileName field. We can apply a filter on the file type but we can also undertake a search by semantic. We can use several different groups of documents for our KBs and there is no reason to suggest using all records in the "documents" table.

ID	Corpora	File Name	File Type	Source Name
1	Correlation between maternal and fetal plasma levels of glucose and free fatty acids. Correlation coefficients have been determined between the levels of glucose and ffa in maternal and fetal plasma collected at delivery. Significant correlations were obtained between the maternal and fetal glucose levels and the maternal and fetal ffa levels.	on-glucose-level.doc	doc	myUSBPen
2	Changes of the nucleic acid and phospholipid levels of the livers in the course of fetal and post-natal development. We have followed the evolution of dna, rna and pl in the livers of rat foeti removed between the fifteenth and the twentyfirst day of gestation and of newly born or weaning young rats.	on-phosfolipid-level.pdf	pdf	myUSBPen
3	Surfactant in fetal lamb tracheal fluid. Lambs delivered by cesarean section with intact fetal circulation have a fluid filling the trachea. Analysis revealed that this fluid contained material high in surface activity in lambs delivered near term, but less surface activity in premature lambs.	fetal-lamb-tracheal-fluid.pdf	pdf	general hospital-webserver

| 4 | Placental and cord blood lipids. Comparison in a set of double ovum twins, a stillborn and a live-born. Determinations of phospholipid, total and free cholesterol, triglyceride and nefa have been made on placental tissue and cord blood in a set of double ovum twins, one stillborn and one live-born. | cord-blood-lipids.ppt | ppt | MyHarddisk |

Table 3.2 - Table related to the application example.

By using LSA in the SQL environment, our analysis has greater flexibility, allowing us to consider different sets of documents such as KB, specifying a WHERE condition in our SELECT statement. This means that for all the subsets of the documents considered we can estimate the similarity between a query and one or more documents. For example, we can consider a KB of only documents that are present on "myUSBPen" resource, and thus we can use an SQL-query such as:

SELECT LSAInfoKB(toLSAInfo (toLSAVector(corpus)))

FROM documents

WHERE sourceName="myUSBPen"

When a KB has been chosen, we can store it in a table for a further similarity query or we can perform a direct similarity query by using a nested query. Consider a query captured by a simple text field from a client application connected to our database. Precisely, a query is a document that can be converted in LSAVector and used to make a similarity estimation. In order to perform a similarity query without a materialized KB, we can submit the following query to our database:

SELECT simCos (toLSAVector(corpus) ,

toLSAVector(. . . text of the query . . .) ,

KB)

FROM documents ,

(**SELECT** LSAInfoMATRIX(toLSAVector(corpus))

FROM docs) AS KB

Without a stored KB, the query is more time-expensive than a query based on a materialized KB. In other words if we store our KB in a table defined as:

CREATE TABLE AS

SELECT L AIn   ATRIX   L AIn   L AVector(corpus))

FROM documents

we can evaluate the similarity level with a query such as:

SELECT simCos (toLSAVector(corpus) ,

toLSAVector(" . . . text of the query . . . ") ,

KB. kb)

FROM documents , KB

Consider the following example in order to appreciate the potential of SQL-LSA fusion. Suppose that we found a natural language query that satisfies a specific knowledge need of our task. We can constantly update the documents by simply using a perspective based on a semantic query such as:

CREATE VIEW myPersonalKnowledgeCollectionOnElectric

AS simCos (toLSAVector(corpus) ,

toLSAVector(" . . . text of the query . . . ") ,

KB. kb)

FROM documents ,

(**SELECT** LSAInfoMATRIX(toLSAVector(corpus)) **FROM** docs)

AS KB

The semantic similarity obtained from the LSA analysis can be used within a sql command such as DELETE or INSERT, including a WHERE clause, in order to manage our KB. Suppose we want to prune our KB, deleting or moving the documents that have a level of semantic similarity under 0.2 with respect to a specific query. This aim is achieved by using the following statement:

DELETE FROM documents WHERE id in

SELECT id ,

simCos (toLSAVector(corpus) ,

toLSAVector (. . . text of the query . . .) ,

KB, kb) < 0 ,2

FROM documents ,

(select LSAInfoMATRIX(toLSAVector(corpus)) fro   s)

as KB

Notice that in the above query, the deletion is based on an LSA analysis executed on-the-fly. The potential demonstrated above is possible since our framework is an extension of the SQL language.

3.6 Conclusions

This chapter demonstrates the key results of the TEKNE project in the business modeling field by focusing on three main aspects: (i) collaborative management of Business Vocabularies and Business Rules to help business communities share a common understanding of the terms and expressions used across multi-language and multi-domain value networks. The approach adopted leverages standard and business-oriented technologies and languages to bridge the gap between the world of business people and IT experts and to enable effective business-to-business collaboration, (ii) the definition of a general-purpose model repository based on the MOF standard and conceived to be deployed in a networked environment. The MOF repository is the key element of the overall model management architecture in that it allows the flexible and customizable definition of a common knowledge base that is accessible, with ad-hoc mechanisms and policies, by any business network stakeholder, (iii) the use of an innovative search and retrieval system. Modern text retrieval systems are mainly targeted at ordinary end users and can be characterized as similarity retrieval systems. They encourage the use of unstructured natural language queries and return lists of texts ranked according to their similarity with the query. Older text retrieval systems, on the other hand, are referred to as Boolean retrieval systems and support Boolean queries. They return texts ordered by date, author etc. but often frustrate users with unsatisfactory results. However, this mechanism does not guarantee superior performance for any query. Our framework made it possible to build applications with sophisticated and customizable search methodologies that combine Boolean with similarity retrieval methods to obtain better results. Furthermore, these results can be attained without previously requiring a human operator to work on the documents.

References

[1] Jin L, Robey D (1999). Explaining Cybermediation: An Organizational Analysis of Electronic Retailing. International Journal of Electronic Commerce, Vol. 3, No. 4, pp. 47-65.

[2] Sarkar M, Butler B, Steinfield C (1995). Intermediaries and cybermediaries: A continuing role for mediating players in the electronic marketplace. Journal of Computer-Mediated Communication, Vol. 1, No. 3.

[3] Sarkar M, Butler B, Steinfield C (1998). Cybermediaries in Electronic Marketspace: Toward Theory Building. Journal of Business Research, Vol. 41, pp. 215-221.

[4] Hedberg B (1991). The role of information systems in imaginary organizations. In: Stamper R, Kerola P, Lee R, and Lyttinen K (ed.) Collaborative Work, Social Communications and Information Systems, Amsterdam, North-Holland,pp. 1-8.

[5] Davidow WH, Malone MS (1992). The Virtual Corporation, New York: Harper Collins.

[6] Mowshowitz A (1997). Virtual Organization. Communications of the ACM, Vol. 40, No. 9, pp. 30-37.

[7] Tapscott D, Ticoll D, Lowy A (2000). Digital Capital, Boston, MA: Harvard Business School Press.

[8] Russell DA (2005). Challenges of the Internet.

[9] Sowa JF, Zachman JA (1992). Extending and formalizing the framework for information systems architecture. IBM Systems Journal Volume 31 Issue 3.

[10] Hildreth S (2005). Rounding Up Business Rules. ComputerWorld Software. IDG.

[11] Szulanski G (1996). Exploring Internal Stickiness: Impediments to the Transfer of Best Practice Within the Firm. Winter, Strategic Management Journal, Special Issue: Knowledge and the Firm Vol. 17, pp.27-43.

[12] Halle B V (2001). Business Rules Applied. Wiley.

[13] Morgan T (2001). Business Rules and Information Systems: Aligning IT with Business Goals, Pearson.

[14] BRG (2003) "The Business Rules Manifesto"

[15] Fox MS, Chionglo JF, Fadel F G (1993). Common-sense model of the enterprise. Proceedings of the Industrial Engineering Research Conference.

[16] Zack M H (2003). Rethinking the knowledge-based organization. Sloan Management Review, vol. 44, pp. 67-71.

[17] Nonaka I, Takeuchi H (1995). The Knowledge-Creating Company. Oxford: Oxford University Press.

[18] Grant RM (1996). Toward a Knowledge-Based Theory of the Firm. Winter, Strategic Management Journal, Special Issue: Knowledge and the Firm Vol. 17, pp.109-122.

[19] Furnas G W, Landauer TK, Gomez LM, Dumais ST (1987). The vocabulary problem in human-system communication. Communications of the ACM, 30(11):964-971.

[20] Charfi A, Mezini M (2004). Hybrid Web Service Composition: Business Processes Meet Business Rules. ICSOC'04, New York.

[21] Chapin D (2008). SBVR: What is now Possible and Why? Business Rules Journal, Vol. 9, No. 3.

Chapter 4 - Model-based service-oriented architectures for Internetworked Enterprises

Devis Bianchini[2], Marco Brambilla[1,] Alessandro Campi[1], Cinzia Cappiello[1], Stefano Ceri[1], Marco Comuzzi[3], Valeria De Antonellis[2], Barbara Pernici[1], Pierluigi Plebani[1]

[1]Politecnico di Milano, Milan, Italy

[2]Università degli studi di Brescia, Brescia, Italy

[3]Eindhoven University of Technology, Eindhoven, The Netherlands

Abstract - Service-oriented architectures (SOA) provide the basis to (re)design business processes in order to develop flexible applications where available services are dynamically composed to satisfy business goals. The adoption of this type of architecture enables the design of information systems that connect IEs to each other to run collaborative business processes. In fact, organizations can design service-based processes based either on simple internal applications or on external services. This chapter provides models and methods for the design and execution of service-based processes able to exploit all the services offered in an IEs registry. This service registry contains services that need to be defined with the same granularity and described via the same functional and non-functional models. The alignment in process and service design and modeling is discussed in this chapter, to enable the adoption of efficient techniques for service sharing, discovery and invocation.

4.1 Introduction

The Internetworked Enterprise (IE) paradigm is based on borderless organizations that share applications, services and knowledge and whose processes are transformed and integrated with those of their partners. This enables the creation of a "virtual corporation" that operates through an integrated network connecting the company's employees, suppliers, distributors, retailers and customers 0. Prior to the advent of the Internet, a number of companies developed their own intranets by using electronic data interchange and client/server computing technologies to simplify communications and document exchanges. Heterogeneity of these collaborative environments implies the adoption of standards and infrastructures to

G. Passiante (ed.), *Evolving Towards the Internetworked Enterprise: Technological and Organizational Perspectives*, DOI 10.1007/978-1-4419-7279-8_4,

communicate. With the advent of Service Oriented Architecture (SOA), organizations use services to develop and utilize simple internal applications or outsource activities by searching for external services, thus enabling more efficient and easier inter-organizational interactions. In particular, IEs now have the possibility to share their own applications by using the Software as a Service paradigm (SaaS). In this scenario, each organization maintains a catalog of available services implementing its functionalities; these services can be shared across IEs and reused to build collaborative processes. In this way, services offered and requested support the design of operating information systems able to connect IEs to each other.

Services are the drivers of enterprise communications and are defined as units of work provided by service providers and offered to the other organizations involved in a collaborative business process. Thus, each enterprise can easily expose some of its own services as well as discover and use the services offered by virtual partners within a network of enterprises based on the IE paradigm. Collaboration should be facilitated by guaranteeing the standardized representation of business processes. This involves modeling different aspects of process and service descriptions, such as functional and non-functional requirements, and QoS parameters. Capturing the business knowledge of each organization and providing a homogeneous view entails semantically enhancing the descriptions of the processes and services of each firm. This requires an enterprise cluster to be provided with a shared and easily extensible business vocabulary. A semantic agreement on process and service representation enables better identification and selection of services across Internetworked Enterprises for collaborative purposes.

In this chapter, methods and models for a semantic description of federated processes, including functional and non-functional aspects, are described. In the MDA approach, which defines system functionality using a platform-independent model (PIM), business process representation has been exploited from different perspectives. Starting from high-level process representation, we present a methodology to guide organizations in the identification of services that compose the process. Once the set of required services has been identified, we also describe methods to support the service selection phase. In fact, the service registry might contain similar services and suitable techniques are needed to define the service that better satisfies the organizations' requirements. Finally, in order to better support the design and realization of a service-based Web application, we envisage the construction of a tool capable of turning a BPMN diagram into a set of WebML diagrams representing the skeletons of the service-based Web applications supporting the process, executable with the selected and available service.

4.2 Modeling service-based business processes

Modeling a business process and its implementation presents several challenges. Complexity increases when it concerns a network of enterprises whose processes have to be redefined and integrated to exploit the opportunities offered by the IE models. Each enterprise describes its own processes using a specific language and has specific requirements on how a process should be executed. In order to allow dynamic service integration among enterprises belonging to a virtual cluster, both technological and semantic interoperability aspects must be taken into account. It is useful to provide a common and shared vocabulary (e.g., ontology) to facilitate effective understanding and sharing of the information involved in business process modeling, leading to benefits such as system interoperability and the reuse and sharing of business knowledge. The main purpose of the adoption of standard terms is to improve the communication process among both people and software systems in order to increase the quantity and the quality of information exchanged.

4.2.1 Processes and services definition

According to the MDA paradigm, processes are first described by starting from the requirements specification and thereafter modeling the activities from different perspectives and granularities. Processes are structured explicitly into Platform Independent Models (PIMs) and Platform Specific Models (PSMs). A business process *BP* is generally defined as a collection of related, structured activities or tasks to serve a particular goal specified by one or more end users. Processes are usually defined at a PIM level using a workflow-based notation (e.g., BPMN), independently from implementation technology and platforms 0. The process designer defines the workflow able to provide the desired output by linking simple tasks through control structures (e.g., sequence, choice, cycle, or parallel) to form complex tasks. Furthermore, the actors participating in the process must also be considered. Actors are represented as abstract entities that interact with the business process, responsible for one or more simple tasks. Actors can be grouped into organizations. In workflow-based notation, task responsibilities are represented through swimlanes. For example, BPMN supports swimlanes with two main constructs: pools, to represent organizations participating in the process, and lanes, that constitute sub-partitions within pools and are used to organize activities that are logically related to each other (e.g., when they are performed by the same department). We can provide the formal definition of a simple task st_i as follows:

$$st_i = \langle n_{t_i}, IN(t_i), OUT(t_i), f_{t_i}, A_{t_i}, \{t_{i-1}\} \rangle$$

where: n_{ti} is the task name; $IN(t_i)$ and $OUT(t_i)$ are the sets of task inputs and outputs respectively; $f_{ti} : IN(t_i) \rightarrow OUT(t_i)$ is the transformation associated with the task; A_{ti} is the actor responsible for the task; $\{t_{i-1}\}$ is the set of tasks that precede task t_i according to control flow dependencies. According to widely accepted data structure diagrams (e.g., UML, XML complex data types) each input $in \in IN(t_i)$ can be described as $\langle n,P \rangle$, where n is the input name and P a set of properties or attributes that further detail the input data. Outputs can be described in the same manner. A task (either simple or complex) can be seen a small procedure able to produce specific outputs by elaborating inputs received by other tasks. A business process *BP* results from the combination of a set T of complex tasks, which correspond to significant portions or stages of the process. In the PSM, which is derived from the PIM, task implementation and execution is specified in a platform-specific way. The operational language we use for process implementation is BPEL. Considering the implementation technology in service-oriented environments, a business process can be executed invoking services that can also be selected at run time 0. The definition of a service imposes a series of constraints such as: (i) a service is self-contained, namely, it does not require context or state information of other services; (ii) a service is connected to other services and clients using standard, dependency reducing, decoupled message-based methods such as XML document exchanges. Moreover, a service is a conceptual unit of work that takes one or more inputs and creates an output perceived by clients as having a tangible value. In this scenario, on a PSM level, a process is described as the composition of one or more services connected by control structures that constitute the orchestration mechanism. Considering the definitions of "service" and "complex task" provided, it is possible to establish a correspondence between these two concepts. More formally, at design time, a complex task t_i can be defined as the abstract representation of the operations of a component service of the business process. At run-time, each complex task t_i (i.e., a component service) has to be bound to a selected concrete service able to provide the desired functionalities. Service selection should guarantee the invocation of the best available concrete services, taking into consideration process constraints, but also end-user preferences and the execution context.

Herewith following we refer to component abstract Web services operations to be executed in the process with the term task t_i, while Web services selected to be executed are called concrete Web services ws_j. When a component service is invoked, the BPEL specification is analyzed and the set of candidate Web services for executing its component tasks is retrieved from the network of collaborative Internetworked Enterprises. Each Internetworked Enterprise can be viewed as a node in a P2P network. In fact, each enterprise both provides and looks for services on the collaborative network. Each enterprise is equipped with a registry, where locally available services are registered. Services are selected from the registries by considering the signature of the operation to be performed and according to the specified local quality constraints of tasks in the process. Herewith following, Web services will be indexed by j and we will indicate with WS_i the set of indexes of Web services ws_j as candidates for the execution of task t_i; with OP_j the set of indexes of operations implemented by Web service ws_j; with $ws_{j,o}$ the invocation of operation $o \in OP_j$ of Web service ws_j. Let I be the number of tasks of the composed service specification and J the number of candidate Web services retrieved from the network of Internetworked Enterprises.

The goal of the service selection phase is to define the optimum execution plan of the composed process, i.e., the set of ordered couples $\{(t_i, ws_{j,o})\}$, indicating that complex task t_i is executed by invoking ws_j for all tasks in the process, such that the overall QoS perceived by the user for the application instance execution is maximized. Both a semantic-enriched service description and a quality model are required for effective concrete service selection. The following sections will address these aspects.

4.2.2 Semantic service description

Semantic descriptions focus on the functional aspects of a service and are based on the WSDL standard for service representation in terms of service functionalities (operations) and input/output messages (parameters). Available Web services ws_j are stored in extended UDDI registries, called *Semantic Peer Registries*; each registry includes: (i) a *Service Category Taxonomy (SCT)*, extracted from available standard taxonomies, e.g., UNSPSC, NAiCS, to categorize services; (ii) a *peer ontology*, providing semantic knowledge related to service description elements and (iii) a *service ontology*, which organizes semantic service descriptions through semantic links.

Concepts in the peer ontology are organized according to semantic relationships, `subclass-of` and `equivalent-to`. Furthermore, the peer ontology is extended by a thesaurus providing the terms and terminological relationships (such as synonymy, hyponymy and so forth) associated to names of concepts in the peer ontology. In this way, it is possible to enlarge matchmaking capabilities when looking for correspondences between elements in service descriptions and concepts in the ontologies. The problem, in fact, is comparing service descriptions in the presence of different terminologies (peer ontologies). The thesaurus is automatically derived by considering the set of terms denoting atomic concepts in the peer ontology and the lexical system WordNet 0 and aims to bridge the gap between different peer ontologies. Management and use of semantic links between semantic service descriptions improve functional service selection and will be discussed in Section 4.4. Moreover, to support adaptive concretization, the authors in 0 propose a set of semantic annotations associated to the process specification to define either the intrinsic characteristics of the process or requirements of the user of the composed service:

- *Probability of execution of conditional branches*: for every switch s, the probability of execution $\{p_1^s, p_2^s, ..., p_{NB^s}^s\}$ of conditional branches is specified ($\sum_{h=1}^{NB^s} p_h^s = 1$, NB^s indicates the number of disjoint branch conditions of s)

- *Loop constraints*: the expected maximum number of iteration NI^l is defined for every loop l

- *Local and global constraints on quality dimensions*: local constraints define the quality of Web services to be invoked for a given task in the process i.e., candidate Web services are selected according to a desired characteristic, e.g., the price of *a single Web service invocation* is lower than a given threshold. Global constraints specify requirements at process level, i.e., constraints posing restrictions over the entire composed service execution can be introduced, e.g. the price of *the composed service execution* is lower than a fixed budget. We assume that quality constraints can be defined on a set of N pre-defined quality dimensions q_n

- *User preferences*: a set of normalized weights $\left\{w_1, w_2, ..., w_N\right\}$, $\sum_{n=1}^{N} w_n = 1$, indicating the user preferences with respect to the set of quality dimensions

- *Web service dependency constraints*: impose that a given set of tasks in the process are executed by the same Web service. This type of constraint allows considering both stateless and stateful Web services in composed services

The probability of the execution of conditional branches and the distribution of number of loop iterations can be evaluated from past executions by inspecting system logs or can be specified by the composed service designer 00.

4.2.3 Quality model

Several quality criteria can be associated with Web services execution. In the present chapter, we assume that quality values are real numbers (associated with a given metric) that vary in a bounded range with a minimum and a maximum value. The quality of a Web service is defined by a set of quality dimensions, each associated to a given quality aspect. In order to annotate a service with quality information, we refer to the quality model proposed in 0.

Given a Web service, its quality is defined by the set $QD=\{qd_k\}$. Quality dimensions are various and can be defined at different architectural levels (i.e., from hardware to user level). The quality dimensions commonly used in current literature are: 000.

- *Execution time*: the expected delay between the time instant when a request is sent (a service is invoked) and the time when the result is obtained
- *Availability*: the probability that the service operation is accessible
- *Price*: the fee that a service requester has to pay to the service provider for the service invocation

- *Reputation*: a measure of the service invocation trustworthiness. It is defined as the ratio between the number of service invocations that comply with the negotiated QoS over the total number of service invocations
- *Data accuracy*: the ability of a data collection to meet user requirements, defined as the proximity of a value v returned by a service operation and a value v' considered as correct

Another class of quality dimensions is tied to the business logic of the Web service and is consequently directly related to a given application domain. Considering our reference example, possible quality dimensions are the delivery time of the supplier, the robustness of the component and the number of colors available to customize the elements. Even if quality is subjective by definition, all can agree on this list of quality dimensions. We formalize this agreement by introducing a new actor called **community**. This actor is not involved in the Web service selection process, but only during the Web service quality description phase. As defined in 0, a community is a group of people with the aim of proposing a specification for a group of objects with some relevant common characteristics. It is worth noting that an example of community was presented above when we mentioned the set of technical quality dimensions (e.g., availability, accessibility). In fact, this set is defined by what we usually call the "Web service community". In a federated environment, community can be explicitly identified as a group of people that represents all the members of the federation. According to the TEKNE vision, the federation reflects the set of companies that operate on the same domain and share the same goals. Therefore, we can assume that these companies agree on the same set of quality dimensions.

According to the characteristics of Service Oriented Computing, providers and users may not previously know each other. Due to the subjectivity of quality, we must be sure that providers and users not only rely on the same language for expressing capabilities and requirements, but also use the same set of quality dimensions to express them. According to this hypothesis, Figure 4.1 shows the main elements and actors involved in our quality model. The Quality Tree (QT) collects all the quality dimensions relevant for a given application domain along with the technical quality dimension identified by the Web service community. Both users and providers rely on the QT to express their requirements and capabilities. In addition, the user also revises the QT and produces a Weighted QT (WQT) reflecting user preferences.

We assume that the communities involved are able to define the relevant quality dimensions QD:

$$QD=\{qd_i\} = \{PQD|DQD\}=\{\{pqd_l|dqd_m\}\}$$

QD can be split into two subsets: PQD and DQD. PQD collects the set of L *primitive quality dimensions* pqd_l, whereas DQD includes the M derived *quality dimensions* dqd_m.

More formally, we define a quality dimension pqd_l as:

$$pqd_l = \langle name, V, ef(V), PC \rangle \; 1=1,...L$$

The *name* uniquely identifies the quality dimension. The element V corresponds to either categorical or interval admissible values. In the former case, the admissible values will be included in a specific vector $V=\{v_h\}$ ($h=1,...,H$) while, in the latter case V will be defined by its extremes, i.e., $V=[v_{min}, v_{max}]$. The function *ef*: $V \rightarrow [0..1]$ represents the *quality evaluation function*, i.e., how the quality increases or decreases with respect to the admissible values: 0 means lowest quality, 1 highest quality. The trend of *ef* is usually defined by a utility function, e.g., linear, logarithmic, exponential, sigmoidal. The admissible value set V is organized in disjoint primitive service classes $PC=\{pc_k\}$ ($k=1,...,K$), obtained as follows:

- in case of categorical values, the primitive service classes coincide with the values that the dimension can assume: i.e., $qd_i.PC \equiv qd_i.V$, $H=K$
- in case of interval values, primitive service classes are obtained by splitting $V=[v_{min}, v_{max}]$ into K intervals, so $PC=\{pc_k = [pc_{kmin}];pc_{kmax}]\}$ where $pc_{kmax} = pc_{(k+1)min}$, $pc_{1min}=v_{min}$; $pc_{Kmax}\}=v_{max}\cdot pc_k$ ranges are obtained as follows: let divide $qd_i.ef(V)$ in K ranges $\{[e_{kmin}; e_{kmax}]\}$, then $p_{kmin}=qd_i.ef^{-1}(e_{kmin})$ and $pd_{kmax}=qd_i.ef^{-1}(e_{kmax})$

A $dqd_m = <name, values, \{qd_j\}>$ is not directly measurable but depends on other quality dimensions, where:

- name: uniquely identifies the quality dimension
- values . [0..1]: defines the admissible values set for the dimension, and
- $\{qd_j\} \in QD$: is the set of quality dimensions - primitive and derived - affecting dqd_m.

Relationships among quality dimensions in QD are identified by the communities involved and are represented as a tree called the **Quality Tree (QT)**. In particular, giving a qd_i its quality tree, i.e., QT (qd_i) is defined as follows:

$$QT(qd_i)= <pqd_h \;|.\; dqd_k \; \{QT\,(dqd_k.qd_j)\}>.$$

We assume that, given an application domain, a qd named "qos" always exists in QD and the related $QT(qos)$ describes the organization of all the dimensions in QD.

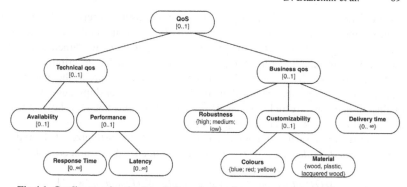

Fig.4.1- Quality tree for the description of a furniture component supplier service

Figure 4.1 shows the quality tree related to a furniture component supplier service sample. Considering this example, *PQD = {availability, response time, latency, robustness, colors, material, delivery time}*. The community states how to measure these dimensions and defines the admissible values regardless of specific service implementation. For example, *availability* can be defined as *uptime/(uptime+downtime)* and its values will be included in a continuous range, i.e., [0..1]. To the contrary, the class quality dimension collects all the possible variants and the range of values will be discrete, i.e., *colors.values = {blue, red, yellow}*. The ranges of values may also be unbounded. For example, delay can assume any positive value: *deliverytime.values = [0..∞]*.

In addition to the primitive quality dimensions, the community also defines the derived quality dimensions DQD. A $dqd_m \in$ DQD describes a higher-level aspect of service quality that depends on other - either primitive or derived - quality dimensions. For example, *performance* depends on *latency* and *response time*.

We decided to model the quality of service according to a tree for two main reasons. Firstly, this structure enables an explicit representation of the influences among quality dimensions. It is worth noting that we only state that this relationship exists and not how it occurs. In some sense, we state a qualitative dependency: the higher the quality of a child, the higher the quality of the father node. Secondly, the tree-based structure also reflects the different abstraction levels according to which the quality can be described. At the highest level, we have a generic QoS dimension that is affected by all quality dimensions that the community considers relevant. Going down the tree to the lowest level, the leaves of a QT identify the primitive dimensions that really determine quality. According to the values that these dimensions assume, quality will increase or decrease. In this way, service providers always work at the bottom level since they need to describe how high the quality really is: they need to state what the values will be for a given quality dimension they are able to offer. To the contrary, final users can work towards the entire tree. If a user knows the exact meaning of a primitive quality dimension, the requirements can be described by a subset of the admissible range *(e.g., colors.values = {red, yellow})*. Otherwise, the user can rely on the derived quality dimensions *(e.g., technicalqos.values $\in [0.7..1]$)* and, in this way, the user can be agnostic with respect to the influencing primitive quality dimensions. Obviously, working at a lower level implies more accurate quality description.

The community, by means of the QT, gives a general picture of the quality description of a given application domain. Here, the relationships among several quality dimensions are only sketched, since the QT does not state how much a $dqd_m.qd_j$ influences the related dqd_m.

In our quality model, we assume that a user is able to customize a QT producing a *Weighted Quality Tree WQT* . Thus, given a quality dimension $qd_i \in DQD$:

$$WQT(qd_i) = \langle pqd_l, e_{pqdl}(value) | dqd_m, WQT (dqd_m), \{w_{m,j}\} \rangle.$$

where e_{pqdl} is the evaluation function of the quality dimension pqd_l and the structures of $QT(qd_i)$ and $WQT (qd_i)$ are the same. Given a dqd_m, the weights $w_{k,j}$ represent how much the related quality dimensions $dqd_m.qd_j$ influence the dqd_m. These values can be obtained manually or even suggested by a recommendation system. It may occur that during the definition of a QT, especially when technical dimensions are involved, the community also performs the weights assignment process, defining a set of weights able to guide the user during final customization.

Along with weights, WQT also includes in its leaves the quality evaluation $e_{pqdl}(value)$ functions. Here, given $pqd_l \in PQD$ the user specifies the best and worst values and how the quality varies with respect to $pqd_l.values$. The evaluation function is defined in different ways according to the kind of admissible values, continuous range vs. discrete range. In case of a continuous range of values, the best and worst values can be easily identified considering the lowest and highest values in $pqd_l.values$ and the semantic of the quality parameter. For example, considering availability, the lowest value corresponds to the worst quality and, consequently, the highest value corresponds to the best quality. On the opposite side, if we consider response time, the higher the value the lower the quality and vice versa. The trend of the quality function is usually defined by a utility function: e.g., linear, logarithmic, exponential, sigmoidal. We assume that the output of a e_{pqdl} is normalized and always included in $[0..1]$. If $pqd_l.values$ is discrete, the evaluation function associates a value in $[0..1]$ to every element: the higher the value, the better the quality.

It is worth noting that each dimension can be associated with a range of admissible values identified regardless of a specific Web service implementation. Therefore, all existing Web services, given a quality dimension, can only offer a subset of the admissible values defined by the community and users can request levels of service quality according to their preferences. In the following section, we describe, respectively, how the capabilities and the requirements can be defined.

4.2.3.1 Quality offering

Capabilities reflect the quality offered by a Web service provider. Focusing on the service description, the provider before publishing its Web service will define a document expressing the functional aspects. WSDL represents the *de-facto* standard that identifies the set of available operations and exchanged messages. Along with functional aspects, the service provider also needs to attach a document in which the quality offered is described. At this stage, the literature does not include a language for quality description with the same consensus as WSDL does for functional aspects. Nevertheless, we think that the capabilities as introduced in the following section can be simply expressed according to languages such as WSOL 0 or WS-Policy 0.

According to our quality model, a capability $c(pqd_l)$ is an instance of a $pqd_l \in PQD$ where:

$$c(pqd_l).name = pqd_l.name$$
$$c(pqd_l).values \subseteq pqd_l.values$$

Thus, a capability expresses, for a given primitive quality dimension, the real values that the provider is able to support during the Web service execution. This range of values will always be a restriction on the values defined in pqd_l, since, by definition, the latter has been defined by the community and collects all the possible values regardless of a specific service. Moreover, a capability can refer only to primitive quality dimensions since they are the only ones that can be measured.

A service provider, for each $pqd_l \in QT$ declares throughout the $c(pqd_l)$ the quality that will actually be supported. The collection of all these capabilities is organized in a Service Level (*SL*).

$$SL(QT) = <\{c(pqd_l)\}, price> \quad \forall pqd_l \in PQD$$

In detail, an *SL* includes the definition of both the benefit and the cost to the service provider. The cost corresponds to the set of capabilities offered, whereas the benefit coincides with the price of the service.

An SL determines a possible configuration of values of the primitive quality dimensions. In this way, an SL can be monitored since all the elements are measurable by definition. A provider, for each Web service, can define several of these configurations and collect them in the Service Levels Document (*SLD*).

$$SLD(QT) = \{SL_s(QT)\}$$

4.2.3.2 Quality request

Once a user has identified the QT collecting all the relevant quality dimensions, a customization process produces the related WQT. User requirements $r(qd_i)$ are defined starting from $WQT(qos)$:

$$r(qd_i).name = qd_i.name$$
$$r(qd_i).values \subseteq qd_i.values$$

Differently from a constraint c, a requirement r can operate a restriction on both primitive and derived quality dimensions. This allows the user to express her/his requirements at different levels of abstraction, as previously mentioned. If a requirement predicates on a primitive quality dimension, then the user is aware of the meaning of the dimension and its possible values. On the other hand, if a requirement predicates on a derived quality dimension, then the user does not care about the real values of the measurable quality parameter. In this way, users only know that a value close to 1 means higher quality and vice versa.

In the same way as capabilities, requirements are also collected in a Requirement Level (RL), which expresses a configuration of requirements along with the amount of money that the user is willing to pay to exploit the service. In this case, as discussed in 0, the requirements reflect the benefit for the user and the price corresponds to the user cost. The selection process aims to mediate between the two contrasting user and provider perspectives.

Finally, the set of alternative RLs are grouped in the Requirement Levels Document (RLD).

$$SL(QT) = \langle \{c(pqd_l)\}, price \rangle \quad \forall pqd_l \in PQD$$

$$RL(WQT) = \langle \{r(pqd_{lr})\}, \{r(dqd_{mr})\}, cost \rangle$$
$$pqdl_r \in P\,QD, dqd_{mr} \in DQD$$
$$HR \leq H, KR \leq K$$

$$RLD(WQT) = \{RL_r(WQT)\}$$

It is worth noting that in a RL a user can include a dqd_m and even qd_j influencing the dqd_m itself. We assume that the requirements entirely cover the quality tree. This means that for each quality dimensions the requirements are clear. It also means that for each $pqd_l \in QT$ either a direct requirement is expressed $r(pdq_l)$ or an indirect requirement is expressed by $r(dqd_m)$ where dqd_m is affected by the pdq_l.

4.3 Service identification methodology

To move from the workflow-based representation of the business process at the PIM level (e.g., BPMN) toward its specification at the PSM level as an orchestration of available concrete services (e.g., BPEL), a methodology is required to identify component abstract services in the original process 0. These component services will be matched against concrete services during the selection phase to compose the best services (from the functional and QoS perspectives) into the final executable business process. We propose a methodological framework for component service design starting from process descriptions. The methodology brings together Semantic Web technologies, process modeling techniques, ontology building and semantic matching. The phases of the methodology are the following (see Figure 4.2):

- **Semantic process annotation** – concepts defined in the peer ontologies adopted by the Internetworked Enterprise are used to semantically annotate business process elements (inputs and outputs, task names) to enable better service identification in distributed heterogeneous environments
- **Identification of candidate services** - candidate component services must be identified ensuring the same decomposition granularity, thus enabling better service comparison for sharing and reuse purposes
- **Reconciliation of similar services** - component services must be clustered on the basis of the similarity of their tasks and I/O data, in order to identify similar services on different processes and enable the design of reusable component services.

Most workflow-based notation tools allow the designer to represent the process in terms of tasks and control structures. Information on the data flow between tasks and between actors is not provided. In order to identify component services, a preliminary step before applying our methodology is the completion of the task representation with the definition of inputs and outputs, the associated operation and responsible actors and organizations as described in 0.

The methodology also requires the specification of dependencies among tasks and the description of data exchanges between actors. This latter information is useful since a service is recognized as a recurrent communication pattern, where the service requester sends a request and receives a response that is of value to the requester himself/herself. On the other hand, the provider can invoke other services to execute his/her tasks, becoming the requester for those services. Therefore, the overall business process can be viewed as a complex structure of nested and chained service invocations connected by control structures.

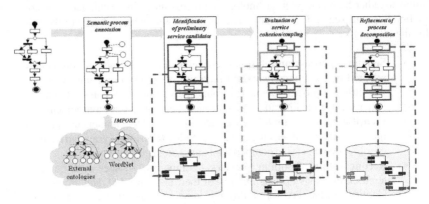

Fig. 4.2 - Methodology phases.

Semantic process annotation. The first phase of the methodology aims to solve terminological discrepancies (e.g., synonymies or homonyms) between names of business process elements by exploiting the peer ontologies and the thesaurus introduced in Section 4.2.2. The thesaurus constitutes the pre-existing, domain independent terminological knowledge that relates each term that is not already included in the peer ontology to atomic concepts by means of synonymy (SYN) and broader/narrower term (BT/NT) relationships properly weighted. It is possible to quantify the name affinity between two generic terms n_1 and n_2 (either atomic concepts or not) as the product of weights associated to the chain of relationships that relate n_1 to n_2.

Identification of candidate services. A major goal of our methodology is to enable homogeneous identification of services by analyzing process description. For the identification of candidate component services, we propose some heuristics deriving from empirical observations on the features and definition of services found in literature. According to definitions given in 0, services constitute units of work that are invoked by one of the actors involved in the process to obtain a tangible value. For each actor *A*, the outgoing and incoming data flows (that is, data transfers towards and from other actors respectively) are considered as service requests/invocations and responses/values respectively. Therefore, for each request/response pair, the set of tasks that could be associated with the component service can be identified by considering all the tasks that are involved in the portion of the process that is activated by the request and in charge of producing the response.

Once the candidate services have been identified, services are further analyzed in terms of defined cohesion/coupling criteria to better define service structure and granularity. Homogeneous granularity is a strong requirement for effective collaboration. Specifically, identified services must ensure high internal cohesion and low coupling. The cohesion/coupling metrics adopted were inspired by their well-known application in the software engineering field 0 and are used to evaluate the degree of similarity correspondence between I/O flows among tasks 0. The cohesion coefficient evaluates how much the tasks within a single service contribute to obtaining a service output. The coupling coefficient evaluates the extent to which tasks belonging to different services need to interact. The ratio between coupling and cohesion coefficients must be minimized. This is used to guide iterative service decomposition until we obtain maximum intra-service cohesion and minimal inter-service coupling.

Reconciliation of similar services. The set of services resulting from the previous phases includes all the component services of a considered business process. It is possible that some services in this set denote the invocation of the same service in different points of the process. Similarity of component services is evaluated and similar services are proposed to the process designer to be merged and to be considered as different invocations of the same service. In order to evaluate the similarity between services, coefficients introduced in 0 are applied. Summarizing, two services S_1 and S_2 are similar if their *Global Similarity GSim(S_1,S_2)* $\geq \delta$, where δ is a threshold set by the process designer. The global similarity is obtained as the linear combination of two coefficients: (i) an *Entity-based Similarity* coefficient that evaluates the extent to which two services work on the same data; (ii) a *Functionality-based Similarity* coefficient that evaluates the extent to which two services perform the same functionalities.

4.4 Service Discovery

The output of the methodology described in the previous section is the definition of the sets of tasks that can be associated with services to invoke at run-time. The service discovery phase enables process execution and is usually defined as the process for identifying the Web services able to satisfy both the functional and quality requirements expressed by users. Service discovery mechanisms usually start from the analysis of the functional requirements to identify that, given a set of available services, match the request. A finer analysis is performed by analyzing this set with respect to the quality requirements to enable a ranking for the identification of the best available service with respect to user requirements.

The main goal of this section is to describe models and methods able to guarantee an optimized discovery both from a functional and non-functional perspective.

4.4.1 Semantic-driven service discovery

In the Internetworked Enterprise scenario, a collaborative business process is configured and executed as an orchestration of suitable Web services that are registered in an underlying distributed service catalog. The distributed catalog is made up of the service registries belonging to the enterprises involved, with semantic links that are dynamically established and maintained between those registries providing similar services. The overall distributed semantic structure enables the following functions:

a) *Automatic service discovery.* Aggregation of collaborative partners based on service sharing is facilitated by automatic service discovery based on the use of semantic-enriched service descriptions and advanced servicematchmaker.

b) *Representation of semantic neighborness.* Each single registry is enabled to define semantic links towards other registries, over the logical network topology, that provide semantically related functionalities (semantic neighbors). In particular, it is possible to keep track of similar services throughout the network and speed up process composition. Semantic neighbors are classified and ranked according to the similarity between functionalities provided.

c) *Implementation of distributed search policies.* To support collaborative internetworked enterprises looking for an external service to be integrated into their own business processes, different search policies are defined according to similarity properties. These policies implement different collaboration scenarios and guide request forwarding throughout the network (forwarding policies).

d) *Management of network evolution.* Since in the ever-changing environment considered, new services can be published or removed and new internetworked enterprises can join or leave the collaborative network at any moment, an up-to-date representation of semantic neighborness is maintained.

As stated in Section 4.2.2, each Internetworked Enterprise represents a peer on a collaborative P2P network able to provide and use the available services. Each peer presents the architecture shown in Figure 4.3.

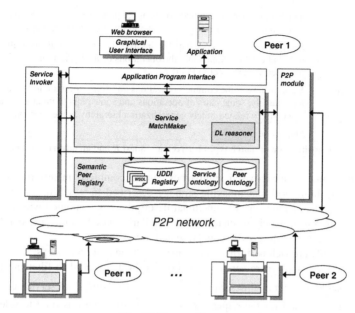

Fig. 4.3: Peer architecture

In the following sections, we focus on the Semantic Peer Registry and the Service MatchMaker, without details on the Application Program Interface, the Service Invoker and the P2P module handling inter-peer communications.

4.4.1.1 Semantic service matchmaking

According to several efforts in literature, ontology-based service matchmaking can be performed to find different kinds of relationships between semantic service descriptions. Deductive service matchmaking approaches 00 rely on logic-based techniques that give a qualitative ranking of the match type between a request *R* and a service advertisement *S*, as summarized in **Table 4.1**.

In literature, similarity-based approaches 00 have been applied in combination with deductive approaches, thus merging the high precision of the latter with the high recall of the former.

Match(R,S)	Description
Exact	*S* and *R* have the same capabilities, namely: (i) equivalent operations (ii) equivalent output parameters (iii) equivalent input parameters
Plug-in	*S* offers at least the same capabilities as *R*, i.e., names of the operations in *R* that can be mapped into the operations of S and, in particular, the

	names of corresponding operations, input parameters and output parameters that are in any generalization hierarchy in the peer ontology
SUBSUME	R offers at least the same capabilities as S, i.e., names of the operations in S that can be mapped into the operations of R; this is an inverse kind of match with respect to PLUG-IN
INTERSECTION	S and R have some common operations and some common I/O parameters, namely, some pairs of operations and some pairs of parameters are respectively related in any generalization hierarchy in the peer ontology
MISMATCH	Otherwise

Table 4.1: Classification of match types between a request R and an advertised service S

Deductive and similarity-based approaches can be combined in different ways. We rely on the hybrid matchmaking strategy described in 0, where a *deductive model* for matchmaking service functional descriptions is combined with a *similarity-based model*, which evaluates service similarity based on the peer ontology and the thesaurus via the coefficients presented in Section 4.3.

The hybrid approach performs service matchmaking as a set of steps:

- *Pre-filtering*, where service categories in SCT are used to filter out mismatching functional descriptions; given the set $\{cat_R^i\}$ of service categories specified for the request R, the pre-filtering phase is used to select a set of advertised services, called *candidate services*, which have at least one associated category that is equivalent or more specific than one of the categories of R, according to the SCT;

- *Deductive matchmaking*, where the deductive model is applied among service descriptions to establish the type of match;

- *Similarity-based matchmaking*, to quantify the degree of similarity between service descriptions; EXACT and PLUG-IN match denotes that the advertised service completely fulfills the request and service similarity is set to 1.0 (*full similarity*); if MISMATCH occurs, the similarity value is set to 0.0; finally, SUBSUME and INTERSECTION match denotes partial fulfillment of the request and, in this case, similarity coefficients are actually applied to evaluate the degree of partial match.

The matchmaking algorithm can be applied between two service descriptions S_1 and S_2 to identify if there is a semantic link between them.

Definition (Semantic links). *Given a pair of services S_1 and S_2, a semantic link between S_1 and S_2 is denoted with the following 4-uple:*

$$< S_1, S_2, \text{MatchType}, Gsim(S_1, S_2)>$$

where MatchType $\in$ {EXACT, PLUG-IN, SUBSUME, INTERSECTION, MISMATCH} *and* $Gsim(S_1, S_2) \in [0,1]$.

We distinguish between two situations:

(i) S_1 and S_2 belong to the same node p, thus generating an *intra-peer semantic link*, denoted with $sl_p(S_1, S_2)$, evaluated with respect to the peer ontology PO and the thesaurus TH built for node p;

(ii) S_1 and S_2 belong to two different nodes p_1 and p_2 respectively, thus generating an *inter-peer semantic link* between collaborative partners, denoted with $isl_{p1 \to p2}(S_1, S_2)$, evaluated with respect to peer ontology PO_1 and thesaurus TH_1 built for p_1, source of the semantic link.

A necessary and sufficient condition such that a semantic link between S_1 and S_2 can be established is that the pre-filtering phase based on service categories gives a non-empty set, match type is not MISMATCH and $Gsim(S_1, S_2)$ is equal to or greater than a given threshold δ.

When a node p joins the network of interoperating partners, it produces a *probe service request* for each service S_p^i it wants to make sharable; this probe service request contains the description of the functional service interface of S_p^i and the IP address of p and is sent to the other nodes connected to p in the P2P network. A node q receiving the probe service request matches it against its own service descriptions S_q^j by applying the matchmaking techniques based on its own peer ontology and thesaurus and for each comparison obtains the `MatchType` and the similarity degree. If the `MatchType` is not MISMATCH and the similarity degree is equal to or greater than the predefined threshold δ, an inter-peer semantic link $isl_{q \to p}(S_q^j, S_p^i)$ is established between the two nodes that become *semantic neighbors* with respect to the linked services. In future, if a request R matching with S_p^i reaches node q first, the inter-peer semantic link is used to forward the request directly to p, avoiding flooding the entire network of interoperating enterprises, as shown in the next paragraph. Intra-peer semantic links are established between services registered on the new peer p, without sending any probe request and thus avoiding propagation of messages on the network. When a new service S_n is published on a node already connected to the network, intra-peer semantic links are established with other services on p, while only a probe request is generated containing the functional description of S_n.

4.4.1.2 P2P service discovery

When a requester looks for a new service R, it sends the service to a p to which it is connected together with its own IP address. The request is processed according to a two-step strategy, consisting in a *local* and a *distributed* search. The request is matched locally and subsequently forwarded to the other nodes connected to p according to different forwarding strategies exploiting inter-peer semantic links. Partners finding relevant matching services will send them directly to the requester to avoid network overload. The hybrid matchmaking model is applied to R and each service description published in the Semantic Peer Registry of the nodes. Matching results are only those services where the match type is not MISMATCH and the **GSim** value is equal to or greater than the similarity threshold δ. Experimental results have shown that application of the hybrid matchmaking model produces better precision and recall values 0. However, optimization strategies are required to reduce the number of service comparisons by exploiting semantic links. Intra-peer semantic links are used during service discovery on the node p that first receives the request (*local search*); inter-peer semantic links are used to efficiently forward the request to the semantic neighbors of the node (*distributed search*).

Local search. Given a service request R sent to a node p, the peer searches for suitable services in its own registry and retrieves a list $CS = \{<S_1, GSim_1, mt_1>, ...<S_n, GSim_n, mt_n>\}$ of candidate services with corresponding similarity values $GSim_i = Gsim(R, S_i)$ equal to or greater than the threshold and type of match mt_i differing from MISMATCH. The purpose of intra-peer semantic links is to avoid the application of the hybrid matchmaking model when not strictly necessary. Therefore, the expected result of the optimization process during local search is a further improvement of performance in the proposed approach. From an operative point of view, we suppose that the match type between the request R and a candidate service $S_i \in CS$ offered on a given peer has already been established. Now intra-peer semantic links relating S_i with other services locally provided can be considered. Given a service S_i matching the request R, only the local services S_j that present intra-peer semantic links with S_i are considered among candidate services for the request R. In particular, according to the semantics of match types explained in Table 4.1, the following rules are applied:

- if match(R, S_i) = EXACT, then R and S_i are the "same" service and, for each S_j that presents an intra-peer semantic link with S_i, match(R, S_j) = match(S_i, S_j) and $GSim(R, S_j)=GSim(S_i, S_j)$
- if match(S_i, S_j) = EXACT, then S_i and S_j are the "same" service and match(R,S_j)=match(R,S_i) and $GSim(R,S_j)=GSim(R,S_i)$
- if match(R,S_i) = PLUG-IN and match(S_i,S_j) = PLUG-IN, then the capabilities of R are "included" among the capabilities of S_i, which in turn are "included" among the capabilities of S_j, that is, match(R,S_j) = PLUG-IN; according to the hybrid matchmaking model, $GSim(R,S_j)$ is directly set to 1.0
- in all the other cases, the match between R and S_j must be evaluated

According to this strategy, R is compared with each S_i on node p until a matching service is found; at this point, each S_j that is not related to S_i by means of intra-peer semantic links is discarded. To improve performance, services S_i that are related with several other local services S_j must be compared first with R, that is, local services are sorted decreasingly with respect to the number of outgoing intra-peer semantic links.

Distributed search. After performing a local search on peer p, local matching services $S_i \in CS$ are considered as starting points to select the best semantic neighbors to which the service request R can be forwarded. Semantic neighbors are selected on the basis of inter-peer semantic links starting from each $S_i \in CS$. A list SN of semantic neighbors is returned, where each $sn \in SN$ is defined as

$$<n_{sn}, \{<S_1, GSim_1, mt_1>, ...<S_k, GSim_k, mt_k>\}>$$

where n_{sn} is the identifier for the semantic neighbor sn (i.e., its IP address), S_1 ...$S_k \in CS$ are the semantic service descriptions that are sources of an inter-peer semantic link from p towards sn, mt_j and $Gsim_j$, with j = 1, . . . k, are the type of match and similarity degree labeling the j-th inter-peer semantic link respectively. Semantic neighbor selection is made according to the type of match between $S_i \in CS$ and R and the type of match that labels the inter-peer semantic link starting from S_i. Semantic neighbor selection is performed according to different forwarding policies: a *minimal* and an *exhaustive* policy.

According to the minimal policy, search of the collaborative network stops when matching services that fully satisfy the service request have been found. This strategy is performed according to the following rules:

- service request R is not forwarded towards neighbors that have no semantic links with services Si∈ CS that match locally
  service request R is forwarded towards neighbors whose services Sj could provide additional capabilities with respect to services Si∈ CS that match locally (according to the semantics of the match types shown inTable 4.1)

- if it is not possible to identify semantic neighbors for any service $S_i \in CS$ that matches locally, service request R is forwarded to a subset of all semantic neighbors (randomly chosen), without considering local matches, or to a subset of network peers if no semantic neighbors have been found at all.

According to these criteria, if a service $S_i \in CS$ presents an EXACT or a PLUG-IN match with the request R, then S_i completely satisfies the required functionalities and it is not necessary to forward the request to semantic neighbors with respect to S_i. Otherwise, if S_i presents a SUBSUME or an INTERSECTION match with the request R, the peer p forwards the request to those peers that are semantic neighbors with respect to S_i. Peer p does not consider semantic neighbors that present a

SUBSUME or an EXACT match with S_i, since this means that they provide services with the same functionalities or a subset of functionalities of service S_i and they cannot add further capabilities to those already provided by S_i on peer p. According to the exhaustive strategy, the search does not stop when a relevant matching service is found. In fact, if a service $S_i \in CS$ presents an EXACT or a PLUG-IN match, the service request R is forwarded to semantic neighbors with respect to S_i, since the aim is to find other equivalent services that could present better non-functional features. The search stops by applying a time-out mechanism. For the same reason, peer p also considers semantic neighbors that present a SUBSUME or an EXACT match with S_i. If the CS list of locally matching services is empty, peer p is not suitable to serve the service request. On the other hand, if the list of selected semantic neighbors SN is empty, peer p is not able to guide the request propagation on the network. In both these cases, peer p randomly selects a subset of peers connected in the underlying P2P network to which the request is forwarded.

Selected semantic neighbors are ranked according to their relevance to the service request R. The relevance of a semantic neighbor sn of a peer p equally depends on both the similarity degree labeling the inter-peer semantic links between p and sn and on the similarity degree between R and each $S_i \in CS$. Therefore, the relevance of the semantic neighbor sn is defined as the harmonic mean that combines these two contributions:

$$r_{sn} = \frac{1}{k} \sum_{i=1}^{m_k} \frac{2 * GSim_i * GSim(R, S_i)}{GSim_i + GSim(R, S_i)}$$

A ranked list $RSN = \{< sn_1, r_{sn1}>, \ldots < sn_h, r_{snh}>\}$ of semantic neighbors of p with the corresponding ranking values is obtained. Ranked semantic neighbors can be further filtered according to a threshold-based mechanism.

A number of tokens A_p is then assigned to the peer p on which the service request R has been formulated. These tokens are proportionally distributed among selected semantic neighbors, according to the relevance value calculated for each semantic neighbor. The number of tokens assigned to the semantic neighbor sn with relevance value r_{sn} is determined as:

$$A_{sn} = \left| \frac{A_p}{\sum_{i=1}^{|RSN|} r_{sni}} * r_{sn} \right|$$

Tokens represent the number of replies the peer p expects from the semantic neighbor sn. When a peer receives R and the assigned number of tokens A_{sn}, if it finds locally semantic service descriptions that match the service request, it consumes a token and distributes the remaining tokens among the selected semantic neighbors. If the peer does not find matching semantic service descriptions or candidate semantic neighbors to which the service request could be sent, it (randomly) selects a subset of peers to which it is connected in the underlying P2P network and equally distributes available tokens amongst them. Request propagation stops when $A_{sn} = 0$. The adoption of the token-based strategy is useful to limit the propagation of service requests over the network thus preventing network overload. On the other hand, this strategy allows for more relevant semantic neighbors (that is, semantic neighbors associated to higher relevance values) to provide more answers, that is, the token-based mechanism is used to better guide service request propagation.

4.4.2 Quality-aware matchmaking

Web service discovery refers to the activity that is able to identify the best Web service from a set of available services. Often in literature, this activity only considers the functional aspects while quality aspects are not usually taken into account. In our opinion, the lack of a common, shared and flexible quality model implies the lack of a quality driven selection process. With the quality model presented in Section 4.2.2 we aim to fill this gap and in the following section propose an approach to selecting Web services according to this quality model. Here we suppose that a set of functionally equivalent Web services has been already identified with the techniques explained in the previous section. Thus, the selection process described in this section only refers to the quality aspects.

Our selection process is composed of two main activities. First of all, for every functionally equivalent available Web service, a *quality matchmaking* step is performed to state if user requirements are met; if so, the Web service is included in the **Selected Web Service set (SWS)**. This set represents the input of the second activity, i.e., *Ranking*, which performs a cost-benefit analysis and returns a sorted list of Web services in SWS.

Quality matchmaking receives user requirements and the service capabilities for each Web service as inputs. The matchmaking process is composed of two main steps: *low-level evaluation* and *high-level evaluation*. Both of these steps are performed comparing an *UR* with every C_j.

Roughly speaking, low-level evaluation activity identifies which C_j is able to fulfill all the requirements of the primitive quality dimensions in *UR*. Thereafter, exploiting the WQT, the high-level evaluation performs the same verification on derived quality dimensions and included in $RL_r(WQT)$.

The result of this two-steps evaluation process will be, for each Web service, the list of Service Levels Selected $SLS_w = \{SL_{w,a}(QT)\} \subseteq SLD_w(QT)$ passing both evaluation steps. If $SLS_w = \varnothing$ then at least one service level provider offering is able to satisfy one of the alternative user requirements $RL_r(WQT)$ and the related Web service w can be selected.

4.4.2.1 Low-level evaluation

An $RL_r(WQT)$ may contain, by definition, requirements of both primitive and derived quality dimensions. In the former case, the user strictly identifies the measurable aspects that the provider must support. This usually occurs for quality dimensions that are more related to the use of the Web service: e.g., *material = {wood, lacquered wood}*. Thus, given a user requirements $RL_r(WQT) \in RLD(WQT))$ and a provider offering $SL_{w,s}(QT) \in SLD_w(QT)$, the low-level evaluation aims at stating whether $SL_{w,s}(QT)$ satisfies $RL_r(WQT)$ where:

$$SL_{w,s}(QT) \text{ satisfies } RL_r(WQT) \Rightarrow (\, \forall r(pqd_{lr}) \in RL_r(WQT), \, \exists c(pqd_c) \in SL_{w,s}(QT)|$$
$$pqd_{lr}.name = pqd_c.name \wedge c(pqd_c).value \supseteq r(pdq_{lr}).value) \wedge$$
$$max(SL_{w,s}(QT).price) \leq max\,(RL_r(WQT).cost)$$

Generally speaking, the low-level evaluation verifies that the offering is able to provide a wider range of values than the user requires. In this phase, cost and price are also compared: the highest offering price must be less than or equal to the maximum amount of money that the user is willing to pay.

For example, the $c(delTime).values$ is satisfied by $SL_{A,2}$ and $SL_{B,1}$. This means that both services are able to support this requirement. If we consider *price*, we can easily state that WS_B is asking a higher price (see $SL_{B,1}$). For this reason, the Web service WS_B cannot be further analyzed and will not be included in the SWS.

4.4.2.2 High-level evaluation

The second step of the quality matchmaking process considers the quality dimensions derived in $RL_r(WQT)$. According to our quality model, the range of values of a dqd_m is always $[0..1]$, and the $r(dqd_m) \subseteq [0..1]$. In this way, the user indicatively defines the quality required for a high-level parameter that actually cannot be measured, but depends on other quality dimensions. Similarly to the low-level evaluation, given a $SL_{w,s}(QT) \in SLD_w(QT)$, the high-level evaluation aims at stating whether $SL_{w,s}(QT)$ satisfies $RL_r(WQT)$, where:

$$SL_{w,s}(QT) \text{ satisfies } RL_r(WQT) \Rightarrow \forall r(dqd_{mr}) \in RL_r(WQT)$$
$$q(dqd_{mr}, SL_{w,s}(QT), WQT) \in r(dqd_{mr}).values$$

In this case, a $SL_{w,s}(QT)$ - which only includes primitive quality dimensions - satisfies a requirement on a derived quality dimension $r(dqd_{mr})$, if the required range of values on this quality dimension ($r(dqd_{mr}).values$) includes the result of the quality function q defined as follows:

$$q(dq_i, SL(QT), WQT) = \begin{cases} \sum_{j=1}^{l+m} [q(qd_i.qd_j, SL(QT), WQT) \cdot w_{i,j})] & qd_i \in DQD \\ \min(e_{qdi}(c(qd_i).values)) & qd_i \in PQD \end{cases}$$

where $c(qdi) \in SL(QT)$, $e_{qdi} \in WQT$. This function quantifies the quality of a primitive or derived dimension qd_i calculated with the capabilities in $SL(QT)$, with respect to the user preferences WQT. In detail, if the quality dimension is derived, the quality function is the weighted sum of the quality of the influencing dimensions $qd_i.qd_j$. To the contrary, in case of a primitive quality dimension, we consider the quality evaluation function defined in WQT and associated to this dimension. In particular, we consider the worst quality associated to the values offered by the provider, which corresponds to the minimum values obtained invoking e_{pqdi} for each value in the $c(qd_i).values$.

Considering our example, in the user requirements we have $r(technicalqos).values = [0.4..0.7]$. Starting from the capabilities expressed in $SL_{A,1}$:

$q(technicalqos, SL_{A,1}, WQT) = min \ (e_{availability}(c(availability).values)) * 0.3 + q(performance, SL_{A,1}, WQT) * 0.7 =$
$min \qquad (e_{availability}(c(availability).values)) \qquad * \qquad 0.3 \qquad +$
$[min(e_{responsetime}(c(responsetime).values) * 0.1 +$
$min(e_{latency}(c(latency).values) * 0.9] * 0.7 = 0.489$

In this way, we can state that in the worst case $SL_{A,1}$ offers the quality of technical aspects (0.489) included in the range required by the user ($[0.4..0.7]$). Skipping further computations, in our example both $SL_{A,1}$ and $SL_{A,2}$ satisfy all the requirements on the derived quality dimensions, so that WS_A belongs to SWS.

Thus far, we have understood which Web services are able to satisfy user quality requirements. Every member of SWS can be used for the user's purpose and if the provider actually supports what has been promised in the SL, no problems will occur. Actually, since the capabilities are different for every Web service, one of these ought to be better than others. The goal of the last step of the selection process is to rank the service levels of the Web service included in the SWS. The order relationship ($\prec_q$) is obtained by performing a cost-benefit analysis (CBA). In detail, regardless of the Web service to which service levels SL_a and SL_b are related:

$SL_a \prec_q SL_b \Leftrightarrow CBA(SL_a) > CBA(SL_b) \equiv$

$\frac{w_{cost}}{max} * SL_a(price) + w_{ben} * q(qos, SL_a, WQT)) < \frac{w_{cost}}{max} * SL_b(price) + w_{ben} * q(qos, SL_b, WQT))$

According to this formula, the ranking depends on the weights on the cost (w_{cost}) and benefit (w_{ben}). During the ranking activity we can thus understand the extent to which money saving is more important than quality for the user. For example, for a user who really requires a high quality service and is not concerned about money, $w_{cost} < w_{ben}$.

Even in this step, we take into account the worst-case scenario and for this reason consider maximum price and minimum quality. Concerning the latter, the quality evaluation is performed according to the expression (12) considering the overall quality tree identified by the derived quality dimension *qos*. According to our example, we have:

$$q(qos, SL_{A,1}, WQT) = 0.5 * q(technicalqos, SL_{A,1}, WQT) +$$
$$0.5 * q(businessqos, SL_{A,1}, WQT) = 0.57$$
$$q(qos, SL_{A,2}, WQT) = 0.5 * q(technicalqos, SL_{A,2}, WQT) +$$
$$0.5 * q(businessqos, SL_{A,2}, WQT) = 0.55$$

Consequently, assuming that the user assigns the same importance to cost and benefit, i.e. $w_{cost} = w_{ben} = 0.5$, then:

$$CBA(SL_{A,1}) = 0.5 / 200 + 0.5 * 0.57 = 0.31$$
$$CBA(SL_{A,2}) = 0.5 / 200 + 0.5 * 0.55 = 0.27$$
$$\Rightarrow SL_{A,1} \prec SL_{A,2}$$

Thus, with respect to user requirements, Web Service WS_A provided with service level $SL_{A,1}$ has better quality then the same Web service with service level $SL_{A,2}$.

4.5 Service Interaction Design

The starting point of a data-intensive workflow modeling language is WebML 00. In this section, we show how to extend WebML with standard process modeling concepts (BPMN) and with standard application distribution primitives (based on Web Services). Developers can model their business processes using their favorite BPMN editor, manually transforming the process models into a set of WebML specifications according to the desired distribution architecture and co-ordination policy, and thereafter use WebRatio to specify the hypertexts and automatically generate the code that implements the applications to be installed at the various nodes of the selected architecture. The "explicit" design styles are amenable to automation, therefore we envisage the construction of a tool capable of turning a BPMN diagram into a set of WebML diagrams representing skeletons of the Web applications supporting the process.

The main ingredients of the WebML hypertext model are site views, areas, pages, units, operations, links and session/application variables. A site view is a graph of pages, possibly grouped into areas, allowing users of a given group to perform their specific activities (e.g., users browse the information, while managers update it). Pages contain content units connected by links, which represent atomic pieces of information to be published.

Consider for instance a simple scenario: users browse a Home Page, from which they can navigate to a page showing an index of loan products. After choosing one loan, users are lead to a page with the loan details and the list of proposals for the chosen loan. The WebML specification for the described hypertext is depicted in Figure 4.4.

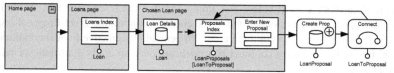

Fig. 4.4-WebML specification of a simple hypertext for browsing loan information.

The Home Page contains only some static content, which is not modeled. A link from this page leads to the Loans page, containing an index of all loans, graphically represented by means of an index unit labeled Loans Index. When the user selects a loan from the index, he is taken to the Chosen Loan page, showing the loan details. In this page, a data unit labeled Loan Details, displays the attributes of the loan (e.g. the company, the total amount and the rate) and is linked to another index unit labeled Proposals Index, which displays all the plan options of the loan. In general, a unit displays some of the attributes of one or more instances of a given entity; the entity name is specified at the bottom of the unit. Below the entity name, a predicate (called selector) can be specified to express a filter condition on the instances of the entity to be shown.

Contextual links. The content of units displayed in a page is often related to that of other units; this connection is achieved by contextual links, carrying data between the related units. An example of a contextual link is the link from the Loans Index unit to the Loan Details unit in Figure 4.4: it transports the ID of the loan chosen in the index unit and displayed in the data unit. The data carried by a contextual link is not always explicitly shown in a WebML diagram, since in many cases it can be inferred from the context. For example, a link exiting from an index unit always carries the identifier of the chosen object, a link going out from a data unit carries the identifier of the object displayed by the unit etc. Thus, links exiting from the Loans Index and Loan Details units in the example implicitly carry as context a Loan ID.

Transport links. WebML distinguishes between normal links (denoted by solid arrows) and transport links (denoted by dashed arrows). Normal links enable navigation and are rendered as hypertext anchors or form buttons; they can be contextual or not. For example, from the Home page in Figure 4.4, a user can follow the link to the Loans page. This particular link is not contextual, since it carries no information and simply enables a change of page. By contrast, transport links are always contextual. For example, the link from the Loan Details data unit to the Proposals Index unit is a transport link: when the user enters the Chosen Loan page, the Loan Details unit is displayed and, at the same time, the content of the Proposals Index unit is computed and displayed without the user's intervention. No navigable anchor is rendered for transport links.

Selectors. The content of a unit may depend on selectors, which are (possibly parametric) predicates. The Loan ID transported from the Loan Details to the Proposals Index unit is used to select the options associated with the loan by the relationship role LoanToProposal. This selection is expressed by the selector condition [LoanToProposal] below the unit's entity, which ensures that only the LoanProposal instances connected to the chosen Loan via the Loan-Proposal relationship are retrieved to build the index. In general, conjunctive logical conditions can be used where each conjunct is a predicate over an entity's attribute or relationship role.

Operations. WebML allows specifying update operations on the data underlying the Web application. Basic update operations are: the creation, modification and deletion of instances of an entity, or the creation and deletion of instances of a relationship. Other operations may include sending e-mail or, as we will see, invoking Web services. Unlike units, operations do not display data and are therefore not included in a page.

Figure 4.4 also illustrates an example of entity creation. The Chosen Loan Page contains an entry unit, representing a form collecting user data. When the user submits the data by clicking on the outgoing link of the entry unit, the entered data is used to create a new LoanProposal instance in the data repository. Data creation is represented by a create operation. After the creation, the new instance is connected to the currently selected Loan by means of a connect unit. Connect units create a new instance of a relationship.

WebML includes several other units and operations (such as the Modify unit for data updates and the Disconnect unit for relationship removal), a customizable mechanism to deal with run-time failures, extensible by the user who can add his/her custom units.

Enforcing process constraints via hypertexts requires conditional navigation. This is needed, for instance, to implement XOR and AND gateways and to evaluate logical conditions before/after activity execution.

The basic WebML primitives do not provide this capability. Therefore, we introduce two new WebML units: the If unit and the Switch unit (the latter being, of course, syntactic sugar based on the former). The behavior of the If and Switch unit is similar to the equivalent programming language constructs, but they govern the navigation in a WebML hypertext. The If unit has one or more incoming links and one associated logical expression; only one of the two outgoing links is activated, depending on whether the logical expression evaluates to true or false. Notice that there is no guard condition on the outgoing links, but a single Boolean condition is associated to the unit; therefore, only one of the two outgoing links can be enabled. The Switch unit has an associated expression and each outgoing link has a guard condition testing the equality of the expression to a given value;

only one of the outgoing links whose guard condition is true is followed as the result of the navigation, possibly selected non-deterministically.

4.5.1 Modeling processes IMPLICITLY with hypertext design primitives

When building applications involving process and hypertext constructs, process enactment rules (the process structure) are in many cases hard-wired in various ways within the Web interface itself and/or the application data. We call this approach implicit process control. The implicit encoding of process control may use the topology of hypertext links to control user interaction in simple sequential processes and data sharing for encoding more complex multi-actor processes. We now discuss each mechanism in detail.

A natural means of controlling processes within Web applications relies on hypertext links. The principle is to associate each activity to one or more Web pages, and then show users a link to the starting page of the activity only when the process specification allows the user to perform that activity. This is the usual solution to enforce sequential navigation: the topology of the hypertext is used to enforce the desired precedence constraint between activities. This simple constraint enforcement mechanism is built into many useful applications where a single user performs the business process in a "linear" way, following a well-defined sequence of steps. This is the case of on-line wizards, questionnaires and application forms.

Other structures are enabled by this approach: OR splits may be modeled by using one anchor for each possible process branch to follow; joins are obtained by making the navigation converge to a same page; iterations, pre- and post-conditions can also be expressed when conditional units are used. Links are instead insufficient to enforce AND-split and AND-join process constraints. The reason is that, within a given site view, the user's navigation always follows a single path at a given time and thus parallel execution is not possible. More generally, the main limitation of link-based control is that it cannot be used alone to enforce constraints between activities assigned to different users, since link topology is relative to the set of pages browsed by a specific user.

An alternative mechanism for implicitly enforcing multi-actor process constraints in a Web application relies on the shared information repository, e.g., the database underlying the application. The key idea is to encode case advancement, i.e., the activation and completion of activity instances in the application data. Thus, synchronization within each site view can be achieved via hypertext links as in the previous case, while synchronization across site views is obtained by having activities record their progress in the database using conditional navigation (based on the values actually found in the database).

The precise way in which process advancement information can be encoded in the database depends ultimately on the relationship between the process and the data model. Consequently, there are as many possible way of encoding process advancement as there are ways of modeling the application data. In this section, we discuss some frequently used design patterns and show how process control can be achieved using these data models.

Process control using activity-isomorphic entities. In some processes, for any activity A that is part of the process specification, an entity EA exists that is part of the application data model, such that an instance of EA is created exactly as the effect of successfully executing an instance of activity A. This entity is activity-isomorphic and the Web application simply tests for the existence of its instances in order to understand if activities following A can be started in a given case.

Process control using case-isomorphic entities. In some cases, the application data model contains a single entity that encapsulates all information on case advancement. Each case is associated with exactly one instance of this entity, and each activity modifies that entity instance to mark activity completion. In this case, the entity is said to be case-isomorphic. An example can be drawn from the loan request process described in Figure 4.4. In the data model, the LoanRequest entity encodes all the data associated to the case, and case evolution is represented by the attribute Status of the LoanRequest, which can take only one value from among: "ToBeValidated", "Validated", "Checked", "Accepted" and "Rejected". The status of the LoanRequest instance records the case advancement.

Application and process data are connected only when the need arises to correlate an activity with the data instances on which it is performed. The hypertext model is extended with ad hoc WebML primitives for delimiting the start and end of activities, assigning work items to activities and retrieving the application data relevant to the execution of a given activity. These extensions can be regarded as macros, i.e., combinations of elementary WebML concepts (e.g., operation units, and unit selector conditions) to retrieve and update the instances of the process reference model, which encapsulates the hypertext features stemming from the process model.

The process reference model and the process management units endow WebML with a clear method for specifying and deploying process-driven hypertexts as sets of interconnected Web pages and operations. The entities and relationships of the process reference model are shown in Figure 4.5: Entity Process is associated with entity ActivityType, representing the kinds of activities that can be executed in a process. Both entities describe general data on processes and activities that need not be replicated for each process/activity instantiation. Entity Case denotes an instance of a process, which has a name, used as a label for communicating with the user, a start time, an end time and a status. Entity Case is related to entity Process (relationship InstanceOf) and to entity ActivityInstance (via relationship PartOf), denoting the occurrences of an activity instance in the case.

Entity ActivityInstance is associated with entity ActivityType (via relationship InstanceOf), to denote the class of an activity instance.

Entities User and Group represent the process actors as individuals clustered in groups. A user may belong to different groups, and one of these groups is chosen as his default group, to facilitate access control when the user logs in. Entity ActivityType is related to entity Group, (via relationship AssignedTo) to denote that the users of the group are entitled to perform the specific kind of activity. Concrete activity instances are associated with individual users (via relationship AssignedTo) to express the more refined assignment of activity instances to the individual users who can execute them; an activity instance is also connected to the specific user who actually executes it (via relationship ExecutedBy).

Advancement information is encoded in status attributes. The status of a case can be: initiated, active (when at least one activity has started) or completed. The status of an activity instance can be: inactive, active or completed. The designer can specify an arbitrary number of relationships between the process reference model and the application data, which may be required to connect the process activities to the data items they use.

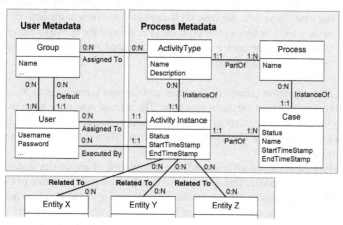

Fig. 4.5- Process reference model and its interconnection with the application data model.

The WebML hypertext model can be extended with primitives (called process management units) to record the advancement of a particular case in the process reference model. Process management units are convenient macros that simplify the hypertext; they could equivalently be expressed with conventional units applied to the reference model.

Three operation units are introduced:

- Start Activity/End Activity: respectively used to denote the initiation and termination of an activity instance within a case
- Assign: to model the allotment of work items, represented by suitable application entity instances, to activity instances
- Process-aware content units: used to denote the retrieval of content that depends both on the application data and on the process reference model

The Start Activity primitive starts the execution of an activity instance. The type of activity instance being started is specified as a label below the operation icon. The Start Activity operation has two (optional) input parameters:

- The first parameter is an activity instance identifier. When this is not null, the activity instance to start already exists (as the effect of the completion of a previous activity); the Start Activity operation simply records the activation timestamp of the activity instance and sets the status to "active". When the parameter is null, the activity instance to start does not exist when the operation is executed, but is created by the Start operation, and connected to the proper Activity Type and Case. Thereafter, the Start Activity operation records the activation timestamp of the newly created activity instance, marks its status to "active", and sets the session variable CurrentActivity to the ID of the newly created and activated activity instance.
- The second parameter is a case identifier. When this parameter is not null, a new activity instance must be created in the context of an already existing case; therefore, the case ID is exploited to connect the activity instance to the case it belongs to. If both the case ID and the activity instance ID are null, a new case and a new activity instance must be created (as in the "start case" situation explained next).

The first operation creates the Request activity and connects it to the appropriate activity type; it also creates a new case. The second operation starts the Choice activity (which already exists as effect of an Assign operation); the operation receives an activity instance identifier as input and its effect is to set the corresponding status to "active".

The End Activity primitive records the termination of an activity instance in the process reference model. The operation icon is labeled with the name of the activity type being terminated. The operation requires as input the ID of an activity instance; its execution sets the status of the activity instance to "complete", records the completion timestamp and resets the CurrentActivity session variable to NULL.

The start activity operation can be tagged as the start of the case, when the activity to be started is the first in the entire process. Similarly, the end activity operation can be tagged as the end of the case, when the activity to be terminated is the last in the process. The graphic decoration of the Start Activity and End Activity operations used to denote the starting/ending of cases consist in a small white dot and in a small black dot respectively. At case start, a new activity instance is created and connected to the activity type specified in the operation label, a new case instance is created with "active" status, an internal case name and a proper start time. The case instance is connected to the newly created activity instance (using the relationship PartOf) and to the process of the activity type (using the relationship InstanceOf). The session variable CurrentCase is set to the ID of the newly created case. At case termination, the activity instance status and the case status are set to "complete", the termination timestamps are recorded and the CurrentCase variable is reset to NULL.

The assign operation associates activity instances with instances of application entities or with instances of the User entity. Its purpose is to record the work items associated to a specific activity instance or the users in charge of executing it. If the activity instance target of the assignment does not exist, the operation creates it and connects it to the relevant parts of the process reference model. The operation icon is labeled with the name of the activity type involved; it receives as input parameters the ID of the current case, the ID of an activity instance (optional), the ID of an application entity instance (optional) and the ID of a user (optional).

The following situations are possible:

- If the activity instance ID parameter is null, the operation creates a new activity instance, with status set to "inactive", and connects it to the appropriate Activity Type and Case. The creation of a new activity instance models the frequent case when, in the context of a given activity, it is possible to anticipate the next activity to be performed in the case and to assign application objects to it. The creation of the activity instance enables its future selection (from a task list of "inactive" activities or from the listing of application objects connected to "inactive" activities) and activation (by a start operation).
- If the operation receives as input the OID of an application entity, it connects the target activity instance and the input entity instance (using the RelatedTo relationship).
- If the operation receives as input the ID of a user, it connects the target activity instance and the input user instance (using the AssignedTo relationship).

The assignment of an application entity instance and a user are not exclusive; each of them is denoted by an assignment expression below the activity name ("[Entity=EntityName]" and "[AssignedTo=UserID]" respectively).

Process-aware content units are regular WebML content units (e.g., index and data unit) augmented with special-purpose selector conditions concisely expressing the retrieval of data objects related to the process reference model. The icons of process-aware content units are identical to those of the corresponding regular WebML content units, but icons of process-aware units are tagged with a "W" symbol, denoting the retrieval of process-related data. For example, a process-aware index unit can retrieve:

- All the activity instances of a particular activity type (using the InstanceOf relationship) belong to cases in a specific state (using the PartOf relationship), are assigned to specific users (via the AssignedTo relationship) and executed by the specific users (via the ExecutedBy relationship). The unit will be rendered as an index over the identifiers of the activity instances matching its input parameters and selector conditions, and its outgoing link has an output parameter associated with the identifier of the selected activity instance.

- All the application entity instances that are related to activity instances in a specific state (via relationship RelatedTo), of a specific activity type (via the InstanceOf relationship), belonging to cases in a specific state (via the PartOf relationship) are assigned to specific users (via the AssignedTo relationship) and are executed by the specific users (via the ExecutedBy relationship). The unit will be rendered as an index over the identifiers of the entity instances matching the input parameters and selector conditions, and its outgoing link has an output parameter associated with the identifier of the selected entity instance.

Note that, in both cases, the unit provides as an output parameter an ActivityInstance identifier, but the selector conditions can be applied either to the Entity or to the Activity connected to the Activity Instance.

4.6 Conclusions

Service-oriented architectures (SOA) provide the basis to (re)design business processes in order to develop flexible applications where available services are dynamically composed to satisfy business goals. In this chapter, we show that the adoption of this type of architecture enables designing information systems that connect IEs to each other to run collaborative business processes. In fact, organizations can design service-based processes based either on simple internal applications or on external services. Aside from improving business competitiveness, a collaboration based on the service-based approach is also valuable as it eliminates the need to install and run the application on the customer's own computer and consequently alleviates the customer's burden of software maintenance, ongoing operation and support. For this reason, the adoption of SOA technology also enables small and medium enterprises (SMEs) to join IE networks, since it promises to reduce both costs and the complexity of connecting systems and business processes.

In order to enable more efficient and easier inter-organizational interactions, service-based collaboration imposes the use of standards in the process and service design phases. Service registry should contain services that need to be defined with the same granularity and described via the same functional and nonfunctional models. An alignment in process and service design and modeling enables the adoption of efficient techniques for service sharing, discovery and invocation as presented in this chapter.

References

[1] D. Ardagna and B. Pernici, "Adaptive service composition in flexible processes". IEEE Transaction on Software Engineering, vol. 33, no. 6, pp. 369–384, 2007.

[2] D. Bianchini, C. Cappiello, V. De Antonellis and B. Pernici, "P2S: A Methodology to Enable Inter-organizational Process Design through Web Services". Proc. of 21st International Conference on Advanced Information Systems Engineering (CAiSE'09), pp. 334-348, 2009.

[3] D. Bianchini, V. De Antonellis and M. Melchiori, "Flexible Semantic-based Service Matchmaking and Discovery". World Wide Web Journal, 11(2):227-251, 2008.

[4] A. Calì, D. Calvanese, S. Colucci, T. Di Noia and F.M. Donini, "A Logic Based Approach for Matching User Profiles". in Proc. of the 8th Int. Conference on Knowledge-Based Intelligent Information & Engineering Systems (KES'04), pp. 187–195, 2004.

[5] C. Cappiello, M. Comuzzi and P. Plebani, "On Automated Generation of Web Service Level Agreements". Proc. of the 19th Int. Conference on Advanced Information Systems Engineering (CAiSE'07), pp. 264-278, 2007.

[6] G. Canfora, M.di Penta, R. Esposito and M. L. Villani, "QoS-Aware Replanning of Composite Web Services". Proc. of the 3rd Int. Conference on Web Services (ICWS'05), pages 121-129, Orlando, Florida, 2005

[7] S. Castano, V. De Antonellis and S. De Capitani di Vimercati, "Global Viewing of Heterogeneous Data Sources". IEEE Transactions on Knowledge and Data Engineering, 13(2):277-297, 2001.

[8] S. Ceri, P. Fraternali, and A. Bongio, "Web Modeling Language (WebML): a modeling language for designing Web sites". WWW9/Computer Networks 33(1-6): 137-157, 2000.

[9] S. Ceri, P. Fraternali, A. Bongio, M. Brambilla, S. Comai, and M. Matera, "Designing Data-Intensive Web Applications", Morgan-Kaufmann, December, 2002.

[10] S. H. Chang and S. D. Kim, "A service-oriented analysis and design approach to developing adaptable services". Proc. of the International Conference on Service Computing, pages 204-211, Salt Lake City, UT, 2007.

[11] J.L.G. Dietz, "The Atoms, Molecules and Fibers of Organizations". Data&Knowledge Engineering, 47(3):301-325, 2003.

[12] X. Dong, A. Y. Halevy, J. Madhavan, E. Nemes and J. Zhang "Similarity Search for Web Services". Proc. of the 30th Int. Conference on Very Large Data Bases (VLDB'04), pages 372–383, Toronto, Canada, 2004

[13] C. Fellbaum. "Wordnet: An Electronic Lexical Database". MIT Press, 1998

[14] B. Fries, M. Khalid, M. Klusch and K. Sycara "OWLS-MX: Hybrid OWL-S Service Matchmaking". Proc. of First Int. AAAI Symposium on Agents and Semantic Web, Arlington, VA, USA, pages 77–84, 2005.

[15] I. Horrocks and L. Li "A Software Framework for Matchmaking Based on Semantic Web Technology". International Journal of Electronic Commerce, Special Issue on Semantic Web Services and Their Role in Enterprise Application Integration and E-Commerce, 2004.

[16] P. Hung and L. Haifei, "Web services discovery based on the trade-off between quality and cost of service: a token-based approach". SIGecom Exch., 4(2):21–31, 2003.

[17] C. Marchetti, B. Pernici and P. Plebani, "A quality model for multichannel adaptive information". Proc. of the 13th international World Wide Web conference on Alternate track papers & posters, pages 48–54, New York, NY, USA, 2004.

[18] J.A. O'Brien, "Introduction to Information Systems: Essentials for the Internetworked Enterprise". McGraw-Hill Education, 2000.

[19] V. Tosic, W. Ma, B. Pagurek and B. Esfandiari, "Web Service Offerings Infrastructure (WSOI) - a management infrastructure for XML Web services". Proceedings of Network Operations and Management Symposium, pages 817–830, 2004.

[20] I. Vanderfeesten, H.A. Reijers and W.M.P. van der Aalst, "Evaluating workflow process designs using cohesion and coupling metrics". Computer in Industry, 59(5):420-437, 2008.

[21] A. Vedamuthu, D. Orchard, M. Hondo, T. Boubez and P. Yendluri, "Web Services Policy 1.5 – Primer". Available on line: http://www.w3.org/TR/2006/WD-ws-policy-primer-20061018, 2006.

[22] L. Zeng, B. Benatallah, M. Dumas, J. Kalagnamam and and H. Chang, "QoS-Aware Middleware for Web Services Composition". IEEE Trans. on Software Engineering, 30(5):311-327, 2004.

Chapter 5 - A technological infrastructure to sustain Internetworked Enterprises

Ernesto La Mattina[1], Vincenzo Savarino[1], Claudia Vicari[1], Davide Storelli[2], Devis Bianchini[3]

[1] Engineering Ingegneria Informatica S.p.A.

[2] eBMS S.S. ISUFI - University of Salento

[3] Università degli studi di Brescia, Brescia, Italy

Abstract - In the Web 3.0 scenario, where information and services are connected by means of their semantics, organizations can improve their competitive advantage by publishing their business and service descriptions. In this scenario, Semantic Peer to Peer (P2P) can play a key role in defining dynamic and highly reconfigurable infrastructures. Organizations can share knowledge and services, using this infrastructure to move towards value networks, an emerging organizational model characterized by fluid boundaries and complex relationships. This chapter collects and defines the technological requirements and architecture of a modular and multi-Layer Peer to Peer infrastructure for SOA-based applications. This technological infrastructure, based on the combination of Semantic Web and P2P technologies, is intended to sustain Internetworked Enterprise configurations, defining a distributed registry and enabling more expressive queries and efficient routing mechanisms. The following sections focus on the overall architecture, while describing the layers that form it.

5.1 Introduction

Today P2P networks focus on specific issues: file sharing, distributed computing, knowledge and information sharing. To support these heterogeneous scenarios, P2P Infrastructures [1], Semantic Web and Service-oriented technologies are taken into account. In dynamic P2P networks, it is essential to adopt flexible techniques for searching and accessing shared information. To this end, semantics in P2P systems [2, 3, 4] can be helpful in searching for information and services that better fulfill the user's requests. In particular, Semantic Web technologies, applied to P2P networks, facilitate defining clustering techniques to create and maintain the network and integration models for knowledge and service sharing, query processing and routing.

Within the TEKNE project, one of the research activities concerning the specifications of the technological infrastructure aims at creating a general purpose, modular and extensible semantic P2P overlay network infrastructure.

This overlay enables the integration of heterogeneous systems such as SOA, Knowledge Base and Information Management systems. Structured and semantically enriched queries are submitted to these systems and are propagated across the network, taking into account the semantics extracted from the request message and its payload. Combining the Semantic Web and P2P paradigm helps probe the P2P network by means of more complex and expressive queries. Semantic P2P networks enable better localization, routing and forwarding of static resources, with Web Services adopted as a technological paradigm for service and data interchange interfaces.

The objective is the integration of content and service semantics, according to domain ontologies within a P2P architecture, where each entity involved is represented as a network node. Therefore, specification of the Technological Infrastructure must involve the definition of:

- the technology for distributed services and information discovery, based on a semantic description of each
- an efficient and scalable algorithm for peer selection and request routing

In order to achieve these goals each peer is characterized by an explicit semantic description of services provided and own competence/knowledge according to the shared ontologies [5, 6, 7].

The above considerations lead to the definition of a multi-layer network, constituted by a P2P infrastructure providing services enriched with semantic annotations and a semantic layer that enables efficiently grouping and forwarding requests to semantically analogous peers: the request is not forwarded to all peers or to a random subset, but only to those peers whose resources have a high probability of being related to the request according to peer resource semantic descriptions.

In this context, the term "probability" is not linked to its traditional meaning in the probability theory sense, but to the fact that the peers to whom the request is forwarded are characterized by a common set of concepts semantically close to the request, according to the defined metrics. To this end, peers are clustered according to the similarity of their resources. The request is then propagated through these clusters of peers. The basic idea is that each peer is able to serve a request, but other peers belonging to the same cluster are also able to fulfill the request at the same time. To establish clusters of peers and implement semantic-driven resource discovery, peers are equipped with a knowledge base where the semantic descriptions of their resources, as well as knowledge on other nodes hosting similar resources, are maintained.

Knowledge is not transferred among peers of the same cluster; they only know that those peers with the same set of concepts are grouped together in that cluster.

Generalizing these considerations, each request follows paths characterized by nodes with semantically close knowledge bases. This semantic layer can be built through explicit semantics, linked to a specific ontology consisting of concepts and relationships between concepts, or generated by latent semantics, without excluding that the two approaches can coexist. The adoption of one approach over another or their coexistence drives the choice of search mechanisms based on different search and retrieval algorithms.

By extending this paradigm, the semantic layer can take into account an explicit semantic that could be made up of n ontologies. In fact, depending on the application context, the semantic description of each peer could refer to different ontologies and the cluster could be made up of peers whose knowledge base is linked to concepts belonging to several ontologies - without excluding that the semantics of the request could also be linked to concepts belonging to different ontologies.

The approach of a semantic layer consisting of multiple clusters connected to each other, decouples the semantic network organization from the P2P physical network. This semantic layer can be applied whatever the nature of the network: from networks based on partial or total flooding to structured networks based on rooting tables, and from completely decentralized to partially centralized architectures based on super peers.

In the following section, we describe the overall architecture implementing the multi-layer technological infrastructure, focusing on the functionalities of each module and on the interactions between modules.

5.2 Overall Architecture

TEKNE technological architecture allows Internetworked Enterprises to publish and retrieve resources (data and services) and knowledge from well-established repositories and service registries such as UDDI, ebXML or other XML-based registries and repositories distributed across the network [9]. The technological infrastructure is a semantic based P2P network made up of three main layers (Fig. 5.1).

The lower layer, *P2P Infrastructure* is the *logical overlay* and *network layer* of a traditional P2P architecture. It covers all communication activities such as access to the network, connection of nodes and propagation of the request across the network. The P2P Infrastructure consists of a JXTA infrastructure where communication channels are implemented via JXTA Pipes [10, 11].

The second layer, *Semantic Layer*, takes care of all network semantic issues: clustering activity, node registration and semantic annotation, semantic-driven request propagation and semantic matchmaking of services and other information. During the node-cluster association phase, this layer communicates with the *P2P infrastructure* in order to gain network information such as network balance and full connection between nodes. The Semantic Layer, which will be described more in depth hereafter, is composed of several modules that provide the following functionalities:

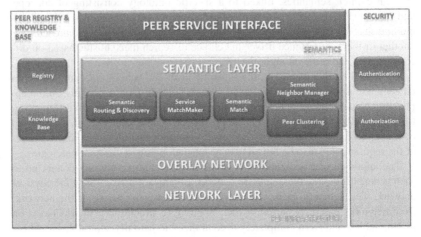

Fig. 5.1 The three-layer architecture

The *Semantic Match* module calculates the type and degree of similarity between the domain ontology concepts formalized in OWL [12].

The *Peer Clustering* module defines the set of concepts of each cluster and the way to assign a new node to one or more clusters according to their semantic description. This module, through the invocation of the Semantic Match component, generates a ranking of candidate clusters, also taking into account network balance issues.

Semantic Routing & Discovery is the module that enables resource discovery and semantic-driven request propagation. Each node is able to discriminate the type of incoming request, execute the related response behavior and propagate it in a semantic-aware manner. This module relies on the *Semantic Neighbor Manager* that is invoked during the request propagation on the P2P network in order to efficiently forward service requests towards the most suitable nodes based on the semantic similarity between peer contents, thus enabling a more focused search and avoiding network overload.

The *Service MatchMaker* module is responsible for matchmaking between a service requests and the services provided by organizations belonging to the network. This module implements the service matchmaking techniques expounded in Chapter 4.

The highest architecture layer, **Peer Service Interface**, manages interactions with end users for the invocation of peer services, the formulation of the request and the visualization of responses. Descriptions, semantic annotations and relations among nodes, resources and services are stored in distributed registries, whose interfaces are provided by the Peer Service Interface.

Each node implements the three architectural layers described above. In particular, all nodes implement both the JXTA communication channel by means of the P2P Infrastructure in order to access the semantic network and the Peer Service Interface to enable end users to perform peer service discovery via peer Web-Clients or UI-Clients.

5.3 Peer Registry and Knowledge Base

Each peer registry plays an important role in the TEKNE platform operational scenario with the task of maintaining the knowledge of each peer in terms of: (i) resources (data and services) exposed by each enterprise appropriately annotated with semantics by means of reference ontologies; (ii) knowledge on other nodes, for example, collaborative partners who share similar resources. The aim is to describe each resource regardless of its nature and the format of its descriptor. For example, UDDI provides specifications for a publishing services registry through their interface described in WSDL and does not allow full freedom to extend the metadata to be used for the description of those services. An important aspect is to extract the services semantics from the inputs, outputs, preconditions and effects of the request and related response (IOPE:Input-Output-Precondition-Effect). These semantics are based on domain ontology, or generally, on several ontologies.

In the definition of the registry architecture, ebXML Registry and Repository specifications are adopted. These specifications provide the implementation of a repository that can be extended, by means of an extensible metadata model (RIM-Registry Information Metamodel), to include the entire semantic services descriptions, namely, their syntactic interface, semantic annotations and semantic model (i.e., the ontologies).

The fact that each node provides a registry describing the organizations and services leads to the creation, from a logical perspective, of a distributed registry and repository where the services of each Internetworked Enterprise are published and searchable through queries submitted to the semantic network (Fig. 5.2).

EbXML Registry & Repository 3.0 specifications [13, 14] provide a federation and cooperation model by means of a metadata model (metadata federation) that enables creating a relationship among registries. This allows registry&repositories to be federated in such a way as to behave like a single virtual registry&repository, delegating the local control of their registry to each individual organization.

In the distributed network of nodes of the TEKNE technological infrastructure, the relationship among registries is not built explicitly through the federation metamodel provided by RIM but by means of the process of association of each node of the P2P network to one or more semantic clusters. Hence, each node and its registry are characterized by the descriptions of each organization belonging to the same node.

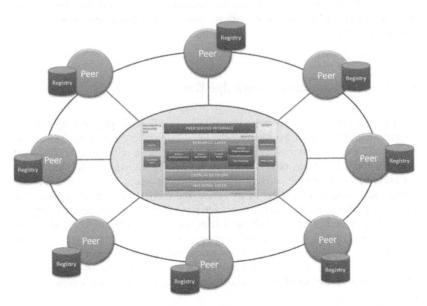

Fig. 5.2 The technological infrastructure of the TEKNE Platform. Each node contributes to building a distributed registry that enables information sharing.

The approach adopted for resource sharing and the interoperability between organizations enabled by the TEKNE platform provides the following macro phases:

Annotation of resources through metadata. In order to search for shared resources among organizations, the first step is to annotate these resources with information describing the domain, their semantics and links to other resources.

Through the slot mechanism, classification hierarchies and, in general, by means of the extensibility of RIM, it is possible to define profiles dependent on the application domain, or a set of metadata related to each other.

In particular, as concerns services that a generic peer X publishes on the P2P network, the peer is equipped with a knowledge base constituted by: (a) *local knowledge* on services that the peer advertises on the network; (b) *network knowledge* on other members of the clusters that peer X is classified in and, within those clusters, other peers that provide similar services with respect to those locally advertised (*semantic neighbors*).

Peer knowledge on services is expressed in OWL-DL and stored in the peer service registry as instance of ebXML OWL Profile (concept instances).

The above considerations on the profile/metamodel result in the need for profiles and models to be shared among the network nodes to ensure their interoperability within a given domain or among different domains, and for information relating to metadata to be searchable across the network. The metadata associated to resources allow defining their semantics and structure for resource discovery.

Retrieval of resource metadata through query facilities. The process of annotation makes it possible to seek information within the registry by means of their associated semantics. In fact, the metadata associated with resources that have been published on the registry can be queried via standard mechanisms provided by the ebXML Registry, for example Filter Query and SQL Query, or through the navigation of a related metamodel.

Complex queries can be structured and saved as a stored query during the model definition phase. In this last case, during the discovery phase, all stored queries are listed according to the model selected by the user.

Retrieval of resources. After finding the metadata instances, it is necessary to retrieve the associated resources. An instance contains the *RegistryObject ID* and by means of the "GetContent" ebXML query the RegistryItem containing the resource can be retrieved.

In general, it is possible to associate to each resource a set of metadata defining the service, and therefore the contract, that provides that resource. In this way, all aspects relating to the storage of resources can be separated from those related to their discovery and retrieval, and in general, from an architectural point of view, the registry and the repository of each organization can be considered as two separated systems. This separation also allows delegating all access policies and query of resources to the registry.

5.4 Semantic Layer

The Semantic Layer is in charge of reorganizing the P2P nodes by associating each of them with one or more semantic clusters. The association of a node to two or more clusters creates an *inter cluster semantic link* among them, namely a possible semantic path to forward a request. For example in Fig. 5.3, an inter-cluster semantic link is set between Cluster 3 and Cluster 4 that share peer N10.

In this way, while in the underlying layer of the overlay network, namely the traditional P2P network, requests are forwarded following the connections among nodes, in the Semantic Layer requests are routed through the *inter-cluster semantic links* resulting from the membership of a node to multiple clusters. For example, peer N9 and N10 (Fig. 5.3) are characterized by a hop equal to 3 in the P2P network and, after their reorganization, by a hop equal to 1 because they belong to the same cluster (Cluster 3). A request submitted by Peer N9 could be forwarded to Cluster 4 by means of the above-mentioned inter-cluster semantic link between Cluster 4 and Cluster 3.

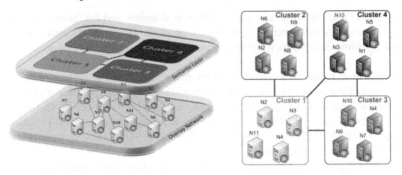

Fig. 5.3 Semantic Layer and inter-cluster semantic links.

The Semantic Layer is thus responsible for the following tasks:

Clustering. Each cluster is characterized by a set of concepts belonging to an ontology, or, more generally, to *n* ontologies. Clustering is based on the partition of the ontology according to its specific structure and the relationships among its concepts. To perform this task, the Peer Clustering module is invoked.

Peer Registration. Each node, after having joined the network, has to register itself with its semantic description (i.e. an XML fragment containing a semantic description of enterprise and services provided) so that the Semantic Layer identifies the clusters that a node belongs to. The task of the Semantic Layer is, therefore, the extraction of the semantics from the node description and matching of concepts associated with each cluster. To perform this task, the Semantic Match and the Peer Clustering modules are invoked.

Balance and connectivity of the network. During the cluster allocation phase, the Semantic Layer also has to take into account the current state of the network, avoiding that certain clusters become much more populated than others and that disjoined clusters of nodes are created without any link between them, thus ensuring full connectivity of the network. In other words, it has to guarantee that there is always a path linking any pair of clusters. This task is performed by the Peer Clustering module.

Semantic-driven resource discovery. Resource discovery throughout P2P networks involves both matchmaking of requests (for services and other resources) and their efficient propagation on the network. Once a request is submitted to a node, the Semantic Layer provides procedures for semantic-driven matchmaking of the request against locally available resources to find suitable search results. To perform this task, Semantic Match and Service Matchmaker modules are invoked. Moreover, the Semantic Layer performs effective request propagation based on peer knowledge of other network nodes. In particular, the request is spread along the network by following inter-cluster links; the choice of a path for request propagation is suggested through a semantic comparison between the request and semantic description that characterizes each cluster that the peer belongs to. To perform this task, Semantic Routing&Discovery and Semantic Neighbor Manager modules are invoked.

A particular peer, the Group Dispatcher, is in charge of defining clusters and performing peer registration. Moreover, the Group Dispatcher is in charge of maintaining the semantic representation of clusters and peers belonging to them, as well as maintaining inter-cluster links. The registration of a new node is implemented through a specific request to the Group Dispatcher. The new node joins the P2P network and looks for available Group Dispatchers. Once a Group Dispatcher has been identified, the peer sends a registration request containing its description.

On receiving the request, the Group Dispatcher extracts information on the peer, performs a cluster rating and sends a registration confirmation that contains information on the clusters to which the new peer belongs. The Group Dispatcher plays an important role in the semantic network infrastructure. This particular peer may be a single point of failure. To avoid this, more than one Group Dispatcher is expected to exist in the network. This solution involves a redundancy of knowledge on the state of the network. Any change in the network triggers a notification process between active Group Dispatchers. In this way, each Group Dispatcher maintains updated knowledge of the network and in particular on the connectivity of clusters. To summarize, the Group Dispatcher:

- defines the clusters that make up the semantic layer;
- establishes the clusters that a new peer belongs to following a registration request, taking into account the state of the network;
- updates knowledge on the state of the network and spreads it to the other Group Dispatchers.

Moreover, the Group Dispatcher plays the role of "hub" in spreading the request toward the islands of clusters. The possible creation of islands of clusters results in a network that is not completely connected. This event occurs when few peers characterize the network and their later abandonment weakens the existing links up to their complete cancellation between some clusters.

A high number of peers allows full connectivity of the semantic network and a greater weight (i.e. number of peers that belong to the same couple of clusters) of each inter-cluster semantic link.

In the following section, we provide details on modules invoked to perform the above-mentioned functionalities.

5.4.1 Semantic Match

In the semantic web context, evaluation of a measure of semantic similarities among ontological concepts is a key component for techniques such as clustering, data-mining, information indexing and filtering [15].

In the Semantic Layer, the Semantic Match module is crucial in the peer registration process and in the request propagation phase. It is designed to provide a measure of comparison among the sets of concepts that characterize clusters, peer descriptions and requests. This measure provides the type and degree of match and is based on measuring the semantic similarity between two sets of concepts.

A natural approach to defining a measure between two concepts in an ontology is to consider the ontology as a hierarchical graph where the edges represent the relations between concepts and the nodes represent the concepts themselves. The approach to evaluate the degree of match between sets of concepts is based on the mutual discretization position between two concepts in the hierarchy. Formally, an ontology is defined as a tuple $O = \{C, R, H\}$ where:

C : represents all the concepts c;

R : represents all the relationships r among concepts;

H : represents ontology hierarchy.

Let Sr and Sa be two set of concepts, respectively:

$$S_r = \{c_r \in C, r = 1,...n\} \tag{1}$$

$$S_a = \{c_a \in C, a = 1,...m\} \tag{2}$$

Semantic Match SM between S_r and S_a is defined as:

$$SM(Sr, Sa) \mapsto (MatchType, DegreeOfMatch) \in [0, DMT] \times [0,1] \tag{3}$$

The *MatchType* is obtained through the following formula:

$$MatchType = \min_r \left\{ \max_a \left\{ match(c_r, c_a) \right\} \right\} \tag{4}$$

where $match(c_r, c_a)$ returns a discrete value according to the following algorithm:

```
match(cr,ca){
    if (cr.isDifferentFrom(ca)
        OR cr.isDisjointWith(ca))
    return FAIL;
```

```
if (cr≡ca
    OR cr.isEquivalentTo(ca))
return EXACT;
if (cr.subClassOf(ca))
return PLUGIN;
if (cr.anchestor(ca))
return SUBSUMES;
if (ca.ancestor(cr) AND NOT cr.subclassOf(ca))
return SUBSUMED_BY;
if (exists a relation r belonging to R such
    that r(cr,ca))
return NEARBY;
return FAIL;
}
```

A descending order is determined among the above discrete values, enabling the computation of *MatchType* according to equation (4):

```
EXACT>PLUGIN>SUBSUMES>SUBSUMED_BY>NEARBY>FAIL
```

DMT is the max value of the discrete range of $match(c_r,c_a)$. In this case DMT = 6. The *DegreeOfMatch* is evaluated according to the following formula:

$$DegreeOfMatch = \frac{1}{|n \cdot DMT|} \sum_r \max_a \left\{ \gamma \cdot match\left(c_r, c_a\right) \right\} \qquad (5)$$

The multiplication factor γ provides a contribution that takes into account the number of relations between the two concepts c_a and c_r:

$$\gamma = \begin{cases} \dfrac{N_r}{N_t} & match\left(c_r, c_a\right) = nearby \\ 1 & otherwise \end{cases} \qquad (6)$$

where N_r is the number of relations between c_r and c_a and N_t is the number of all relations that belong to R.

5.4.2 Peer Clustering

The Peer Clustering module is invoked by the Group Dispatcher to create the clusters that constitute the Semantic Layer. The modality of cluster creation, and consequently, the set of concepts of each cluster, is based on ontology partitioning. This partitioning depends on the structure of the ontology and relations among the concepts (SubClassOf, Equivalence, Restrictions, etc...). The basic idea is that each ontology concept is part of more than one set of concepts that characterize each cluster. The fact that two clusters are characterized by a subset of common concepts will determine, during the registration phase of a new node, a possible relationship (semantic link) or a possible path in the propagation of a request process.

The cluster creation process is based on work presented in [16], namely the creation of the so-called Semantic Overlay Network (SON). Specifically, a Semantic Overlay Network (SON) is defined as a virtual cluster of peers that is associated with an ontological concept in a hierarchy. The descriptions or contents of each peer must be associated with the concepts of a given taxonomy, so that the peer can be assigned to the corresponding SON. During the peer registration phase, the Peer Clustering module calculates, by means of the Semantic Match module, the match degree between the set of concepts that characterize the peer description and the vector of concepts related to each cluster. The result of matchmaking (i.e. Semantic match ranking) is used by the Group Dispatcher to reply to the peer registration confirmation and contains the list of clusters in which the new peer must be included as well as related pipe IDs to instantiate the communication channel (input and output pipe).

5.4.3 Service MatchMaker

The Service MatchMaker module adopted in the three-layer peer architecture implements the service matchmaking approach detailed in [22] and described in Chapter 4.

The Service MatchMaker module receives a service request from the Peer Service Interface, expressed in a WSDL-S document, together with a set of desired service categories used to filter out irrelevant search solutions. To perform the matchmaking task, the Service MatchMaker module communicates with the Peer Registry and Knowledge Base and executes the following steps:

1. retrieval of semantic descriptions of services stored in the underlying registry;
2. for each service, the retrieval of associated service categories;
3. selection of services whose list of associated categories contains at least one of the categories specified for the service request or a more specific category according to the service category taxonomy (see Chapter 4);

4. for the selected services, application of the service matchmaking algorithm;
5. filtering of matching results whose degree of similarity is equal to or greater than the threshold specified in the request;
6. ranking of matching results according to the kind of match (EXACT > PLUG-IN > SUBSUME > INTERSECTION > MISMATCH) and the degree of similarity.

5.4.4 Semantic Neighbor Manager

The Semantic Neighbor Manager is invoked during the distributed search and is in charge of supporting the Semantic Routing&Discovery module during request forwarding over the P2P network and updating the peer service ontology according to answers received to previous requests sent on the network.

This module implements the distributed search described in Chapter 4. The requester peer collects the incoming responses, characterized by the identifier of the service that meets the request, the peer to which the service is registered, the kind of match and the similarity degree. The peer modifies the peer service ontology by updating the inter-peer semantic links according to the following procedure:

- if the request coincides with one of the local service descriptions, the service descriptions are set in the peer service ontology as "source" of inter-peer semantic links;
- if the request does not coincide with one of the local service descriptions, the peer service ontology is updated by adding a new service description corresponding to the request. This service description is defined as *abstract*, since it does not coincide with any locally registered service. This new abstract service description is set as source of the inter-peer semantic links.

Semantic links are then labeled with the type of match and similarity degree, as formalized in Chapter 4. The update of the peer service ontology is useful in order to lead the propagation of future service requests. In fact, when peer X receives a new request, the request is compared with local service descriptions (both abstract, namely, corresponding to previous requests, and concrete) and for each description, the following options are possible:

- the new request does not match the local descriptions or the local descriptions matching the new request are not "source" of any inter-peer semantic link; in this case, the request recipients are peers belonging to the same clusters as peer X, according to inter-cluster semantic links;
- the new request coincides with one of the local service descriptions (exact match), that are "source" of inter-peer semantic links; in this case, this set of semantic neighbors is chosen as the request recipients;

- the new request partially coincides with one of the locally available service descriptions (partial match) that are "source" of inter-peer semantic links; in this case, a combination of the previous strategies of forwarding is applied.

Every time a new service request is served, peer X updates its own peer service ontology.

The Semantic Neighbor Manager module receives the locally found list of service interfaces from the Peer Service Interface. The service request is matched by means of the Service MatchMaker that produces a list of peers to which the request has to be forwarded.

5.4.5 Semantic Routing & Discovery

The Semantic Routing&Discovery module is responsible for request propagation across the network. In particular, it is in charge of normalizing the messages that will be submitted to the network by means of the Peer Service Interface. In detail, the Semantic Neighbor Manager provides the path that the request must follow, namely, the clusters to which the request must be forwarded. The Semantic Routing&Discovery is in turn responsible for enveloping and forwarding the message to the communication channel (propagate pipe).

Another task implemented in this module is to decide, according to the semantics of the request, which application has to elaborate the request. The related response is forwarded to the requester node through the communication channel.

From a logical-architectural perspective, the Semantic Routing&Discovery is composed of:

- an interface responsible for normalizing requests from the Peer Service Interface and forwarding them to the Semantic Neighbor Manager;
- an interface responsible for collecting requests;
- a set of behaviors that will be activated according to the semantics of the request in order to interact with the applications responsible for processing the request.

5.5 Distributed Authentication and Authorization System

The accreditation system of the TEKNE technological platform is based on two main sub-systems. The first is the authentication system, which identifies the user who logs onto the platform, while the second sub-system is responsible, via a profiler, to determine if a previously logged user has permission to access a particular service provided by the platform.

The above platform, in the context of Internetworked Enterprise, is highly distributed, consisting of nodes that expose applications and information services. In this context, the adoption of an architectural model, characterized by a monolithic and centralized system consisting of the above sub-systems, is unsuitable for a variety of reasons that will be highlighted. To this end, consider the figure below (Fig. 5.4) which shows the architecture of a hypothetical Centralized User Profile.

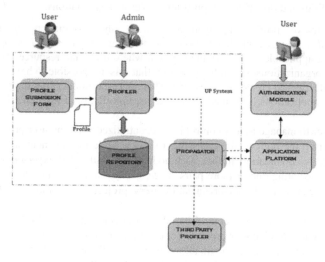

Fig. 5.4 Hypothetical architecture of a Central User Profiling System

The Profile Submission Form creates a user profile containing personal data and preferences on interactions with the platform services:

- **User Personal Information**:
    - permanent personal data;
    - variable information (dependent and independent on the system);
- **User Preferences:** some preferences are related to the system, others are personal information (e.g. type of gadget to display);
- **Information on user behavior** (rules and behavior patterns).

This information is inserted into a *profile repository*. Specifically, the Profile Submission Form codifies the profile form data in order to be available to the *profiler*, which in turn creates a user profile to be stored in a repository. This User Profile, to be used by the application platform, is incomplete since the administrator needs to complete the registration process with the role association, and when relevant, the necessary functionality authorization. Moreover, the Profile Submission Form, asynchronously connected with a profiler, inserts or updates user data within the third party profiler. All user information is retrieved by the profiler repository, which interacts with almost all platform modules offering various services. In particular:

- it interacts with application modules providing the available functionalities according to the specific user role;
- it automatically takes a census of incoming users, according to the information received by the Profile Submission Form;
- it modifies and inserts new applications, roles and associations.

In the above profile management system, the association *application-functionality-user* is centralized, moreover defining a tuple *<application ,user>* that is not applicable in a distributed system where users and resources belong to different organizations, generally expecting that it is not possible to have information on all users to create an access list. This approach implies that the policy for access to applications is defined within the user profile, or at least closely related to it.

In order to manage access control in a decentralized way, the user profile is separated from the policies for accessing a service while management stays within the respective boundaries. In fact, each node of the platform is expected to have a profiler associating one or more pairs *<role, group>* to each user where the term "group" means a set of inter-organization users (project, collaboration, partnership etc.).

In the context of access control based on user roles, the use of ontologies can help define all possible user profiles. For example, the use of an ontology of actors operating within a certain domain allows managing all the possible user profiles in that field. A specific role can be assigned to each profile and a set of permissions on resources to each role. The possibility ensues of "semantic" permission management by means of inheritance and a semantic relationship among the actors' concepts of the ontology. Hence, it is crucial to define and manage common ontologies, shared within internetworked enterprise configurations, which enable a unique identification and interpretation of the associations of roles and actions, without any *misunderstanding*.

Below we outline the vocabulary, expressed in SBVR, created to define and describe the key concepts of a taxonomy of roles, actions and basic notions for the construction of the accreditation system. This vocabulary, appropriately extended, is used in different application contexts for access control to distributed resources available within the TEKNE platform.

organization

Definition:	group of people or organizations united for a purpose
Source:	OSM (OMG)

enterprise

Definition:	an organization that exists to perform a specific mission and achieve the associated goals and objectives.

	Source:	TEKNE Project
user		
	Definition:	person who uses the platform
group		
	Definition:	set of enterprises involved in a collaboration. In order to be actively part of a group, enterprises must enter the technological platform defined in the TEKNE Project and share/use services and models. Once a collaboration is established between two or more enterprises, it is possible to define a group based on the technological platform defined in the TEKNE Project. The group will be composed of all the enterprises that take part in the collaboration. Any user of the platform is by default a member of the predefined group called "Default-group".
role		
	Definition:	a collaboration is defined in terms of the roles that workers of the enterprises have within it, thus a group, representing a collaboration within the TEKNE technological platform, must allow the definition of roles. The "Default-group" has exactly one role called "Default-role".

group _has_ role

user _plays_ role _in_ group

	Note:	A user can play different roles in different groups.
access level		
	Definition:	the user can access resources with some levels of permissions, defined in terms of actions they are allowed to perform on them.
administrator		
	General Concept: **user**	
	Definition:	a user who defines groups and roles. Each enterprise has an administrator.

administrator _creates_ group
administrator _creates_ role

The administrator is a particular user who has the task of managing the platform and updating it according to the needs of the different communities. A key task is to manage groups and roles that come about through a collaboration between organizations that adopt the Internetworked Enterprise paradigm.

Each role generally refers to a shared taxonomy among the entire digital district (network of nodes), and is extensible at group level, i.e., valid specializations can be defined to be available at group level (role scope). The definition of a profile allows more flexible policies to define access rules at multiple levels of granularity: at user level, role and organization, within or external to the service node.

This profile is not closely related to the services that a user can access. In fact, once a user has selected a resource, the system will determine the specific access policy according to the user profile and the type of action that the user wants to perform on that resource (e.g. read, write, link, etc).

It is thus possible to manage a rule that states:

"Only Project Managers can download TEKNE project cost tables". In this case, Project Manager refers to a role defined on a TEKNE group level, an inter-organizational group where any organization that is member of it has defined its own project manager. This example shows how the definition of the access policy is independent of the user profile, since the owner of the resource/service can change the rules on possible actions that can be undertaken, for example, by changing the rule:

"Only Project Managers can view TEKNE project cost tables", without changing any profile.

The general scenario is therefore the following. Each node of the Internetworked Enterprise has an accreditation module that allows each user to access the platform. Each user, after the registration phase, will be characterized by a profile, containing *<role, group>* tuples that will be used, depending on the context, in the platform interaction process (access to services). These tuples will be updated throughout the life cycle of the registered user (e.g., user belongs to a new working group). Therefore, each node generally has several registered users, characterized by a profile, and provides several services regulated by access policies. When a generic user belonging to a node makes a request for a service provided by another node, the request is formulated in order to provide the contextualized information of the user profile according to the service request. In particular, the most suitable tuples *<role, group>* will be provided in order to allow the node that exposes the service to identify the access policies and to determine whether to perform the requested action.

The accreditation system (Fig. 5.5) is able to:

- manage user registration and profile lifecycle;
- manage access to the platform and user requests, ensuring confidentiality, non-repudiation (trusted), and primarily user identification;
- manage service access policies;
- manage group lifecycles and collaborations.

When a new project or a new collaboration is established among the organizations of a digital district, the administrator of the organization who is in charge of initializing the collaboration creates a new group in order to outline the scope of collaboration within the distributed accreditation system. He also defines a set of roles for the new group. Once this phase is completed, the administrator sends an invitation to all participant organizations in order to replicate the same group and role within their accreditation system. Each administrator in turn assigns the above roles to users who will actively participate in that collaboration.

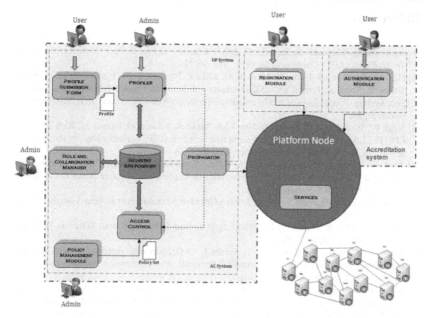

Fig. 5.5 **Architecture of the accreditation system of the Platform**

5.6 Conclusions

This chapter presents the TEKNE technological infrastructure, consisting of a multi-Layer P2P infrastructure. It is characterized by a semantic layer that enables grouping the network nodes into clusters, according to their semantic description, and to efficiently propagate queries by means of semantic links amongst clusters. The general nature of the proposed semantic layer allows applying this infrastructure to heterogeneous contexts, where a semantic description according to shared ontologies can be associated to each network node. In the TEKNE scenario, this infrastructure enables different organizations to share knowledge and service descriptions in order to move towards Internetworked Enterprise configurations. This chapter also describes a distributed and ontology-based authentication and authorization system, aimed at ensuring security and access control on resources of Internetworked Enterprises.

Ongoing work focuses on the evaluation of the benefits of applying the TEKNE infrastructure to a real-life context, namely Value Networks in the aerospace domain.

References

[1] Androutsellis-Theotokis S, Spinellis D (2004) A Survey of Peer-to-Peer Content Distribution Technologies. ACM Computing Surveys., Vol. 36, N.4.

[2] Haase P, Broekstra J, Ehrig M, Menken M, Mika P, Plechawski M, Pyszlak P, Schnizler B, Siebes R, Staab S, Tempich C (2004) Bibster - A Semantics-Based Bibliographic Peer-to-Peer System. Proceedings of the International Semantic Web Conference (ISWC2004), Hiroshima, Japan.

[3] Nejdl W, Wolf B, Qu C, Decker S, Sintek M, Naeve A, Nilsson M, Palmer M, Rish T (2002) EDUTELLA: a P2P Networking Infrastructure based on RDF. In Proceedings of the 11th International World Wide Web Conference, Hawaii, USA.

[4] Aberer K, Datta A, Hauswirth M (2005) P-Grid: Dynamics of self-organization processes in structured P2P systems. Peer-to-Peer Systems and Applications, Lecture Notes in Computer Science, LNCS 3845, Springer Verlag.

[5] Haase P, Agarwal S, Sure Y (2004) Service-Oriented Semantic Peer-to-Peer Systems. WISE Workshops: 46-57.

[6] Haase P, Siebes R, Harmelen F (2006) Expertise-Based Peer Selection. Semantic Web and Peer-to-Peer, Part II, pp. 125-142.

[7] Paolucci M, Payne TR, Kawamura T, Sycara K (2002) Semantic matching of web services capabilities. In: ISWC2002: Ist International Semantic Web Conference, Sardinia, Italy. Lecture Notes in Computer Science, Springer.

[8] Sung LGA, Ahmed N, Blanco R, Li H, Soliman MA, Hadaller D (2005) A Survey of Data Management in Peer-to-Peer Systems. School of Computer Science, University of Waterloo.

[9] Sun Microsystems (2005) Effective SOA Deployment Using an SOA Registry and repository: A Practical Guide, Sun Microsystems.

[10]Gong L (2001) Project JXTA: A technology overview. Technical report, SUN Microsystems, http://www.jxta.org/project/www/docs/TechOverview.pdf.

[11]JXTA: https://jxta.dev.java.net/

[12]ebXML Registry Information Model Version 3.0, OASIS Standard, 2 May, 2005, http://docs.oasis-open.org/regrep-rim/v3.0/

[13]OWL Web Ontology Language, W3C Recommendation 10 February 2004, http://www.w3.org/TR/owl-features/

[14]ebXML Registry Services and Protocols Version 3.0, OASIS Standard, 2 May, 2005, http://docs.oasis-open.org/regrep-rs/v3.0/

[15]Blanchard E, Harzallah M, Briand H, Kuntz P (2005) A typology of ontology-based semantic measures. In Open Interop Workshop on Enterprise Modelling and Ontologies for Interoperability.

[16]Crespo A, Garcia-Molina H (2002) Semantic Overlay Networks in Peer-to-Peer Networks. Technical report.

[17]Lumineau N, Doucet A, Defude B (2004) Cluster Entries for Semantic Organization of Peer-to-Peer Network. In proc. of Semantics for Grid Databases.

[18]Nejdl W, Siberski W, Wolpers M, Schmitz C (2003) Routing and Clustering in Schema-Based Super Peer Networks. In Submitted to the 2nd International Workshop on Peer-to-Peer Systems.

[19]Vazirgiannis M, Nørvåg K, Doulkeridis C (2006) Peer-to-Peer Clustering for Semantic Overlay Network Generation.

[20]Verma K, Sivashanmugam K, Sheth A, Patil A, Oundhakar S, Miller J (2005) METEOR-S WSDI: A Scalable P2P Infrastructure of Registries for Semantic Publication and Discovery of Web Services, Journal of Information Technology and Management, Special Issue on Universal Global Integration, Vol. 6, No. 1 pp. 17-39.

[21]Akkiraju R, Farrell J, Miller J, Nagarajan M, Schmidt M, Sheth A , Verma K (2005) Web Service Semantics - WSDL-S. A joint UGA-IBM Technical Note, version 1.0.

[22] Bianchini D, De Antonellis V, Melchiori M (2008) Flexible Semantic-based Service Matchmaking and Discovery. World Wide Web Journal, 11(2): 227-25.

[23] Bussler C, De Brujin J, Feier C, Fensel D, Keller U, Lara R, Lausen H, Polleres A, Roman V, Stollberg M (2005) Web Service Modeling Ontology. Applied Ontology, IOS Press, pages 77-106.

[24] Vella G, Liotta M, Santangelo A, Ingraffia N, Gentile A (2007) XPL, a Presentation Language based on User Interface Design Pattern. Accepted for publication at 6th IEEE International Conference on Computer and Information Science.

[25] OASIS Web Service Security –WS-Security
http://www.oasis-open.org/committees/tc_home.php?wg_abbrev=wss

[26] Nebel IT, Paschke R, Smith B (2003) User Ontologies for adaptive interactive software systems. University of Leipzig.

[27] Middleton S, De Roure D, Shadbolt N (2006) Capturing knowledge of user preferences: ontologies in recommender systems, Department of Electronics and Computer Science, University of Southampton.

[28] Brainard J, Juels A, Rivest R, Szydlo M, Yung M (2006) Fourth Factor Authentication: Somebody You Know. In ACM CCS, pp. 168-78.

[29] Josephson W, Gun Sirer E, Schneider FB (2004) Peer-to-Peer Authentication with a Distributed Single Sign-On Service. In Proceedings of the International Workshop on Peer-to-Peer Systems.

Chapter 6 - Monitoring Business Processes

Valerio Bellandi, Paolo Ceravolo, Ernesto Damiani, Fulvio Frati

Università degli Studi di Milano

Via Bramante 65, 26013 Crema (CR). Italy

Abstract In this chapter, we introduce the TEKNE Metrics Framework that performs services to monitor business processes. This framework was designed to support the prescription and explanation of these processes. TEKNE's most innovative contribution is managing data expressed in declarative form. To face this challenge, the TEKNE project implemented an infrastructure that relies on declarative Semantic Web technologies designed to be used in distributed systems.

6.1 Introduction

The TEKNE project aims to make Business Process Management (BPM) available to Networked Enterprises. One of the project's main objectives is to propose a framework that is able to monitor the process through an integrated representation of the specifications, the objectives and the execution. This chapter introduces the approach implemented in the TEKNE project and discusses the capabilities supported. Approaches aimed at supporting business process monitoring through an execution layer are not new in literature. Workflow mining [1] is one example of this long tradition. In web services literature, several approaches deal with monitoring communication over service enabled business processes [14][15]. Typically, monitoring has the task of verifying the correct execution of the prescribed flow, although different studies focus on how state conditions can be reached, specifying coordination with other applications or internal response time [13][21][27]. Advanced researches propose dedicated policy languages to describe conditions. The WS-Policy framework [26] provides a general-purpose model to describe a broad range of service conditions and preferences.

Other studies focus on the introduction of a metadata layer supporting an enriched description of the process. Various authors [3][24] propose adopting planners over service description in DAML-S. DAML-S is a language for the description of Web Services attempting to complement the protocol description with a vocabulary supporting services such as discovery, invocation, composition and monitoring. In [11] a complete architecture for the analysis, prediction, monitoring, control and optimization of process executions in BPM Systems is presented. A Description Logic layer provides different services including support to monitor this system. In [12] we have one of the first proposals directed

G. Passiante (ed.), *Evolving Towards the Internetworked Enterprise: Technological and Organizational Perspectives*, DOI 10.1007/978-1-4419-7279-8_6,

towards integrating Semantic Web technologies and BP. In [22][2] we have a definition of the mature developments of this approach. The SUPER project [25] is a European research project specifically focusing on the adoption of Semantic Web technologies in BPM systems.

In comparison with the existing research, our work explores a particular approach based on the idea of directly using business rules as indicators in monitoring activity.

6.2 Monitoring to Change

In the last decade, a great deal of work has been conducted on integrating Business Processes and Informative Systems. The improvements sought are related to business process prescription and explanation capabilities. On one side, the information system can prescribe the business process, imposing a specific structure to the execution, enforcing the implementation of specific tasks in a specific order.

Yet more importantly, the information system can support the explanation of the process, tracking its execution and monitoring whether the specific instances of the process are consistent with the organizational requirements and business objectives. In particular, monitoring is a key activity in advancing the methodology of change introduced in Chapter 3. Only through the implementation of a system that gives the current state of the process can we verify the achievement of objectives and the effects of the changes introduced.

6.2.1 Performance Measurement

Numerous approaches have been proposed to monitor the business process. In the management area for instance, Balanced Score Cards [19] and the Goal Question Metric (GQM) [4] are the most popular. However, these approaches are general and do not specifically take integration between the components of the information system into account. In addition, the evaluation of the measures supported in these approaches is qualitative and not quantitative. Discussing these approaches is outside of the scope of this chapter, although more details can be found in Brun et al's [6] analysis.

In restricting our interest to approaches proposing quantitative measurements, we distinguish two families of approaches. The first focuses on the identification of the general properties of a business process and mainly works on discovering the structure of the process. The second focuses on the evaluation of ad-hoc requirements and measures have a validity limited to the process under analysis.

In other words, distinguishing the two families are the logical frameworks adopted therein.

We can provide a formal definition of the first approach with the expression in formula 6.1. Where CF is the control applied on a process P and p_i is a value, binary or continuous, assigned to a property detected within the structure of the process. For example, the complexity measure proposed by Cardoso [9] is a specification of formula 6.1, where the union operator is implemented by a sum and the p_i values are computed based on the split structures present in a process[1]. Another example of a specification of formula 6.1 is the analysis performed by Petri Nets to verify the absence of anomalies and behavioral inconsistencies (such as deadlock, live-lock, imperfect termination and multiple task repetitions) [23]. In general, formula 6.1 generalizes all the operations that can be performed on the topology of graphs or metagraphs [5].

$$CF(P) = \bigcup_p^n p_i \qquad\qquad (6.1)$$

The second approach is constructed around the notion of conformance to requirements. It can be formally defined referring to [17], where the problem of evaluating performances is captured with formula 6.2:

$$S, W \rightarrow R \qquad\qquad (6.2)$$

where S is a specification of the behavior that must result from the execution of the process to be developed, W represents a set of world properties, i.e. the context in which the process is executed, and R represents a set of requirements or rules to be met by the process. Proving that the specifications will satisfy the requirements in a specific world context requires showing that this implication holds. The effectiveness of a system described by S can therefore be assessed by showing, formally or informally, that this relationship holds among the three descriptions.

6.2.3 The TEKNE approach

We have developed both the above-mentioned approaches in the TEKNE project: the Metrics Framework contains metrics capable of capturing the general

---

[1] When a split (XOR, OR, or AND) is introduced in a process, the business process designer has to mentally create a map or structure that accounts for the number of states that can be reached from the split. For AND-splits, the control-flow complexity is simply 1, since only one state has to be analyzed after an AND-split. The higher the value of XOR-split, OR-split, the more complex a process design is, since developers have to handle all the states between control-flow constructs (splits) and their associated outgoing transitions and activities.

properties of the business process but also allows defining metrics based on ad-hoc requirements and rules. In both approaches, we endeavored to achieve the maximal level of generality to reduce the personalization costs for a specific process as much as possible. The prototypes developed in the TEKNE project contain metrics that can be functional in providing a useful quantitative view on the state of the process. This quantitative view is able to provide an indication on the achievement of the objectives. In particular, we relate our approach to literature on performance indicators.

Description metrics modality

In the TEKNE project, metrics are described using a definition grid that permits explaining several particular and essential properties necessary to design any specific metric function.

We have subdivided metrics into two main categories:

- **Ex-ante.** Metrics that can be evaluated using the project specification.
- **Ex-post.** Metrics that can be evaluated using the project specification in conjunction with data collected from the process execution.

Furthermore, we have identified, for each metric, the **data models** from which the inputs required by the metric function and **preconditions** derive (in terms of data model available) to be used in the evaluation of the function.

Performance Indicators

Performance indicators (PI) are important instruments to control and improve organizations [16]. Their role is to define what requires monitoring, measuring and evaluating. According to [8] we can distinguish 'Performance Measures' that are descriptions of something that can be measured (e.g. number of reworks per day) from *Performance Indicators,* which are descriptions of something that is calculated from performance measures (e.g. percentage reworks per day per direct employee). In other words, PI is composed of a measure plus a condition to be applied to the measure.

Using this definition, the distinction between performance indicator and rule can be eliminated. Generally, a *rule* is intended to define a condition that the process has to comply with, while a *performance indicator* must highlight the trend of a process, if possible considering the simplest set of information. However, when we distinguish between what to measure and the condition to be applied we can include both these definitions in a single definition by simply modulating the degree of application of the condition.

This definition is also compatible with the formulae 6.1 and 6.2 since they both represent a way to implement measures. The conditions on a measure determine the degree of consistency that is required for a measure. In the TEKNE project, we distinguish between conditions applying to a single process execution and conditions applying to aggregated process executions.

- Conditions on *single process execution* may impose an alethic or a deontic modality on the measure. Alethic rules are used to model necessities (e.g., implied by physical laws), which cannot be violated, even in principle. For example, an alethic rule may state that an employee must be born on at most one date. Deontic rules are used to model obligations (e.g., resulting from company policy), which ought to be obeyed but may be violated in real world scenarios. For example, a deontic rule may state that it is forbidden that any person smokes inside any company building. It is important to recall that widespread domain modeling languages, such as the Unified Modeling Language (UML), typically express alethic statements only. When drawing a UML class diagram, for instance, the modeler states that domain objects belonging to each UML class MUST have the attribute list reported in the class definition, implicitly taking an alethic approach to domain modeling. In business practice, however, many statements are deontic, and it is often important (e.g., for computing metrics) to know if and how often they are violated.

- Conditions on *aggregated process executions* are not applied to single activities but to trends. The applied condition insists on the comparison between a specific set of executions of the process (for instance all the executions within a given timeframe) and an objective to be achieved. For example, a rule on aggregated executions could state that the number of missions with daily board expenses above 50 Euros cannot exceed 60% of the total number of missions.

6.3 The Metrics Framework

As proposed in [2], process-monitoring techniques can support two services: discovery and conformance. In the TEKNE project, we provide a formal definition of these approaches with the introduction of formulae 6.2 and 6.3. In the following section, we detail how the two approaches have been implemented.

6.3.1 Discovery

Discovery is about deriving a process model from data in the event log. Using an inductive approach, the process executions are generalized in a model consistent with all the recorded instances. An interesting example is complexity. In literature, the best way to measure the complexity of a business process is by basing it on the graph-theoretical approach. In fact, starting out from this point, in [26] a graph theory applied to business processes is proposed. In particular, the author gives some detailed and formal definitions of different metrics able to calculate the complexity process. Table 6.1 shows these metrics and their description, together with the formulae used to calculate the values.

Coefficient of Network Complexity (CNC)	$CNC = A^2/N$	Defines complexity in such a way that for a fixed number of nodes (activities) (N), a higher complexity results in an increasing number of arcs (A), and therefore in the greater connectedness of the network. It has been shown that many network problems become easier with increasing CNC values.
Cyclomatic Number (S)	$S = A - N + 1$	Gives the number of independent cycles in a graph. The cyclomatic number is independent of the process graph size and only measures the underlying structure, i.e. the cyclomatic numbers of homeomorphically equivalent graphs have the same value. Splitting a process step into two successive smaller components, or joining two smaller activities into a larger one, does not affect S, where a larger graph allows for more structural complexity. The value of S of two successive process graphs is simply the sum of the complexities of the individual graphs.
Restrictiveness estimator (RT)	$RT = \dfrac{2\sum r_{i,j} - 6(n-i)}{(n-2)(n-3)}$	The formula contains an element of the reachability matrix and is confined to the interval [0,1]: it is equal to 0 for parallel digraphs, and 1 for series digraphs. The value of RT could be multiplied by the size of the graph to measure its complexity. This measure could be used to compare the complexity of graphs of different sizes.
Number of trees in a graph (T)	$T = \sum D_{ij}$	Classifies the graphs by the number of distinct trees they contain. Let A be the adjacency matrix of the graph, i.e. associate a variable a_{ij} with the directed arc from node V_i to node V_j. Put $a_{ij} = 0$ if there is no such arc, otherwise set $a_{ij} = 1$. Then, define D as the matrix in [26]. The number of trees in a graph grows dramatically quickly as the connectivity of the process graph increases.

Table 6.1 Complexity measures and metrics.

6.3.2 Conformance

Conformance is about verifying if the executions follow the prescribed control flow or comply with external directives such as business goals, rules and standards etc. In the TEKNE project, we developed a conformance approach by extending the approach introduced in [17]. In particular, we introduced a more defined definition of the components constructing the implication. The problem of evaluating performances can be described by the following implication:

$$S, W, L, \rightarrow R \qquad (6.3)$$

where S is a specification of the behavior that must result from the execution of the process to be developed, W represents a set of world properties, i.e. the context in which the process is executed, L is the log that contains the track of the specific execution of S, and R represents a set of requirements to be met by the process. Proving that the specifications will satisfy the requirements in a specific world context requires showing that this implication holds. The effectiveness of a system described by S can therefore be assessed showing, either formally or informally, that this relationship holds among the three descriptions.

The aim of our system is to verify that implication 1 holds, which can be done both ex-ante and ex-post. Ex-ante is acting on the process specification only, for instance by constraining the naming of objects in conformance with the entities declared in the business context, or verifying that the overall set of business rules is consistent. A typical method adopted to implement conformance indicators is to identify a set of requirements and verify which executed instances of the process violate it. The notion of violation is very useful because it provides a simple criterion of measurement. Given a set of requirements R, if the Implication (2) does not holds, S, W and L violate R. Note that this notion has an important property. By pointing out violations, we obtain a measure of the process performance with a method that is completely independent from the specific semantics of R, so we can support as many indicators as the number of sets of requirements R are able to represent. The notion of violation is also compatible with the notion of the indicator provided since different controls can be applied on the violations detected. For example, you can state that some violations when detected generate an invalid process while others can be accepted with a degree of tolerance. In other words, our methodology is independent of the specific requirements to be evaluated. A methodology that is independent from requirements is crucial for our goals, since, as mentioned, one of the aims of the TEKNE project is to directly use business rules to derive performance indicators. However, this methodology is not the only condition to be supported to directly use business rules and directives as performance indicators. The other condition is providing an algorithm, which is able to conjunctively evaluate S, W, L, and R as a single knowledge base. This algorithm has to work as a black box, taking in input S, W, L, R, computing the consistency of the knowledge base and in case of inconsistency, point out a violation. This algorithm is compatible only with a representation of S, W, L and R in declarative form, and assumes a uniform naming space.

6.3.3 An Approach based on Logics

A theorem prover representing the knowledge base S, W, R, as a set of logical assertions, executes the algorithm verifying violations. This approach is compatible with the standards adopted. BXModeller represents the process in Business Process Modeling Notation (BPMN) [7]; this notation is based on a flowcharting technique that is tailored to creating graphical models of business operations. A straightforward way to translate it into logical assertions is to represent it using logic-based formalism (specifically, OWL DL data structures). We use the Business Management Ontology (BMO) [18] as a means to express the structural properties of the process.

XBeaver directly adopts a declarative approach since the business rule language implemented by the tool (SBVR) was natively designed to be represented in First Order Logic. One of the well-known limitations of theorem provers is detecting the causes of inconsistency [20].

Given a knowledge base, the prover can detect inconsistent assertions. However, in the complex path of dependencies between assertions, it is often impossible to distinguish a single source of inconsistency. For this reason, adopting a theorem prover to detect violations requires a specific methodology. The idea is that violations are tested for a single set of directives. When a knowledge base is analyzed for the first time, the system verifies its consistency. Then it adds to the knowledge base a first set of directives R_i that the model should conform to. If no inconsistency is detected, the process conforms to R_i, and a new set of directives R_{ii} are analyzed, otherwise R_i is split into parts and a new execution of the prover is launched until finding the directive causing inconsistency. This process is iteratively applied, until a report on all the directives violated by the knowledge base is generated.

6.3.4 Implementing Performance Indicators

At first glance, the notion of violation could appear poor, since it is related to the evaluation of a Boolean condition. However, in considering the occurrence of a specific violation it is possible to develop more complex indicators. In [10] some of us discussed the adoption of an approach based on violation to evaluate alethic and deontic conditions with either relative or absolute thresholds.

Alethic directives are used to model necessities that cannot be violated, even in principle. Deontic directives are used to model obligations (e.g., resulting from company policy) which ought to be obeyed, but may be violated in real world scenarios. In order to support indicators expressing both alethic and deontic directives two behaviors are to be implemented. The former must highlight the non-conformity of the process any time a violation is detected. The latter must report on the occurrence of a violation. A directive expressing an absolute threshold prescribes the exact occurrence of a given event; while a directive expressing a relative threshold prescribes that the occurrence of a given event must be in relation (i.e. a percentage) to another event. For example, a directive stating that a maximum of one hundred customers can obtain a promotional price, expresses an absolute threshold. A directive stating that 30% of products are expected to be bought by credit card expresses a relative threshold. Unfortunately, representing this category of model constraints in a logical format suitable for a theorem prover it is not straightforward. Indeed, it is well acknowledged that the introduction of modalities and inequalities in a logical language lead to hard computational complexities. In order to confront this problem we dissociate the representation of constraints from the logical assertions representing directives. In other words, starting from a directive expressed as a business rule we derive a twofold representation: (i) a logical assertion in universal form, to be evaluated by the theorem prover, plus (ii) a constraint representing the suitable modality or threshold to be supported. In particular, we generate a constraint function f of the cardinalities of the facts generated by the process flow to be used as an indicator of the process performance. Thereafter, this cardinality is linked to thresholds expressed by directives. Equation (6.3) formalizes this point as follows:

$$f(Card_{A1}, Card_{A2}, \ldots, Card_{An}) \leq \alpha \tag{6.4}$$

This equation is not evaluated directly by the theorem prover but in a module dedicated to constraint functions.

Considering for example a business rule such as:

all <u>customers</u> *apply* for a <u>Premium Card</u>   (6.5)

This can be represented by the universal assertion:

The number of <u>customers</u> that *apply* for a <u>Premium Card</u> **must** be at least 90% of the number of <u>customers</u> that do **not** have a <u>Premium Card</u>   (6.6)

plus a constraint in the form of inequation:

<u>customers</u> that *apply* for a <u>Premium Card</u> $\geq 0.9 *$ <u>customers</u> that   (6.7)
do **not** *have* a <u>Premium Card</u>

In particular, Figure 6.1 demonstrates how the system interrelates the theorem prover with the module tasked to represent constraints and the module tasked to evaluate them. Basically, given a specific execution of the process Sj, the system starts evaluating all the directives violated by a knowledge base composed of Sj plus the business context W. In parallel, a directive is translated into a constraint in the form described by equation (6.2). When the prover evaluates all instances of the execution of process S, the system compares for each directive the occurrences of violations with the constraint and generates an indicator on the compliance of the process execution.

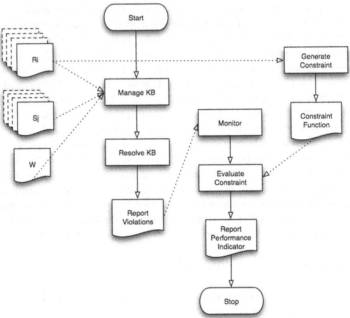

Fig. 6.1 - The module generating performance indicators

6.3.5 The TEKNE Architecture

The proposed architecture is based on three key parts. It addresses the specification of a process, the execution and monitoring of a process, its business context and expected requirements. Each part is self-consistent and is linked to the others by well-defined interfaces and input/output transformations provided by an ESB (Enterprise Service Bus). The first part supports the business engineer at design-time. It provides components and tools to model any business process together with its context and directives from a conceptual perspective. The control flow of the business process is defined through the BXModeller, a collaborative web-application that is compliant to the OMG BPMN (Business Process Modeling Notation), currently the de-facto standard notation for business process modeling. This tool exports the designed process to a standard format for workflow execution: the XPDL 2.0 (XML Process Definition Language). This XML-based language is a widely adopted standard maintained by the WfMC (Workflow Management Coalition) and supported by a number of workflow-engines, including mature open-source implementations such as Bonita and Shark. The business context and the directive are described through another web-application, Xbeaver, which adopts a declarative approach, leveraging SBVR (Semantics of Business Vocabulary and Business Rules), another OMG standard. The adoption of SBVR is motivated by two features: i) SBVR models can be expressed by means of SBVR Structured English, a natural-language-like notation designed to enable process/knowledge owners to directly and easily represent their tacit or explicit knowledge; ii) the SBVR metamodel is compliant and mapped to first order logic, thus fully supporting automatic interpretation and reasoning upon its assertions.

The combination of both features is a key element to address the last objective of the design-time part: the definition of automatable metrics that can be referred directly to business policies and business rules. Indeed, the architecture provides a tool for coupling elements of a business domain (i.e. SBVR business rules) with activities of a business process, thus binding generic logical assertions to generic operations. The entire information described above is stored in a specific repository called the Model Repository. In short, the Model Repository holds the models representing the business process through XPDL2.0, the business domain through a proprietary XML-based representation of the SBVR vocabulary and the mapping information among the elements of the two models.

The run-time environment in which the XPDL representation of the process is executed and the workflow operations are recorded in an ad-hoc log repository constitutes the second part of the architecture. This allows making important information available for analysis and metrics measurement. For example, the name of the activities, the identity of the related participants, the activities' input/output parameters and time scheduling are directly available from the workflow engine context.

Thanks to the previous mapping phase among elements of the BPMN and the SBVR models, it is possible to derive rules from actual instances of process activities. Given a certain rule defined in a vocabulary, a rule can be defined a real-world instance of another rule. For example, "Mario Rossi elects Paolo Verdi" is a rule that is an instance of the rule "Operator elects Customer". Assuming that the workflow-engine is aware of roles, one can for instance derive from the login logs that Mario Rossi is an Operator and that Paolo Verdi is a Customer.

The resolution of rules is the responsibility of the third key part of the proposed architecture: the Metrics Framework described in the previous sections.

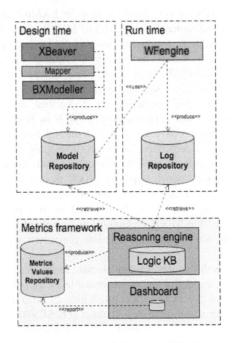

Fig. 6.2 – A synthetic view on the proposed architecture

6.4 Conclusions

The literature on BPM has today attained huge dimensions. In spite of this strong development, very few lines have been written on criteria for evaluating the complexity of Monitoring Systems. In this chapter, we discuss the TEKNE Metrics Framework designed to provide the maximal level of generality and thus minimize the complexity of personalization on a specific process. This has been achieved by implementing two approaches:

- Identification of the general properties of a business process. It mainly works on discovering the structure of the process.
- Evaluation of ad-hoc requirements, with measures having validity limited to the process under analysis.

The most innovative contribution of the TEKNE project is related to the second approach. To achieve generality requires managing data expressed in declarative form. To face this challenge the TEKNE project implemented an infrastructure that relies on declarative Semantic Web technologies designed to be used in distributed systems.

References

[1] Van der Aalst W, Van Dongen B, Herbst J, Maruster L, Schimm G, Weijters A (2003) Workflow mining: A survey of issues and approaches. Data & Knowledge Engineering. 46:237–267

[2] Alves de Medeiros A, Pedrinaci C, Van der Aalst A, Domingue J, Song M, Rozinat A, Norton B, Cabral L (2007) An Outlook on Semantic Business Process Mining and Monitoring. In R. Meersman, Z. Tari, P. Herrero et al. (Eds.): OTM2007 Ws, Part II, LNCS 4806:1244–1255.

[3] Ankolekar A, Burstein B, Hobbs j, Lassila O, Martin D, McDermott D, McIlraith S, Narayanan S, Paolucci M, Payne T, Sycara K (2002) DAML-S: Web Service Description for the Semantic Web. In the Proceedings of the International Semantic Web Conference (ISWC).

[4] Basili V, Caldiera G., and Rombach H (1994) Experience Factory, Encyclopædia of Software Engineering. Wiley, 469-476.

[5] Basu A, Blanning R (2000) A Formal Approach to Workflow Analysis, Information Systems Research.

[6] Brun A, Cagliano R, Caniato F, Fahmy Salama K, Sianesi A, Spina G (2005) Supply chain performance measurement systems: how to evaluate their performance? In Second European Forum on Market-Driven Supply Chains. EIASM, Politecnico di Milano.

[7] Business process modeling notation (BPMN) (2006) OMG. http://www.bpmn.org/Documents/BPMN%20V1-0%20May%203%202004.pdf.

[8] Caputo E (2009) Performance Management System in MDA . Formal Definition of KPIs. Degree of Philosophiæ Doctor (PhD) in "e-Business", eBUSINESS MANAGEMENT SECTION SCUOLA SUPERIORE ISUFI UNIVERSITY OF SALENTO.

[9] Cardoso J (2006) Process control-flow complexity metric: An empirical validation. In the Proceedings of IEEE International Conference on Services Computing (SCC'06), Chicago, US, Sept. 18-22:167–173.

[10] Ceravolo P, Damiani E, Fugazza C, Mulazzani F, Russo (2008) Business Process Monitoring via Ontology-based Representation Models. Journal Computers in Human Behaviour, (24) Elsevier.

[11] Grigori D, Casati F, Castellanos, Dayal U, Sayal M, Shan M (2004) Business Process Intelligence. Computers in Industry 53-3:321–343.

[12] Hepp M, Leymann F, Domingue J, Wahler A, Fensel D (2005) Semantic business process management: A vision towards using semantic web services for business process management. In: ICEBE, 535–540.

[13] Lazovik M, Aiello M, Papazoglou M (2003) Planning and monitoring the execution of web service requests. In Conf. on Service- Oriented Computing (ICSOC-03), Lecture Notes in Computer Sciences 2910, pages 335–350. Springer.

[14] McDermott D (2002) Estimated-regression planning for interactions with Web Services. In 6th Int. Conf. on AI Planning and Scheduling. AAAI Press.

[15] McIlraith S, Son T. C (2002) Adapting Golog for composition of semantic web-services. In the Proceedings of the Conference on principles of Knowledge Representation (KR).

[16] Offen R.J, Jeffery R (1997) Establishing Software Measurement Programs, IEEE Software, IEEE Computer Society, 14-2:45-53.

[17] Jackson M (2001) Problem Frames: Analyzing and Structuring Software Development Problem. Addison-Wesley.

[18] Jenz, Partner (2004) Business Management Ontology (BMO). Technical report.

[19] Kaplan R.S, Norton D.P (1996) The Balanced Scorecard: Translating Strategy into Action, Harvard Business School Press.

[20] Parsia B, Sirin E, Kalyanpur A (2005) Debugging OWL ontologies. In the 14th international World Wide Web conference (WWW2005).

[21] Pistore M, Barbon F, Bertoli P, Shaparau D, Traverso P (2004) Planning and Monitoring Web Service Composition. In ICAPS'04 Workshop on Planning and Scheduling for Web and Grid Services.

[22] Sell D, Cabral L, Motta E, Domingue J, Pacheco P (2005) Adding Semantics to Business Intelligence. In: DEXA Workshops, pp. 543–547. IEEE Computer Society Press, Los Alamitos.

[23] Sivaraman E, Kamath M (2002) On The Use of Petri Nets for Business Process Modeling. In the Proceeding of the 11th Annual Industrial Engineering Research Conference.

[24] Srivastava B, Koehler J (2003) Web Service Composition - Current Solutions and Open Problems. In the Proceedings of ICAPS'03 Workshop on Planning for Web Services, Trento, Italy.

[25] Semantics Utilised for Process Management within and between Enterprises (SUPER). http://www.ip-super.org. Accessed 23 July 2008.

[26] WS-Policy. Web Services Policy Framework (2003) http://www-106.ibm.com/developerworks/library/ws-polfram/.

[27] Wu D, Sirin E. Hendler J, Nau D, Parsia B (2003) Automatic Web Services Composition Using SHOP2. In the Proceedings of ICAPS'03 Workshop on Planning for Web Services, Trento, Italy.

Chapter 7 – SuperJet International case study: a business network start-up in the aeronautics industry

Angelo Corallo, Marco De Maggio, Davide Storelli

eBMS S.S. ISUFI – University of Salento

Abstract - This chapter presents the SuperJet International case study, a start-up in the aeronautics industry characterized by a process-oriented approach and a complex and as yet evolving network of partnerships and collaborations. The chapter aims to describe the key points of the start-up process, highlighting common factors and differences compared to the TEKNE Methodology of Change, with particular reference to the second and third phase, namely, the design and deployment of new techno-organizational systems. The SuperJet International start-up is presented as a case study where strategic and organizational aspects have been jointly conceived from a network-driven perspective. The chapter compares some of the guidelines of the TEKNE Methodology of Change with experiences and actual practices deriving from interviews with key players in SJI's start-up process.

7.1 Introduction

Methodology of Change, one of the results of the TEKNE project (see Chapter 2), aims to guide companies towards the adoption of the Internetworked Enterprise organizational paradigm in order to exploit the opportunities offered by ICTs in value network scenarios. The methodology of change is divided into three phases: the first is the AS-IS analysis of the company in terms of its business model and its organizational, technological and strategic characteristics. The second phase identifies and formalizes the requirements that the company must satisfy to fully adopt the IE organizational paradigm and designs a detail TO-BE in terms of a new business model, a new strategy and a new techno-organizational approach. The last phase aims at enacting and deploying the new systems and new approaches, taking into consideration the risks and opportunities of value network scenarios. This chapter presents the SuperJet International case study, a start-up in the aeronautics industry, characterized by a process-oriented approach and a com-

G. Passiante (ed.), *Evolving Towards the Internetworked Enterprise: Technological and Organizational Perspectives*, DOI 10.1007/978-1-4419-7279-8_7,
© Springer Science+Business Media, LLC 2010

plex and as yet evolving network of partnerships and collaborations. The chapter aims to describe the key points of the start-up process, highlighting the common factors and differences compared to the methodology of change, with particular reference to the second and third phase, namely the design and deployment of new techno-organizational system. The chapter is organized as follows: section 7.2 provides a classification of networked enterprises highlighting the most important aspects that must be considered in processes of change towards value networks, section 7.3 provides information on the case study plan and interviews of key actors involved in the start-up, section 7.4 presents the SuperJet International case study with an overview of its network and briefly describes the start-up process in terms of strategy and choice of partners. Section 7.5 presents a number of considerations and comments, highlighting the salient aspects of the start-up process compared to the methodology of change guidelines. Finally, section 7.6 concludes the paper.

7.2 Enterprise Networks: characteristics

The "network-based view" of the firm has increasingly gained importance since its birth in the early 80s. Issues relating to this organizational form have been thoroughly examined in literature by numerous authors including Mintzberg [1] (Adhocracy) and Handy [2] (Virtual Organization). Network analysis corrects the tendency in organizational theory to focus excessively on individual organizations rather than on the organization of their actions [3]. The virtual organization (or virtual enterprise) is composed of a number of autonomous or semi-autonomous entities working together to achieve a given objective. The purpose of the collaboration is to share resources, costs, skills and market access enabled by ICT [4]. Networked organizations are a form of coordination of economic activities, distinct and different from market and hierarchy, based on the concepts of complementarity, reputation, reciprocity, interdependence, creation of ties and trust [5]. This section presents the main components of a network: from the formal organizational structure to informal behavior, from the basic technological infrastructure to network governance systems. These components, which are those most affected by the techno-organizational design and deployment of new network management solutions, are analyzed in detail in the next sections by comparing the *TEKNE Methodology of Change* guidelines and actual strategies and operations enacted in the SuperJet International start-up process.

The formal structure
The formal structure of the network is the set of coordination mechanisms and procedures that guide network members towards a common objective. *Tasks* are identified and allocated to the network partners who are then *responsible* for specific parts of the overall network objectives. Moreover, business partners have dif-

ferent *roles* depending on their size, position, responsibilities and capacities (e.g. initiator, coordinator). Responsibilities and roles are strongly related to formalized *business processes* that guarantee the network's operational effectiveness. Partners should agree on the network tasks and procedures in order to control its complexity and performance. Finally, business processes and the network itself are characterized by *interdependencies* among their participants. Thompson [6] distinguishes three different ways in which organizational unit tasks can depend on each other: sequential, pooled and reciprocal. Pooled dependency is characterized by the shared use of common resources (e.g. transportation, high performance computing, data centers) and by independence in any other aspects. In sequential dependency, the output of an organizational unit becomes the input of another organizational unit. This kind of dependency is typical of supply chains or logistic chains [7]. With reciprocal dependency, organizational units iteratively exchange their work products, receiving input and providing each other output. Examples of reciprocal dependencies are multi-disciplinary teams working on the design of complex products (e.g. aircraft, information systems, electronic devices) or research groups collaborating in a research study.

Informal behavior
Network behavior management includes taking care of persons, teams and the social relationships between individuals. Informal interactions must be considered as complementary to structured interactions and the capacities of each single worker in the network impacts on the network's performance. Companies are the institutional actors that form the network, but their employees, each with specific aptitudes, actually carry out the work and maintain relationships with the different stakeholders. It is important to select the right *persons* to represent the enterprise in the network in order to maximize collaborations and partnership opportunities. In addition to physical assets and formally established resources, network management must consider people's capacities in terms of knowledge and behavioural skills (cooperation, communication); it must identify and train people, nurturing their skills in order to meet the network objectives. The development of good social relationships facilitates mutual understanding, information flows and communication. *Social relationships* are crucial to build trust between people, avoiding conflicts and supporting a sense of collaboration. The creation of *social ties* is seen as an investment in social capital [8]. It is important to assess the level of emergent embeddedness and to avoid the excessively high or low values of these factor [9]. Finally, it is important to find a balance between formal and informal interactions; *informal interactions* include actions of trade, transactions and interactions between people that take place outside of the network's formal structure/processes. On one side, informal interactions help build social relationships and social capital, and often have the advantage of being faster and more efficient than formal interactions, thus improving information flows and process performance. On the other, they are difficult to document and control, at times leading to non-governable processes.

Network governance
The governance structure of a network defines the "rules of the game", the framework in which network members can conduct their business: roles and responsibilities, mechanisms for conflict resolution, as well as the protection of property rights [8]. The governance structure includes formal rules and regulations, but also informal aspects such as culture and identity. Indeed, trust and shared values between members of a network usually sustain the effectiveness of the governance structure enactment. An umbrella organization is usually responsible for network management. These organizations must combine flexible institutional arrangements, limited power and medium-term participant commitment. In order to become part of the new governance structure and the new network boundaries, participants must give up some power and control of their organizational boundaries. To enable effective coordination and alignment of policies within the network, content, values and interpretation of the rules should be clearly disclosed and assimilated by participants.

Inter-organizational information system
An inter-organizational information system supports and enables inter-organizational processes, providing tools and instruments to manage information flows, communications, transactions, collaboration and coordination among the participants of a networked organization. There are two main strategies to provide a network with an information infrastructure: (i) starting from scratch and developing ad-hoc systems involving high costs and high complexity (ii) linking existing infrastructures and establishing virtual ties among network nodes by leveraging on a common set of standards, protocols and interfaces. The second strategy is more commonly adopted due to lower complexity and costs, relying on SOA-based infrastructures and solutions in order to orchestrate each network node's contribution.

7.3 Case study plan and interviews

The primary focus on one single organization and the particular industrial setting led to a qualitative investigation to address the needs of the specific context of analysis. In particular, a case study approach is appropriate to study contemporary events and non-controllable units of analysis [10, 11]. The study was based on different sources of evidence to increase the validity of findings. Aside from the company website and other web sources, most information was collected through a set of interviews with key company referents. Following a "snowball" approach [12], the researchers first contacted a project manager and this key informant provided an extensive overview of topics and helped the research team identify nine other persons to interview. Interviews were held with the use of semi-structured and open-ended questions to stimulate perspectives, views and opinion sharing [13]. The ten interviews included the following profiles:

- 4 persons belonging to the ICT area (3 in Venice and 1 in Rome);
- 2 persons belonging to the CTO and Know-How Improvement area (in Turin);
- 1 person belonging to the Operations area (in Venice);
- 1 person belonging to the Corporate Strategy area (in Venice);
- 1 person belonging to the Customer Service area (in Rome);
- 1 person belonging to the CEO area (in Venice).

The research was structured in three phases: a) questionnaire design and research focus identification (March 2009); b) interview and data collection (April 2009); c) draft case creation and review (May 2009). To check the validity of findings, the research team adopted the use of member-checking [13] and a key informant reviewed the case study report and validated the main results. Beside basic information related to the industry and market positioning and the start-up key phases and actors, the interview covered 6 main areas as follows:

1. *Process Design and Modeling*
2. *Process Management, Performance and IT Platforms*
3. *Information Flows and Privacy Security Policy*
4. *Network Structure and Dynamics of Relations*
5. *Partnership Strategy and Development;*
6. *Competence Management Approach, Systems and Programs.*

These areas were identified based on the aims and focus of the study as well as on the literature review that helped identify the critical issues involved in the creation of a process-based organization.

7.4 SuperJet International: the start-up of a network in the aerospace industry

The organization analyzed in this study is SuperJet International (SJI), a company established in July 2007, which started its operations in February 2009. SJI is the result of an agreement between Alenia Aeronautica, part of the Finmeccanica Group, and Sukhoi, one of the most renowned Russian aviation companies, with a strong background in the military sector. The agreement resulted from the complementary needs and capacities of the two companies and from a common interest in entering the regional jet market. The focus on the regional jet market reflects the current scenario where producers are converging more and more towards 80/100-seat aircraft due to factors such as the oil price increases, cost-per-seat and "total cost of ownership". Companies that previously produced 30/50-seat jets (e.g. Embraer and Bombardier) began to produce 100 and 110-seat versions. Boeing and Airbus are also adapting some of their jets to enter the regional jet market.

Sukhoi developed (by means of its civil branch SCAC - Sukhoi Civil Aircraft Company) a last-generation family of civil regional aircraft, i.e. the Superjet 100 series. However, the Russian company needed support to enter the civil market, particularly the western market. On the other side, Alenia is well known in a similar market (regional turboprops) thanks to the ATR program and has strong competencies in flight certification and well-established relationships with key European and International certification institutions such as EASA (European Aviation Safety Agency) and FAA (Federal Aviation Administration), but the company lacked a suitable product to enter the regional jet segment. The agreement thus aimed to identify the integrative roles of the two companies: Sukhoi/SCAC designs and produces aircraft and sells them in Russia, China and other Eastern markets whereas the newborn SJI buys aircraft from SCAC, does the marketing and sells to western markets and Japan. SJI also provides worldwide after-sales service and support and the training, design and development of customized VIP and cargo versions of the Superjet 100 family. The shareholding structure of SuperJet International and SCAC illustrates the strategy adopted by the two participants (Alenia and Sukhoi) aimed at balancing their strengths and integrating their objectives (see Figure 1). SuperJet International is the result of a joint venture between Alenia Aeronautica (51%) and the Sukhoi Holding Company (49%), whereas Alenia Aeronautica now owns a 25% plus 1 share of SCAC, which existed before the agreement and was wholly owned by Sukhoi. Alenia thus has the power of veto in SCAC's strategic decisions.

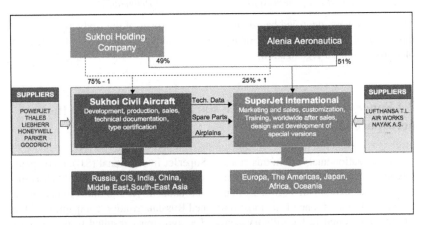

Fig7.1. SuperJet International business network.

SJI is thus "native" to the new market segment, which can be a competitive advantage in the medium/long term. Furthermore, the SJI 100 is a very innovative aircraft resulting from a joint effort between SCAC and international players such as Boeing (supervision), Thales (Avionics), and Powerjet (engines). This aircraft is the state-of-the-art of the regional-jet sector, with a full fly-by-wire system and optimal wing-engine combination guaranteeing substantial fuel savings, pollution and acoustic emission reductions and improved comfort parameters (space per seat, baggage vane, etc.) with respect to competitors such as CRJ, RJ and small versions of the Boeing 737.

As concerns SJI's business network, this is currently under development. In particular, apart from the fundamental partnership with SCAC and involvement in the Finmeccanica Group, SJI has already entered into numerous Letters of Intent with MRO facilities around the world, for example Air Works India Engg Pvt. Ltd, Singapore Technologies Aerospace Ltd., Finnair Plc, Aeroplex of Central Europe Ltd., Nayak Aircraft Services, Aveos Fleet Performance Inc. The search for new potential MRO providers is continuously in progress. Authorized service centers will offer maintenance services as independent contractors. Moreover, SJI has selected Lufthansa Technik Logistik GmbH (LTL) as the exclusive logistics supplier to globally manage Sukhoi Superjet 100 spare parts. SJI is cultivating new competencies in the work force, also through funding scholarships and agreements with local universities.

SJI was the opportunity to create an ex-novo organization and network of enterprises according to a set of specific requirements on a market, customer and process level. However, two big challenges were the absence of consolidated praxes and standardized processes to follow, as well as the creation of a "corporate identity" for two partners with very different management styles, expectations and organizational models.

7.5 Techno-organizational deployment in the SJI case study

This section compares some of the key guidelines for techno-organizational deployment defined in the TEKNE project methodology of change with the experiences collected in the SJI start-up case study analysis.

Project Roles

In a change management project, as well as in a start-up process, the involvement of different organizational roles is recommended, including enterprise leaders and managers, senior and junior IT managers, ICT and KM experts, external consultants and representatives of the partners. These roles form a multidisciplinary team that must support and supervise the entire deployment process, sharing the responsibility of its effectiveness and monitoring the alignment and synchronization of the technological distribution plan, the organizational change management plan and network integration specifications.

In the case of SJI, the enterprise and its techno-organizational deployment were designed by the top management (CEO and Heads of ICT, Operations/Procurement and Customer Services), by external consultants (with particular reference to customer service process design, process integration with SAP and technical data management), by partners (Alenia defined the CBM map for the make-or-buy strategy, SCAC was fundamental in providing technical information on the product while Elsag Datamat provided operational support in the process analysis and design finalization). It is important to highlight that although Sukhoi/SCAC is SJI's primary partner, its involvement in business process design activities was limited since these activities began before the actual legal foundation of SJI and because there were several cultural and organizational gaps that had to be bridged with the Russian partner. Currently, trust relations are gradually being constructed between SJI and SCAC, fostering improved collaboration among their employees.

Use of consultants

It is generally useful to exploit consultants in specific stages, especially in the early diagnosis and capability assessment phases: consultants are usually aware of industry best practices and state-of-the-art approaches and can be more objective in diagnosing and assessing internal capabilities. As the change project moves forward, consultants should play an increasingly marginal role, leaving strategic activities to internal employees.

In the case of SJI, consultants played a key role in identifying business processes through interviews with SJI staff. As outsiders to the Finmeccanica group, they were able to model processes more objectively and contributed innovative ideas to organizing activities and workflows. SJI exploited the excellent skills of several consultants in terms of enterprise organization and strategy during the capabilities assessment and strategy development phase. Other consultants played a less strategic role, since they merely managed the integration of technical data with SCAC at the end of the process design. All consultants, along with SJI top management and Finmeccanica partners, contributed to giving life to the start-up process.

Boundary Spanner and Relationship Promoter

Boundary spanner is a role that contributes to producing a shared interpretation of the common objectives of the network of companies. During techno-organizational deployment, the boundary spanner has the role of supporting, supervising, promoting and ensuring the alignment within the network. Some companies appoint a senior executive as head of external relations. Others allocate alliance responsibilities along functional lines, e.g. marketing alliance to marketing executives or in the case of technology alliance to R&D departments. Still others need an entire business unit to manage their network relationships. Special and critical alliances are sometimes managed by specific managers (senior executive champion) or by collective governance structures, which can help maintain the network's cohesion. Another key role is that of relationship promoter. His objective is to intensively promote inter-organisational exchange processes, leveraging on his good personal relationships with significant players in partner organizations. Relationship promoters must use their relationships to positively influence people and motivate them to collaborate and cooperate with individuals from other organizations.

In the case of SJI, during the process implementation phase, Alenia and Finmeccanica Group Services played the role of boundary spanner, aligning processes to Finmeccanica's network guidelines and directives. Alenia, as a shareholder of both SJI and SCAC, also had the fundamental role of facilitating collaboration between the two companies, organizing periodical meetings and periods spent by SJI employees (mainly from the Customer Service area) at the SCAC headquarters in Moscow in order to work side by side with Russian colleagues. Moreover, SJI's organizational structure and the personnel selected for key roles are a strategic means to aid effective integration among Italian and Russian workers. In particular, Russians and Italians cover several top management positions in SJI and in SCAC respectively, while their deputies are of the opposite nationality. Two key roles in SJI are Assistant Secretary and Head of Customer Service. They are responsible for maintaining official relations in the network and facilitating interactions and collaboration between SJI and SCAC.

Involvement of operative personnel

Organizational processes must be designed together with key operative personnel to ensure the success and adaptability of the solution from an organizational point of view. Among fundamental change management practices is the use of incentive systems to encourage people in their adoption of new approaches and attitudes.

In the case of SJI, the design of each process was not carried out in detail until the respective key roles were covered. Indeed their contribution through direct involvement and brainstorming sessions was considered essential to specify the requirements for low-level activities. As to Customer Service, an open policy towards foreign divisions facilitated the involvement of all employees in the implementation of procedures and sharing of responsibilities. Note that incentive systems where not used during the start-up process.

Networkability principles and standards

Processes should be designed and implemented respecting principles of interoperability and adaptability in order to be easily integrable with their partners'. For example, standard approaches and modeling languages should be leveraged to facilitate collaboration and shared understanding of procedures.

In the case of SJI, the processes where modelled using IDS Sheer Aris Business Architect, the standard BPM Suite adopted by the Finmeccanica Group and following Finmeccanica's guidelines, thus supporting interoperability with its network. Note that at an early stage of the design phase, processes where modelled both with Aris and MS Power Point, thus requiring an additional step to make the models uniform in the final EPC Diagram form in Aris. Another important issue to be solved is the use of units of measure of different technical data and languages in the collaboration between SJI and SCAC. A measure to improve the integration between SJI and SCAC is the use of a common and integrated PLM (Product

Lifecycle Management) System, since technical data provided by SCAC is essential for SJI's services.

Business processes activation time
The activation time of inter-organizational processes depends on the technological and organizational profiles of partners and on their readiness in terms of collaboration technologies and skills. The deployment of the solution can follow two approaches: (i) gradual implementation of cross-organizational processes, starting with the deployment of a key subset and then gradually deploying other processes; (ii) deploying the complete solution to a subset of network partners (partners who are better prepared in moving towards the network paradigm) and thereafter extending it to other partners. The two approaches can be integrated and are not mutually exclusive.

The various SJI business network partners are inserted on a gradual basis, according to business needs. Priority criteria for the activation of SJI's business processes and for the creation of the necessary partnerships depend on actual business needs. Indeed, SJI is now more focused on marketing/sales and customer service partnerships and agreements than the design and development of customized versions of the Superjet 100 family. This is because the product is still not on the market, but sale and after-sale contracts in the Western area are of strategic importance for SJI in order not to depend on SCAC's market performances.

Sponsorship and communication
Sponsorship and high commitment of top management and key persons in an organization is a fundamental condition for the deployment program's effectiveness. Moreover, trust relations must be fostered by creating social ties and setting-up technological infrastructures that enable inter-organizational communication and interaction on a global level.

In the case of SJI, the top management is highly committed and the CEO is highly skilled in communicating the importance of strategic objectives, involving every organizational level in the achievement of these objectives. Trust relations between SJI and SCAC are developed through exchange programs in order to foster common understanding and a shared view of issues and objectives. As concerns the technological communication infrastructure among the network nodes, a VoIP system is used and will be gradually extended to allow voice/video conferences and desktop sharing sessions.

Recruitment
In a networked context, it is essential to assess both the professional competencies and behavioral skills (propensity to cooperation or communication) of individuals. People must be able to operate in the network and collaborate to achieve the network's objectives. When a team is composed of heterogeneous elements, decision processes are more complex and time consuming, although more options and pos-

sibilities are taken into account, thus increasing the possibilities of finding the right solution.

In the case of SJI, given the global scale of its organizational structure, employees were selected from ten different nationalities, especially for Customer Service roles, with some people coming from airline companies and thus highly skilled and aware of client needs and expectations. Moreover, since SJI is part of a global business network, a good level of spoken English is a primary requirement. Finally, many employees were recruited from the Finmeccanica Group partners in order to make the SJI's integration into its network easier and smoother.

Knowledge management

Knowledge management practices support the creation, storage and sharing of valuable information, experience and know-how within and across communities of people and organizations with common interests and needs. Knowledge sharing systems are an important means of facilitating continuous learning practices and to help create a shared understanding of the common environment across the networked organization.

In SJI, process models are shared through a web-based application accessible by any member of the company: this facilitates the exchange of information, communication between departments and helps individuals fully understand the organizational context they operate in. On the network level, there is currently no standardized knowledge management system, but top management intends to consider its creation when the partnerships become more robust and trust-based relations have been established.

Inter Organizational Information System

The difficulties in integrating the information systems of different organizations derive from numerous sources, amongst which: the use of different platforms provided by different vendors, the use of different communication technologies, the use of protocols that are not fully compliant with standards, etc. These types of problems are very common when companies want to create a network and want to make their information systems interoperable. Integrating means defining interfaces, data formats and sources, adapting middleware applications through adapters and connectors, developing transformation and translation of data and information across the network.

SJI has adopted systems and applications that are used as standard by the Finmeccanica Group, thus making SJI fully interoperable with the Finmeccanica network. For example, SAP ERP and IDS Sheer Aris are used to fully manage processes and information across the company. Note that in the future, SCAC will probably use Aris too. Finally, SCAC's PLM (Product Lifecycle Management) System (Teamcenter) will soon be replicated in SJI to share relevant product data.

7.6 Conclusions

In the current competitive scenario, complex and technologically advanced industries highlight a set of problems that have to be faced organically and structurally. Developing and managing the life cycle of more and more complex and innovative products requires the capability to integrate technological skills and scientific disciplines, which is only possible through the greater integration of firms characterized by distinctive and recognizable competences. The aeronautical industry, due to product complexity and the financial and organizational scope of each development plan, has always tested intra and inter-organizational models aimed at simplifying processes and reducing risks. The emergent model is the specialized extended enterprise, where a firm is less and less vertically integrated and is focused on few specific competences, externalizing non-core and non-value-added activities, aiming at inter-organisational collaboration in order to change from the Value-Chain model to the Value-Network model. In this context, competitiveness has to be defended by revisiting business models and business processes according to the value-network perspective.

This chapter presents the start-up of SuperJet International as a case study where strategic and organizational aspects were jointly conceived from a network-driven perspective. The chapter compares some of the TEKNE Methodology of Change guidelines with the experiences and actual practices identified from interviews with key players in the SJI's start-up process. The methodology relates well to the case study, giving a structured view of its strengths and weaknesses.

References

[1] Mintzberg H (1983) Power In and Around Organizations. Prentice Hall

[2] Handy C (1995) Trust and the Virtual Organization. Harvard Business Review 73:40-50.

[3] Salancik G R (1995) Wanted: A good network theory of organization. Administrative Science Quarterly 40:345-349

[4] Byrne J A, Brandt R, Port O (1993) The virtual corporation. Business week. http://www.businessweek.com/@@J1JaMoUQtnJSthEA/archives/1993/b330454.arc.htm. Accessed 18 December 2009

[5] Powel W W (1990) Neither market nor hierarchy: network forms of organization. Research in Organizational Behavior. 12:295-336

[6] Thompson J (1967) Organizations in Action. McGraw Hill

[7] Porter M E, Millar V E (1985) How Information Gives You Competitive Advantage. Harvard Business Review 63:149-160

[8] Riemer K, Klein S (2006) Network Management Framework. In: Klein S, Poulymenakou A (ed) Managing dynamic networks, Springer

[9] Monge P R, Contractor N S (2003) Theories of Communication Networks. Oxford University Press

[10] Stake R E (1995) The art of case study research. Thousand Oaks: Sage Publications

[11] Yin R K (2003) Case study research: Design and methods. Thousand Oaks: Sage Publications

[12] Bryman A, Bell E (2007) Business research methods. Oxford University Press

[13] Creswell J W (2003) Research design. Thousand Oaks: Sage Publications

Chapter 8 - Avio case study: the MRO process

Angelo Corallo[1], Angelo Dimartino[1], Fabrizio Errico[1], Enza Giangreco[2]

[1] eBMS S.S. ISUFI University of Salento

[2] Engineering Ingegneria Informatica S.p.A.

Abstract – This chapter presents the case study of the Avio Brindisi plant where a profound process of change has been in progress for a number of years. We use the TEKNE Project methodology of change to analyze the different aspects of the case, highlighting the firm's strategic, organizational and technological characteristics and the environment it operates in. In particular, we envisage a change in the plant's business model in response to the expansion of its client segments and a potential new approach to MRO operations based on advanced fleet management practices that would radically change the firm's organization and value network with respect to its MRO service offering, thereby yielding extensive global market opportunities.

8.1 Introduction

The aeronautical sector is one of the most significant and complex industries in terms of the high technological content of its products, the high financial risks related to considerable development costs and the complex structure of the supply chain.

On a European level, the aeronautics industry significantly contributes to the EU economic budget and has great political value given its impact on the territory's security and defense. Furthermore, the aeronautics industry is a leading sector on a global level in terms of technological and industrial research and innovation, thus attracting other industry sectors.

A new business model is emerging in which companies focus on a few functions and core competencies and collaborate through dynamic and value-driven business networks, sharing program risks. Indeed, the aerospace industry is composed of a few large global integrators and a number of suppliers and partners that are part of a multi-layer supply chain called the production pyramid. The production pyramid typically includes:

- Program leaders, who design, develop and assemble or manufacture complete units
- Prime partners, who manufacture major assembled parts and/or major aircraft sections (i.e. complete engines, airframes, avionics)

- 1st and 2nd level subcontractors, specialized in the production of components of parts assembled/manufactured by prime partners;
- 3rd level subcontractors, who produce components and subassemblies for second level subcontractors

This sector is characterized by hefty supply chain integration requirements in terms of product design, technology management, resource flows, demand forecast and program management. These requirements led the aeronautics industry to become a leading sector in the adoption of ICT solutions to support the management of business processes[1]. ERP systems and e-procurement solutions are extremely popular, platforms for knowledge management and for e-learning are diffused according to the needs of a heavily knowledge-intensive industry. One of the major obstacles to the actual development of a truly integrated supply chain is the different adoption of ICTs among small and large enterprises respectively belonging to the upper and lower levels of the production pyramid. This leads to a supply chain that evolves at two different speeds, which is extremely dangerous for an industry that requires highly efficient coordination and integration processes within their product development programs.

Although the global aerospace sector is growing impressively, the loss in market share of the American and European aeronautics industry is noteworthy. This has determined, in different proportions, a gain in share in Asia-Pacific and Middle Eastern industries that are playing increasingly important roles in the product development process by ascending levels in the production pyramid. Under such competitive pressure, and given the decrease in product margins with respect to an increase in service margins, Italian firms are obliged to re-position themselves on those processes that precede or follow a product development program that guarantees higher margins.

Thus, the competitive challenge for Italian aeronautics industries is determined by:

- impact capacity on the efficiency, flexibility and integration of a supply chain to sustain a small primary leadership in international program environments
- capability to develop distinctive competences linked to the supply of specific and high value-added aeronautical services in order to strengthen the actual embryonic capacity to become a primary partner.

This chapter presents the case study of the MRO (Maintenance Repair and Overhaul) process in Avio, analyzing its re-design through the Methodology of Change phases defined in the TEKNE project. Given the growing importance of service processes with respect to production processes, the MRO market represents a key enabler for the company's future growth and requires a new approach to compete on a global scale.

---

[1] E-Business Survey 2005, e-Business W@tch

Avio Aerospace Propulsion is an aerospace company on the leading edge of propulsion technology, its headquarters are in Turin, it has several plants in Italy and three facilities in Poland, the USA and Africa. The principal design and manufacturing departments are in Italy as are the military departments. Avio has developed a role as an important subsystem and component manufacturer, participating in key international aeronautical and space programs in all the product life-cycle phases: from research & development to manufacture and assembly, up to service and overhaul. The company is currently engaged in six activity sectors: (i) civil aeronautics (ii) defense (iii) maintenance, repair and overhaul for civil and military aeronautical and aero-derivate engines (iv) space (v) aero-derivate turbines for naval and industrial use (vi) helicopters.

The unit of analysis of this case study is Avio's plant in Brindisi, with particular reference to its MRO activities in military engines. This choice is due to Avio Brindisi's actual need for strategic and operational changes in response to the changing market scenario. Moreover, Avio is part of a value network where information is continuously exchanged and will have to face an integration of information systems in the near future to enable the optimal management of a global market. These characteristics make the case study very relevant to the TEKNE project and to its methodology of change, granting the possibility to apply and evaluate its principles and phases with respect to a real-world scenario.

8.2 As-is: assessment of the unit of analysis

The TEKNE methodology of change's first phase focuses on the identification of those contingency variables that have a direct and indirect impact on the unit of analysis. These variables, influencing firm competitiveness, must be taken into account when undertaking any change process. This contextualization is not only useful in guiding the enterprise in its daily activities, but helps to shed light on future business scenarios. In this case study, a PEST (Political Economical Social Technological) analysis was undertaken to study the macro-environment in which Avio operates, while the micro-environment and its characteristics where studied by assessing Avio's technological, organizational and strategic situation. Note that the assessment refers specifically to a period between the years 2005 and 2008 when the market scenario gradually changed and Avio elaborated and began implementing strategic and operative actions to maintain its competitiveness.

As concerns the macro-environment, the **PEST analysis** highlights a scenario in which the aeronautics industry has to cope with a growing sense of insecurity due to terrorist threats that influence both the civil and military sectors, requiring Airlines to adopt expensive and sophisticated countermeasures and Air Forces to become more efficient and ready to respond to unexpected needs. From a political point of view, strategic international agreements and good relationships between

Italy and other countries play a fundamental role in Avio's business, enabling its participation in international programs and partnerships. Moreover, military expenditure is directly related to peacekeeping missions and thus strongly influenced by strategic alliances and Italy's participation in UN missions. From an economic perspective, services and goods exchanged within the aeronautics industry are characterized by weighty fixed costs, which are strongly affected by interest rates and international monetary policies. Moreover, companies within the industry can be heavily penalized by the fact that they are unable to adapt quickly to the changing environment as a result of the current adverse macroeconomic scenario. Finally, military demand directly depends on defense spending, and thus on institutional funding. In terms of technological factors, the aerospace industry is characterized by the continuous development of new solutions through advanced and innovative R&D activities that are usually financed by public funding. The lifecycle of the final product is very long and the related costs are very high, implicating the maintenance of obsolete machines and technologies.

The micro-environment of the unit of analysis is defined by those contingency variables that impact directly on Avio Brindisi and on its status. In this case study, the micro-environment analysis coincides with the strategic, organizational and technological assessment.

As concerns the **strategic assessment**, the analysis of Avio Brindisi's competitive position is guided by the renowned *Porter's five forces model* [1]. The analysis reported here aims to highlight the key aspects that emerged from the interviews and desk research, without pretending to be complete and exhaustive. For the last few years, Avio's MRO service market of reference has been exclusively the Italian Armed Forces and State Services. This mono-client market bound Avio tightly to the specific necessities and the variable funding of the Italian Ministry of Defense. Thus, when the Italian Government recently decided to cut defense spending, Avio Brindisi faced a profound production crisis that required a drastic strategic change so as to no longer depend on a single and powerful client. With respect to entry of new competitors, the national market has very high barriers and Avio has a monopolistic role. Services on military engines are indeed considered a national strategic asset and the Government decided to permanently assign them to an Italian company. Moreover, conceiving substitute services is not easy since the extensive know-how and expertise acquired by Avio in the MRO of many types of military engines has led to a service that is fine-tuned to customer needs. Finally, Avio Brindisi suppliers provide three different products/services: the supply of spare parts, the servicing of minor accessories, and overhauls requiring technologies that are not available within Avio. The power of suppliers is high due to their high degree of specialization in terms of skills and technologies. The local environment plays a fundamental role in Avio Brindisi's competitiveness, fostering improvement through the growth of the aerospace industry in Apulia resulting from the following drivers: (i) the consolidation of an integrated development model among SMEs in Apulia, including the participation of institutions and the scholastic system (ii) the expanding presence of large firms (iii) attraction of investments from other international companies.

The achievement of strategic objectives is monitored with the measurement of very high-level indicators that are actually related to financial performance. In particular, the two major strategic metrics are the percentage variation of turnover and new orders in a year. The consolidated budget for the years 2005, 2006, 2007 and 2008 show that Avio's MRO of military engines is strongly affected by the Italian Ministry of Defense's persistent budget cuts that in the last few years has led to considerable downsizing of the number and size of orders from the national market and to the decrease of production activities in Brindisi. Order downsizing is actually mitigated by the initiation of MRO activities relating to new engines (EJ200 - Typhoon, AE2100 - C130J and T700/T6A - EH101) and by the gradual enlargement of Avio's market to include the military fleets of other countries.

As concerns **organizational assessment**, the analysis is focused on Avio Brindisi's MRO processes, omitting any other aspect of its business. Avio has worked for over 40 years with leading aero engine manufacturers, acquiring extensive know-how and expertise in the MRO of many types of military engines. Currently, 16 types of engines and more than 32 different versions are supported in Avio's Military MRO Plant located in Brindisi. The plant (54000 m^2) employs around 1000 highly skilled people and its modern layout is optimized to carry out the highest quality and standards of repair and overhaul. Moreover, manufacturing, assembly and test activities are also carried out at the Brindisi Plant, including the final assembly and testing of complete engines (e.g. the EJ200 engine for the Eurofighter Typhoon). The organizational assessment led to a detailed description of the entire business process currently executed in MRO operations. In particular, the process is described in terms of its activities, participants and roles, decision points, key events and control flows through BPMN diagrams. These diagrams are the final result of a series of interviews involving many key actors in the Brindisi Plant and help to highlight criticalities and opportunities for the next re-design phase. The MRO business process can be divided into three sub-processes, each one with specific objectives. A detailed analysis of these processes is outside of the scope of this report, but a brief description of their key issues is important to give a view of Avio's actual needs.

The *Engine Receipt* sub-process has the objective of taking receipt of engines from clients, inspecting them for any issues resulting from transportation or unexpected events and finally stocking them in the warehouse. Problems related to this sub-process are due to the fact that when an engine is received, it is usually put in the warehouse until the client explicitly requires the MRO operations to be undertaken. This can take months, determining high warehousing costs and other side issues resulting from the lengthy stalling process. The *Engine Overhaul* sub-process has the objective of carrying out necessary MRO operations on engines, testing and certifying the quality of results. Since it is currently impossible to make mid-term forecasts on the flow of engines in arrival, it is very difficult to optimize the Engine Overhaul sub-process in terms of resources and time. The flow is indeed highly discontinuous, resulting in periods of under-utilization of human and technical resources, and periods when arrivals exceed the plant's actual capacity, thus determining a bottleneck in the entire MRO process and compromising the service perceived by the client. Note that this situation also affects procurement activities, requiring higher stock levels of spare parts and raw materials to provide an effective buffer to the changing operational needs. Finally, the *Engine Delivery* sub-process has the objective of issuing invoices and delivering the engine to the client.

Avio Brindisi's MRO process thus entails a high degree of complexity since it is composed of many activities, roles and resources that must be managed through effective coordination mechanisms and systems. Business policies, routines, procedures and rules are currently leveraged to control and support decision makers, but there is an emergent need for the standardization and formalization of terms and meanings across the entire enterprise in order to easily share and understand common guidelines and business rules. Given the mono-client approach that Avio Brindisi has pursued up to now, interactions and its relationship with the client are rather informal and its organizational structure is tailored to the needs of the Italian Armed Forces and State Services.

Performance on an operational level is measured with the following set of KPIs:

- *Mean TAT* (Turn Around Time): the average time necessary for the overhaul of an engine or of an engine component;
- *Mean cost of overhaul*: the average cost sustained for the overhaul of an engine or of an engine component;
- *Mean number of penalties*: average number of penalties paid by Avio due to failed contract fulfillment;
- *Number of engines in WIP*: total number of engines with a Work In Progress status at a specific time;
- *Punctuality of delivery*: number of engines delivered in time with respect to contractual specifications;
- *Stocks*: quantity of available stock;
- *Manpower utilization*: indicates efficiency in the utilization of human resources in the process.

The value of these metrics as measured in recent years, has highlighted the need to re-engineer the end-to-end MRO process in order to make it more efficient and controllable in terms of cost and delivery time.

As concerns the **technological assessment**, Avio Brindisi's business processes are currently supported by two IT systems. The first is a SAP platform for Supply Chain Management that enables the coordination of the plant's entire logistics operations. The second system, called MOS, supports contract registration and invoicing. The MRO process actually lacks a tracking system for the real-time monitoring of work in progress. In particular, there is an emergent need to be able to report the status of their engines to clients at any time following receipt and during MRO operations. Moreover, the interviews highlighted the need for a simulation system to optimize the scheduling of operations with respect to specific priorities and available resources. Finally, it is worth noting the existence of an advanced MRO Management system called ISIS (In Service Information System) developed by Avio to provide an integrated and complete fleet management service. ISIS is currently used in only a limited number of programs.

The metric used by Avio to measure the performance of its technological systems are:

- *Disruption of Service*: which counts the number of times that one or more modules of the system are unavailable due to technical problems;
- *ISAC* (Index of anomalies reported by the customer): gives a quantitative measurement of anomalies reported by the client. ISAC is calculated with the formula $ISAC = A \div H \times 100$, where A is the number of anomalies reported by clients and H is the total number of production hours.
- *Buono Subito*: number of engines that pass final certification testing on the first attempt, without requiring further overhaul activities.

The analysis of the macro-environment and micro-environment in which the unit of analysis operates is summarized in the following SWOT table:

Strengths	Weaknesses
• Monopoly of the Italian military market	• Mono-client market
• Growing importance and consolidation of the aeronautical district of Apulia, which includes large national enterprises and a strong network of SMEs	• High power of suppliers
	• Impossibility of making mid-term forecasts on the flow of engines in arrival
• Extensive MRO know-how and expertise in many types of military engines, developed over a 40 year period of activities and collaborations with leading aero engine manufacturers	• Inadequate technological infrastructure in the Brindisi Plant
	• Weak coordination mechanisms in local business networks
• Good experience in fleet management practices and supporting tools	• Incomplete vocational training on a local level
• Stable and trust-based relationships with suppliers	

Opportunities	Threats
• Growth of global demand and start-up of new international programs	• Different adoption of ICTs among small and large enterprises in the aerospace production pyramid
• Slight increase in margins due to after-sales services	• Competitive pressure of emerging countries
• Opening of new markets in emerging countries	• Decrease in Italian Defense operative funding
• Public funding available for European, national and regional R&D projects in the aeronautics sector	

Table 8.1: SWOT table of the Avio scenario

8.3 To-be: business model re-design

The strategic, organizational and technological assessments are fundamental sources of information through which the current business model of the unit of analysis is formalized. In fact, this facilitates re-thinking the key components (building blocks) in such a way as to enable the enterprise to compete in future market challenges. The TEKNE Methodology of Change adopts the Business Model Ontology (BMO) approach based on Osterwalder's study to describe a new and innovative business model. According to Osterwalder, "the business model of a company is a simplified representation of its business logic. It describes what a company offers its customers, how it reaches them and relates to them, which resources, activities and partners it leverages on and finally, how it earns money" (Osterwalder, 2004). Influenced by the Balanced Scorecard approach [2] and more generally by business management literature [3], the approach consists of four main pillars: product, customer interface, infrastructure management and financial aspects. For a more structured analysis, these four pillars are divided into nine interrelated building blocks, thus allowing a simple and schematic description of a business model [4]. Our aim is to briefly show how building blocks are changing in Avio Brindisi and the final goal of this change process, highlighting the type of consequences that are expected on a strategic, organizational and technological level. The business model description gave us the opportunity to align the strategic, technological and organizational layer through a unique and schematic representation, making an improved analysis of internal gaps possible.

8.3.1 Product

This area covers all aspects of what a firm offers its customers. This comprises not only the company's bundles of products and services but also the manner in which it differentiates itself from its competitors. This perspective is described through the value proposition element [4]. The value proposition is the first of nine elements of the business model and can be described as the statements of benefits that the firm delivers to its external constituencies [5]. It is described as the definition of how items of value, such as products and services as well as complementary value-added services, are packaged and offered to fulfill customer needs [6]. In our case study, the strategic decision of opening Avio's market to other countries requires some changes in services offered in order to make them attractive to new clients that have different needs and expectations from those of the Italian Armed Forces. Avio is currently improving the service quality of its MRO offer, allowing clients to monitor the status of their engines while they are in the WIP (Work in Progress) stage. The preceding one-to-one relationship with the Italian Armed Force led to informal monitoring mechanisms that are actually unsuitable for an international market. However, the services offered by Avio Brindisi are fundamentally the same as those offered prior to the market extension: MRO operations provided on client demand. This approach requires the client to schedule the maintenance and send the engine to Avio when maintenance operations are needed, which means that Avio has no foresight on the mid-term arrivals of engines and is unable to optimize MRO plans and procurement processes. This type of problem could be solved if Avio were to offer its clients a complete and effective fleet management service, centralizing engine health monitoring and their MRO operation scheduling, thus optimizing the flow of engines in arrival and dramatically reducing periods of congestion or the underutilization of the Brindisi Plant. A well-organized and technologically advanced fleet management service is actually the only way to confront a global multi-client market where overhaul and maintenance operations must be orchestrated to optimize both client and service provider goals. The former want a guaranteed number of aircraft always available and ready for missions, the latter want to optimize their internal processes and provide a scalable and controllable MRO service.

8.3.2 Customer interface

The customer interface pillar covers all customer related aspects. This comprises the choice of a firm's *Client Segment*, the *Communication and Distribution Channels* through which it gets in touch with them and the kind of *Relationships* the company wants to establish with its customers [4].

Client Segment

Effective segmentation enables a company to allocate investment resources to target customers that will be most attracted by its value proposition.

In our case study, in view of the mono-client market that Avio Brindisi had until a few years ago, the Italian Ministry of Defense's funding cuts led to both considerable downsizing of orders and a serious crisis in the Brindisi Plant. The top management decided to confront this crisis by opening Avio's MRO offering to the military fleets of other countries in order to develop its client segmentation and mitigate dependency on Italian defense expenditure. Market expansion is currently directed towards developing countries and towards those countries that do not have the competencies or the political will to develop their own MRO services. Note that expansion in advanced countries (e.g. France, Germany, USA) is almost impossible since those markets are similar to the Italian market, with very high entry barriers due to strong monopolistic players.

Relevant outcomes of this marketing initiative are:

- a five-year exclusive contract to recondition the Spey MK807 propulsion system of the Brazilian Air Force's entire fleet of AM-X aircraft
- an agreement with the Dutch Ministry of Defense to start a public/private project for the maintenance of military engines. This agreement represents the starting point of Avio's increasing future involvement in military MRO services in North Europe
- a collaboration project with a Polish partner for the supply of military MRO services to the Polish Ministry of Defense
- a contract for the overhaul of forty T64/4D engines that will be provided by the USA Department of Defense to the Afghan Armed Forces.

Other minor contracts have been signed with African and Eastern Europe countries. Expansion of the client portfolio is one of the key strategic factors that have allowed Avio Brindisi to confront the production crisis and to keep the plant operational.

Communication and Distribution Channels

This component describes how a company gets in touch with its customers. Its purpose is to make the right quantity of the right products or services available at the right place and at the right time to the right people [7]- subject of course, to cost, investment and flexibility constraints [8].

A direct and trust-based relationship with the customer has always characterized Avio's communication and distribution strategy. The new global market perspective has not changed this approach but requires strengthening the organization and become more focused on understanding the market and customer needs and if/how they can be satisfied by Avio's capabilities. Two dedicated organizational units are responsible for acquiring new clients and managing the lifecycle of contracts. The Commercial Unit, which is organized by geographical area, analyzes the market, identifies new prospects, formulates offers and negotiates new contracts up to their approval and signature. For every bidding process the Commercial Unit appoints a *bid team*, a cross-functional working group that is responsible for following the entire bidding phase and to support the Commercial Unit in any activity, when required. This allows the offer to be tailored to the specific characteristics of the client and the entire negotiation to be totally client-centric. The Business Unit is responsible for maintaining relationships with the acquired customers and managing the entire lifecycle of their contracts following signature.

Customer relationship

The historical collaboration between Avio Brindisi and the Italian Ministry of Defense has led to a symbiotic relationship where Avio reserves some areas of its plant at no cost to specific MRO activities that are executed directly by Air Force employees. Relationships with other clients, although not as close, are as open as possible, so that important clients such as the Brazilian Air Force have an office and several employees working at the Brindisi Plant.

New and interesting perspectives can be found in advanced fleet management services that will radically change the value perceived by clients. The offer will not be limited to on-demand MRO operations. Via an end-to-end fleet management service, Avio intends to increase the quality of services provided, thus bringing them closer to customers needs.

8.3.3 Infrastructure management

The infrastructure management pillar is about *how* a company creates value. It describes the capabilities a firm needs to provide its value propositions and to maintain its customers interface [9]. Three components characterize this area: *capability, value configuration and partnership*. This pillar outlines the value network that generates economic value through complex dynamic exchanges between one or more enterprises, its customers, suppliers, strategic partners and the community [10].

Capabilities can be tangible (machinery and equipment to implement both engine module maintenance and testing of entire engines), intangible (ability to analyze relevant data, efficient fleet management coordination, licensing and certification, tacit knowledge and experience of employees, repair capability, relationships with partners and suppliers), or human (employee skills and knowledge: 700 employees of which 54% are graduates. R&D employees number 60).

The *value configuration* in Avio Brindisi concerns: engine health state monitoring, planning, scheduling and coordinating maintenance and repair activities, product support and after sales services, R&D activity on new repair methods.

A company's *partnership* outlines which parts of the activity configuration and which resources are distributed among the firm's partners. A partnership is a voluntarily initiated cooperative agreement formed between two or more independent companies to carry out a project or specific activity jointly by coordinating the necessary capabilities, resources and activities [4]. Currently, Avio Brindisi has relationships with three different types of partners in the MRO process:

- suppliers of spare parts (stable and continuous relations);
- small accessories MRO firms (stable relationships, but occasional);
- suppliers who perform repair activities using technologies not used by Avio Brindisi (occasional relationships);

The introduction of a *fleet management service* will radically impact on Avio's resources and activities, requiring intervention on human resources through on-going training. It requires redefining the entire MRO process through the active involvement of partners and suppliers. These suppliers therefore have an active role in carrying out various activities such as engine health state monitoring, planning and scheduling. All this with the ultimate aim of improving the value perceived by clients.

8.3.4 Financial aspects

Financial aspects are the fourth and last area managers have to take into consideration to renew the Avio Business Model. Two main components are considered within this area: the cost structure and the revenue model.
The revenue model measures the firm's ability to translate the value it offers its customers into money and incoming revenue streams. The Avio revenue model is composed of different revenue streams:
- Overhaul of national engines
- Overhaul of international engines
Cost Structure measures all the costs the firm incurs to create, market and deliver value to its customers [9]. It sets a price tag on all the resources, assets, activities and network partner relationships and exchanges that cost the company money. Avio Brindisi's main cost items are:
- Parts and materials
- External repair service
- Workforce
The financial perspective is transversal because all other areas influence it. This perspective is the outcome of the rest of the business model's configuration and for this reason, due to the introduction of fleet management activity, will inevitably be redefined. In particular, the revenue model will be modified on the basis of the new value proposition and the cost structure (cost allocation) will be

influenced by the new relationships Avio creates with customers and suppliers to implement fleet management.

8.3.5 Value flows

After having described the Business Model of Avio through the BMO approach, and after having introduced the main transformations occurring due to the fleet management approach, it is now interesting to analyze the value flows that are generated across the business network of Avio, extending the possible implications to business units other than the one of Brindisi. For this purpose, following the TEKNE Methodology of Change, we used the e^3value ontology, which allows the graphical representation of the exchanges of value objects between actors of a business network. The adoption of the fleet management approach entails a complete change in the value exchange between Avio and its clients (Figure 8.1 represents the current (as is) and the expected (to be) value flows). If with the traditional contracts Avio "sells" MRO operations, thus aiming at maximizing their number in order to improve the turnover, the *pay by the hour* type of contract that characterizes a fleet management strategy requires Avio to deliver reliability and availability of engines to the client, thus radically changing the value object that is exchanged among the actors: Avio guarantees a fixed amount of hours of availability of engines for the fleet of the client, and in return the client pays a fee that is proportional to that amount. At the same time Avio has the possibility to access any information related to the health and working status of the engines in order to monitor their lifecycle and plan a dynamic and optimal maintenance scheduling that reduces both the number of operations and hours of unavailability of the engines.

The scenario can be extended by considering that Avio produces engine components in the plant of Torino and that such components are used to assemble engines and aircrafts bought and used by Air Forces all over the world. In terms of an end-to-end business model that takes in consideration the whole enterprise, it is interesting to make an hypothesis on the possibility that Avio becomes direct partner of Prime Contractors in order to provide Air Forces not only the product, but a complete solution that includes after-sale services, with particular reference to fleet management and engine MRO services. Avio provides capabilities for fleet management services and, on return, Prime Contractors obtain service contracts that are outsourced to Avio Brindisi.

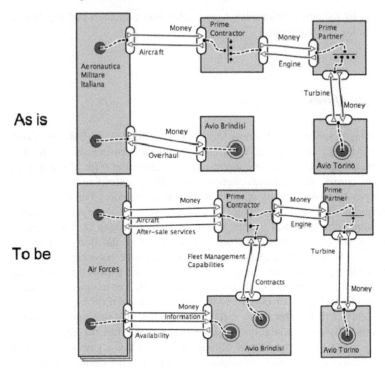

Fig. 8.1 - The as is and to be scenarios of Avio's value flows

Future research work will analyze the correlation that exists among the quantity of engine components sold by Avio and the quantity of fleet management contracts obtained, trying to understand the minimum number of fleet management contracts necessary to achieve a given goal in terms of profit. The scenario depicted in the to-be diagram indeed, considering the higher margins of after-sale services with respect to those of product selling, would lead to an aggressive strategy in which Avio lowers its prices when selling engine parts in order to foster Prime Contractors and Prime Partners to offer Avio's after-sale services boudled to the aircraft.

8.4 Conclusions and future work

This chapter presents the case study of the Avio Brindisi plant where a profound process of change has been in progress for a number of years. We used the TEKNE Project methodology of change to analyze the different aspects of the case, highlighting the firm's strategic, organizational and technological characteristics and the environment it operates in. In particular, we envisage a change in the plant's business model due to the expansions of its client base and a potential new approach to MRO operations based on advanced fleet management practices. The adoption of this approach would radically change the way activities are carried out and would lead to a different perspective of the company and its network performance evaluation. Future studies will be focused on a deeper analysis of the business processes and technological requirements needed to fully support a fleet management strategy. At this stage, it would be interesting to construct some hypotheses on the performance metrics that would fit this approach and that would integrate or substitute the performance indicators used currently.

Fleet management means that Avio schedules MRO operations for every customer's engine. The more effective the scheduling, the more engines are efficient and available for use and the fewer the activities that Avio must perform. However, inconveniences can occur during the lifecycle of an engine. In such cases, the scheduling must be rearranged and Avio's costs increase. A new performance metric is the percentage of MRO operations needed due to inconveniences (non-scheduled) with respect to the total number of MRO operations (scheduled + non-scheduled). This metric provides a measure of the quality of the fleet management system and its capacity to minimize MRO operations, maintaining the efficiency of engines. If 10% is exceeded, then the scheduling algorithm must be revised.

Information about the health status of engines must be sent to Avio's scheduling and control system every N days or every M flight hours. Another new metric counts the instances that information arrives late, allowing monitoring the information flow required for the fleet management system to work properly. If the number of delayed information arrivals exceeds X in a given time period, then the reasons for these delays must be identified.

These are just two examples of how the entire organization and its performance evaluation system would change with a fleet management strategy, but further research and studies must be undertaken to leverage the future opportunities of this perspective, including an integrated approach to the value delivered by business units that provide after-sale services and business units that produce engine parts.

References

[1] Porter M E (2001). Strategy and the Internet. Harvard Business Review.

[2] Kaplan R S, Norton D P (1992). The balanced scorecard--measures that drive performance. Harvard Business Review **70**(1).

[3] Markides C (1999). All the Right Moves. Boston, Harvard Business School Press.

[4] Osterwalder A (2004). The Business Model Ontology - A Proposition in a Design Science Approach. Dissertation. L'Ecole des Hautes Etudes Commerciales de l'Université de Lausanne.

[5] Bagchi S, Tulskie B (2000). e-business Models: Integrating Learning from Strategy Development Experiences and Empirical Research. 20th Annual International Conference of the Strategic Management Society, Vancouver.

[6] Kambil A, Ginsberg A, et al. (1997). Rethinking Value Propositions. New York, NYU Center for Research on Information Systems.

[7] Pitt L, Berthon P, et al. (1999). Changing Channels: The Impact of the Internet on Distribution Strategy. Business Horizons.

[8] Anderson E, Day G, et al. (1997). Strategic Channel Design. Sloan Management Review.

[9] Afuah A, Tucci C (2003). Internet Business Models and Strategies. Boston, McGraw Hill.

[10] Allee V (2000). Reconfiguring the Value Network. Journal of Business Strategy 21(4): 36-39.

[11] Gordijn J, Akkermans H (2003). Value based requirements engineering: Exploring innovative e-commerce idea. vol. 8(2):114-134, 200. In Requirements Engineering Journal, vol. 8, pp. 114–134, 2003.

Chapter 9 - Inter-organizational design: exploring the relationship between formal architecture and ICT investments

Daniela Iubatti, Francesca Masciarelli, Alberto Simboli

DASTA – University G.d'Annunzio – Italy

Abstract - This chapter aims to explore how the information-processing capabilities that emerge from a network structure affect the diffusion of innovation in a multidivisional organization. In particular, this study analyzes the role of firm investments in ICT to facilitate communication and knowledge diffusion. Using a qualitative approach, we investigate the behavior of an Italian multinational firm, Engineering S.p.A., analyzing our data using a content analysis procedure. Our results show the limited role of ICT in favoring knowledge exchange both inside and outside the firm's divisions: traditional communication patterns are generally preferred over the use of technologies for information sharing. Additionally, we find that key individuals who play a central role in the firm's communication network are unable to use ICTs for knowledge transfer. We conclude that this is the result of a strategic decision to keep top management practically unchanged since the firm was established. Therefore, key individuals act as filters to knowledge flows. Knowledge, in particular tacit knowledge, is transferred from key individuals to other actors through face-to-face contacts, thereby creating a diseconomy for the organization.

9.1 Introduction

Over 20 years ago, in a famous article entitled "*Central problem in the management of innovation*", Van de Ven [1] claims that "*to understand the process of innovation is to understand the factors that facilitate and inhibit the development of innovations. These factors include ideas, people, transactions and context over time*".

In this chapter, we aim to contribute to the understanding of the relationship between tacit knowledge and technological change in the networks of key individuals. Networks have been hailed as a potential configuration to compete in ambiguous, uncertain and complex contexts. In support of this assumption, many studies in the field of networks have demonstrated the essential role that networks play in changeable environments [2, 3, 4]. Network theory explains that individuals are key players in defining how interactions take place and how the nodes in network languages are linked to each other [5, 6]. An important contribution to our understanding of the role of personal relationships in economic systems comes from Granovetter [7], who identifies two different transaction forms: arm's length relationships (or "strong ties"), which include business relationships, and embedded relations (or "weak ties"), which are more personal. Embeddedness "refers to that process by which social relations shape economic action in ways that some mainstream economic scheme overlooks or misspecifies, when they assume that social ties affect economic behavior only minimally or, in some stringent accounts, reduce the efficiency of the price system" [8, 7, 9]. In the same way as networks, multi-unit organizations are a particular structure in which nodes relate to each other to exchange information, resources and ideas [10, 11]. Multi-unit businesses are an important example of the so-called intra-firm network, where individuals represent key peers who share knowledge. Some individuals assume particular relevance, according to the role they play in enhancing knowledge flows among other actors belonging to the same network [12, 5]. Cross and Borgatti [13] argue that those key individuals play an essential role in shaping knowledge spread amongst others who promote the generation and diffusion of innovative processes.

In addition to the recognition of the key role played by some individuals, a multilevel approach to the role of networks proposed by Padgett & Powell [14] and by Xiao & Tsui [15] underlines the importance of context in influencing organizations in terms of adoption of new technologies to operate in dynamic environments. Therefore, contexts and key individuals represent important determinants in understanding the structure of an intra-firm communication network and its effects on the diffusion of knowledge among organizational members.

Knowledge sharing assumes a predominant position in network contexts as it enables the generation of innovation and, subsequently, its diffusion among network actors [6, 16]. Today, knowledge spread within a network relies primarily on ICT-based relationships. ICTs are useful tools that increase the quality, quantity and speed of codified information flows.

Several studies support the argument that the information-processing capabilities emerging from a network structure determine innovation [17, 18, 19]. But what form should this pattern of ties take in a multidivisional organization? What type of structure will emerge? What is the role of ICT investments in defining communication and knowledge diffusion? In this chapter, we analyze whether the organization is largely influenced by the presence of ICTs and how the relationship between innovation, network and ICTs has changed over time.

Drawing upon existing contributions, we aim to investigate the link between economic activities and the relationships underpinning them and in so doing provide answers to our research questions. Our hope is to gain a better understanding of the dynamics between relationships and economic activities through the investigation of the role played by ICTs and by personal relationships in the diffusion of knowledge.

This chapter is organized as follows. Section 2 describes the theoretical framework used to define our propositions. Section 3 introduces the empirical context we explored for our analysis. Section 4 explains the methodology used. Section 5 and 6 describe the analytical findings. Finally, section 9 presents our conclusions.

9.2 Theoretical Background

In this study, we explore the relationship between firm ICT investments, organizational networks and knowledge diffusion. Our perspectives are based on three theoretical approaches: theories on network structures, organizational IT architecture and group routines.

Research exploring the nature of network structures dates back 30 years. Burt [12], Granovetter [7] and Williamson [20] provided the first prominent contributions basing their studies on various theories such as resource dependence theories, cognitive theories and theories on organizational forms. Scott [21] partly unified these theories by means of social network analysis.

We start from the assumption that within the organization, the patterns of communication among individuals become institutionalized over time [22, 23]. Specifically, according to DiMaggio & Powell [24], the organization is capable of changing its structure and often does so as it responds to changes that occur in its environment or changes in the available technology.

Today, technological evolution is increasingly affecting communication patterns within an organization. Recent contributions refer to organizational IT architecture as a firm's list of technology standards linked to its business requirements. The mass of complex linkages among technology, IT capabilities and knowledge diffusion is becoming a key determinant of firm innovation: IT technologies are a powerful means of organizing and spreading information and knowledge within the organizational context.

For each organization, innovation is the result of a mosaic of different perspectives developed over time as individual ideas accumulate into a complex set of options. Moreover, the number of people involved in the innovation process also increases: people with different skills, interpretive schemas and frames of reference become involved in the process. When an innovative idea is communicated, it can proliferate into multiple ideas as a result of different frames of reference and interpretive schemas. Organizations are largely characterized by the presence of groups of people that belong to the same network. Groups are essential management tools to develop innovation; firms face innovation issues that can be ambiguous, complex and uncertain. Groups perceptions and interpretation of a problem critically influence managerial strategies [25] and their decision to promote change and innovation depends on their perception of relevant opportunities and constraints.

Moreover, in the same way as individuals, groups can be governed by routines. Most empirical research on routines has been implemented on an individual level of analysis. A group is governed by routines when its members start talking less about actions constantly repeated over time than about actions they rarely undertake. Again, in the same way as individuals, groups do not perceive gradual changes. Internal coordination increases the structural elaboration that creates inertia, reducing the group's capability to perceive the need for innovation and thus maintaining the status quo even when the organization presents clear dysfunctions [26].

Contributions of scholars who explored the importance of networks in economic activities and the role of personal relationships within networks highlight the differing impact of personal and professional relationships on economic activities. However, these contributions have not explored how multi-unit firms respond to the adoption of ICTs and how network ties adapt accordingly.

9.3 The empirical context: Engineering S.p.A.

The empirical context selected for this study is *Direzione Ricerca e Innovazione*, a specific department of a multi-unit firm operating in Rome (Italy) called Engineering S.p.A. and operating in the software and Information Technology (IT) industry. Engineering S.p.A is considered one of the most important Italian firm providing integrated software solutions. It acts as a group of "small firms", also called the Engineering Group, composed of 13 companies and 37 operational departments in Italy and abroad with over 6000 IT professionals. The Engineering Group was founded in 1980 with total revenues today of around 800 million Euros. The Engineering Group's aim is to offer integrated and complete solutions in all the stages of the IT value chain, such as consultancy, system and business integration, outsourcing services and so forth. Six business units represent Italian Engineering S.p.A.: *Finance, Pubblica Amministrazione Centrale (PAC), Pubblica Amministrazione Locale e Sanità, Energy & Utilities, Industria & Servizi* and *Telco & Media*. Furthermore, a separate division, *Direzione Ricerca e Sviluppo*, provides knowledge to all other divisions on innovative processes and practices to implement. Specifically, this division enables the introduction of technological and engineering methods through specific Dynamic Adaptive Distribution (DAD) software and fosters innovation sharing thanks to continuous research to improve overall performance.

In this study, we focus our attention on *Direzione Ricerca e Sviluppo*. This department represents a valuable context for our research: it is structured as a network where each division relates with the other to enhance innovative processes; it has a high presence of skilled IT-related employees, in accordance with the firm's business. In addition, it operates in a dynamic environment, playing a prominent role in both fostering and challenging the firm's competitive advantage through innovation adoption.

9.4 Method

To answer our research questions we used a qualitative approach that is particularly suitable in research aimed at implementing explorative analyses [27, 28, 29, 30].

As a first step, to gather data we conducted open-ended interviews, called explanatory interviews, comprising questions on specific topics and including the interviewee's particular opinion on them [31]. A semi-structured questionnaire consisting of three main parts was developed. The first part inquires into a description of work-flows in the division and the characteristics of relations with other divisions and third parties. This is the generic part where the interviewee is asked to mentally draw up an activity map. The second part focuses on Information Technologies (IT) and their role in this division, placing more emphasis on those technologies, namely, Information and Communication Technologies (ICT) that affect most relationships with other actors within and outside the firm. Finally, the third part explores the characteristics of the firm's external environment, stressing the differences between the firm and its competitors and what the interviewee considers to be the source of the firm's competitive advantage.

Orazio Viele, head of *Direzione Ricerca e Innovazione*, was contacted first. He showed a proactive interest in participating in our project. Subsequently, we presented the project to the heads of the other firm divisions who agreed to be involved and to answer our questions. A total of 7 face-to-face interviews were conducted and each was recorded and transcribed in order to have access to all the details of the conversation and to implement a content analysis. Content Analysis is defined as a "research technique for the objective, systematic and quantitative description of the manifest content of communication" [32]. Following Krippendroff's [33] procedure, we first identified the sampling unit of analysis, in our case, the division. Besides, sentences are considered the context and the recording units of analysis. A list of nodes linking two independent lists was developed, representing the framework for the codification of the transcribed interviews. A set of rules, identified in dictionaries, was subsequently established with the purpose of improving the objectivity of the analysis [34]. Using NVivo7 software, a list of words that appeared more than 10 times was identified in the texts and after deleting articles, auxiliaries and prepositions, joining singulars and plurals; all remaining words were linked to a relevant node, thus generating the final dictionary. Coders worked independently in analyzing each sentence and codifying it according to the specific concept that it expressed.

9.5 Results

In this section, we report the results of the content analysis process. Following the analytical model proposed in Figure 1, we analyzed how the different types of relationships impact on organizational changes and vice versa. Relationships and the propensity/inertia to change highlight different interdependencies that lead to drawing several significant conclusions.

The results of the analysis will be discussed in the remaining part of this section, giving rise to an original contribution allowing us to answer our research questions.

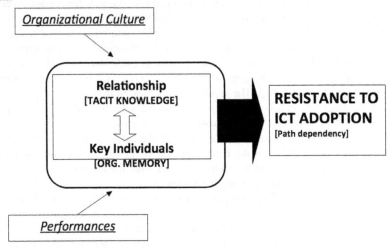

Fig. 9.1– Analytical Model

9.5.1 Descriptive Results

Our findings showed limited adoption of ICT in relating with other actors, both within and outside the division [5, 6]. In *Direzione Ricerca e Innovazione*, traditional communication patterns are preferred over the use of technologies to share information among individuals.

Generally, periodic meetings and face-to-face contact are the predominant ways of relating not only with other members of the division but also with third parties. In addition, phone and web-conference calls and e-mail exchanges constitute key information sharing vehicles.

Efforts have been made to enhance the use of ICT in both internal and external relationships in the division, but they failed to achieve their goal. Notwithstanding the implications of the firm's characteristics, there is strong resistance to adopting new technologies in communications although their introduction is a continuing process.

As pointed out by all interviewees, the main reason why ICT is not adopted is largely related to Engineering S.p.A.'s management style based on personal contacts instead of on more technological tools.

Our empirical findings show, as previously mentioned, that an informal management style influences the adoption of ICT in sharing information and knowledge among individuals within and outside the division – this type of management style reflects the firm's organizational culture, developing informal relationships rather that ICT-based relationships. Furthermore, key individuals play a prominent role in shaping the adoption of communication technologies.

Paradoxically, the more an individual is important in the division and in the entire firm, the greater the obstacle to using ICT in relationships with other individuals.

The reasons for this counterintuitive result can be found in existing literature on organizational routines. Engineering S.p.A.'s management is stable and remains practically unchanged since its establishment and thus key individuals act as filters to knowledge flows.

Tacit knowledge is transferred from key individuals to other actors through informal contacts, demonstrating that the organization's memory is personified in those key actors.

The knowledge diffusion model adopted creates a diseconomy for the organization. In the absence of a codified organizational memory, every new event requires new knowledge to be created. Furthermore, overall high performance tends to enhance a vicious process that enforces the above-mentioned management style, triggering numerous problematic effects on the firm's ability to adapt to a changing external environment. Each of these issues contributes to the inability to use ICT in the firm and in particular in *Direzione Ricerca e Innovazione*, which in turn relies only on informal contacts to share information and experiences to solve problems.

9.5.2 Analytical results

This section discusses the analytical results of the content analysis described in the previous section. Table 9.1 provides the overall descriptive and analytical results.

	Change	Inertia (ICT)	Propensity (ICT)	Inertia (Org)	Propensity (Org)	Tacit Knowledge
Relationships	1929	534	1174	353	0	925
Within the BU	1543	534	888	253	0	828
Outside the BU	484	0	329	155	0	214
Role of individuals	693	224	85	422	0	
Organizational culture	274	0	0	202	72	

Table 9.1 – Relationships, role of individuals and organizational culture vs. Change and tacit knowledge matrix

Strong connection between relationships and change. Table 9.2 shows how the two types of relationships affect the propensity or inertia to change in the division. In particular, there is a propensity to introduce ICTs in order to increase the speed and quality of communications [5] but those technologies are not adopted because of rigid routines that provoke organizational inertia to change. Relationships within the division have a prominent effect on the above mechanism, favoring the introduction of new technologies and, at the same time, inhibiting the adoption of ICTs. This inverse relation is highlighted in Table 9.2, where the propensity to change in terms of ICTs is shown, but people do not use those technologies to iterate and no organizational changes occur.

	Change	Inertia (ICT)	Propensity (ICT)	Inertia (Org)	Propensity (Org)
Relationships	1929	534	1174	353	0
Within the BU	1543	534	888	253	0
Outside the BU	484	0	329	155	0

Table 9.2 – Relationships vs. Change Matrix

The role of key individual affects organizational inertia to change. Cross et al. [6] assert the importance of key individuals in shaping the entire network and its relationships, both internally and externally. Furthermore, Tsai and Ghoshal [35] argue that social interactions among actors of a network enable the production of innovation, implying changes. The matrix in Table 9.3 shows a different trend. The role of key individuals in the division influences the adoption of ICTs to share knowledge and information, enhancing organizational inertia to change. Few trials to introduce new technologies have been undertaken but key players constitute the most important barrier to organizational change given their crucial relevance to other actors in the division and in knowledge sharing processes.

	Change	Inertia (ICT)	Propensity (ICT)	Inertia (Org)	Propensity (Org)
Individuals	693	224	85	422	0

Table 9.3 – Role of individuals vs. Change matrix

Relationships within the division favor tacit knowledge sharing. In line with that argued by many authors, geographical and cognitive proximity mostly affect the flow of information and knowledge between members of a network [36, 37]. Table 9.4 shows that the relationships within *Direzione Ricerca e Sviluppo* enable sharing tacit knowledge to a greater extent than external relationships. Due in part to inertia to change and the role of key individuals as explained above, the importance of face-to-face contacts and a stable environment help develop effective tacit knowledge sharing among actors of the network. The process for generating tacit knowledge is accelerated by relationships within the division due to the geographical proximity of individuals and, no less important, their cognitive proximity [37].

	Tacit Knowledge
Relationships	925
Within the BU	828
Outside the BU	214

Table 9.4 – Relationships vs. Tacit knowledge Matrix

Organizational culture enhances organizational inertia to change. Table 9.5 shows that the firm's organizational culture, basing on informal knowledge sharing patterns, is one of the barriers to organizational change. In fact, the matrix highlights that cultural issues are evident inhibitors of the adoption of ICTs, which would in turn enable organizational changes. Stable management, a strong cultural background and high performance trigger an iterative mechanism that prevents the adoption of new technologies and, as a consequence, organizational change, thus increasing the rigidity and inertia to adaptation to a changing environment.

	Change	Inertia (ICT)	Propensity (ICT)	Inertia (Org)	Propensity (Org)
Organizational culture	274	0	0	202	72

Table 9.5 – Organizational Culture vs. Change Matrix

9.6 Discussion and Conclusions

The different types of relationships that take place among networks members shape the pattern of new technology diffusion and adoption [6]. Furthermore, key individuals in intra-firm networks play an essential role in knowledge sharing processes, generating value for the firm as a whole [35]. In addition, organizational culture influences communications patterns and the propensity/inertia to change.

This chapter demonstrates the difficulties in promoting successful and effective adoption of ICTs in the researched firm. Our investigation shows that investments made to increase the speed and quality of ICTs produce technologies that are then not adopted. The network structure tends to remain unchanged and relationships remain based on personal face-to-face interactions. We find that the main reason for this pattern of social ties is the presence of rigid routines that cause organizational inertia to change. Put differently, despite the firm's efforts, when the organizational culture is based on informal knowledge sharing patterns and the management is stable, the adoption of new technologies becomes ineffective.

Our findings have significant implications for existing literature. First, we bridge social network theories with research that explores the role of IT architecture. This represents a first step towards understanding the role of ICTs in defining the evolutionary patterns of networks. Second, we link literature on IT architecture with research on organizational routines. Our results represent an important contribution to organizational literature since we prove that the effectiveness of IT investments is negatively moderated by the presence of routines that reduce the adoption of new communication tools.

Specifically, our work presents implications for scholars and enhances understanding of network dynamics. In our empirical context, relationships within the division, namely *Direzione Ricerca e Innovazione*, increase inertia to change, in contrast to that argued by numerous authors [38, 14]. The presence of rigid communication routines inhibits the introduction of new technologies. Moreover, key individuals in the networks have a prominent effect on organizational inertia to change, increasing the hostility of other actors to the adoption of ICTs. Cross et al. [6] argue that key players shape knowledge transfer within networks, increasing the possibility of generating innovations. We find that the role of those individuals also has different implications when modeling information flows, indirectly decreasing the propensity to adopt ICTs and to organizational change. Coherently with past literature [36, 37], geographic and cognitive proximities both influence knowledge sharing and networks since relationships within the division mostly determine tacit knowledge exchanges, but they also constitute a limitation to increasing adaptation mechanisms. Finally, organizational culture influences the propensity to change and determines whether firms are flexible or not. In the empirical context analyzed, this inhibits the adoption of new technologies through iterative communication processes.

Furthermore, in this present work we use an original research approach to analyze qualitative data: Content Analysis. This is a technique for the qualitative description of the content of communications in speeches and interviews [32] and has been largely used in sociological and psychological applications, receiving scarce attention in the managerial fields. All the advantages of content analysis explained in the 'method' section, allow us to overcome the difficulties related to the qualitative nature of the data. However, focusing on a single case study is one of the limitations of this study in terms of result generalization. Replications of the same analysis in other case studies would help increase the reliability of our findings and contextualize them according to specific environments and sectors.

References

[1] Van de Ven, A. (1986). Central problem in the management of innovation. Management Science, Vol. 32, No. 5, pp. 590-607.

[2] Burt, R. S. (1992). Structural Holes: The Social Structure of Competition. Cambridge MA, Harvard University Press.

[3] Kogut B., (2000). The Network as Knowledge: Generative Rules and the Emergence of Structure. Strategic Management Journal, Vol. 21, No. 3, Special Issue: Strategic Networks, pp. 405-425

[4] Powell, W. W. (1990). The Transformation of Organizational Forms: How Useful Is Organization Theory in Accounting for Social Change? R. Friedland and A. F. Robertson (eds.), Beyond the Marketplace, Rethinking Economy and Society, New York: Aldine de Gruyter.

[5] Cross, R. and S. P. Borgatti (2000, draft). The Ties that Share: Relational Characteristics that Facilitate Information Seeking.

[6] Cross, R., A. Parker, L. Prusak and S.P. Borgatti (2001). Supporting Knowledge Creation and Sharing in Social Networks. Organizational Dynamics, Vol. 30, No. 2, pp. 100-120.

[7] Granovetter, M. (1985). Economic action and social structure: the problem of embeddedness. American Journal of Sociology, Vol. 91, pp. 481-510.

[8] Uzzi, B. (1996). The Sources and Consequences of Embeddedness for the Economic Performance of Organizations: The Network Effect. American Sociological Review, Vol. 61, No. 4, pp. 674-698.

[9] Crosby L.A. and N. Stephens, (1987). Effects of Relationship Marketing on Satisfaction, Retention, and Prices in the Life Insurance Industry. Journal of Marketing Research, Vol. 24, No.4, pp. 404-411.

[10] Hansen, M. T. (2002). Knowledge Networks: Explaining Effective Knowledge Sharing in Multiunit Companies. Organization Science, Vol. 13, No. 3, pp. 232-248.

[11] Johannisson, B. (1998). Personal Networks in Emerging Knowledge-based Firms: Spatial and Functional Patterns. Entrepreneurship & Regional Development, Vol. 10, pp. 297-312.

[12] Burt, R. (1977). Positions in Multiple Network Systems, Part Two: Stratification and Prestige among Elite Decision-Makers in the Community of Altneustadt. Social Forces, Vol. 56, special issue, 2: 551-575.

[13] Cross, R., A. and S.P. Borgatti (2002). Supporting Knowledge Creation and Sharing in Social Networks. Organizational Dynamics, Vol. 30, No. 2, pp. 100-120.

[14] Padgett, J. and W. Powell (2003). Economic transformation and trajectories: a dynamic multiple network approach. http://home.uchicago.edu/~jpadgett/papers/sfi/intro.chap.pdf

[15] Xiao, Z. and A. S. Tsui (2007). When Brokers May not Work: the Cultural Contingency of Social Capital in Chinese High-tech Firms. Administrative Science Quarterly, Vol. 52, No. 1, pp. 1-31.

[16] Nonaka, I. (1994). A Dynamic Theory of Organizational Knowledge Creation. Organization Science, Vol. 5, No.1, pp. 14-37.

[17] Aitken, M. and Hage, J. (1971). The organic organization and innovation; Sociology Vol. 5, No. 1, pp 63-82.

[18] Edström, A. and J.R. Galbraith (1977). Transfer of managers as a coordination and control strategy in multinational organizations. Administrative Science Quarterly, Vol. 22, No. 2, pp. 248-263.

[19] Woodward, J. (1980). Industrial organization; theory and practice; New York, Oxford University.

[20] Williamson O.E., (1991). Comparative Economic Organization: The Analysis of Discrete Structural Alternatives. Administrative Science Quarterly, Vol. 36, No. 2, pp. 269-296.

[21] Scott, J. (1988). Social Network Analysis. Sociology, Vol. 22, No. 1, pp. 109-127.

[22] Burkhardt, M. E., and Brass, D. J. (1990). Changing patterns or patterns of change: The effect of a change in technology on social network structure and power. Administrative Science Quarterly, Vol 35, pp. 104 –127

[23] Carley, K. (1991). A theory of group stability. American Sociological Review, Vol. 56, pp. 331–354.

[24] DiMaggio, P, and W. W. Powell (1983). The iron cage revisited: Institutional isomorphism and collective rationality in organizational fields. American Sociological Review, Vol. 48, pp. 147-160.

[25] Dutton, J. E. and Duncan, R. B. (1987). The Creation of Momentum for Change through the Process of Strategic Issue Diagnosis. Strategic Management Journal, Vol. 8, pp. 279-295.

[26] Tushman, M. L., and Romanelli, E. (1985). Organizational evolution: A metamorphosis model of convergence and reorientation. In L. L. Cummings & B. M. Staw (Eds.), Research in organizational behavior, vol. 7, pp. 171–222. Greenwich, CT: JAI Press.

[27] Eisenhardt, K. (1989). Building theories from case study research. Academy of Management Review, Vol. 14, No. 4, pp. 532-550.

[28] Leonard-Barton, D. (1992). Core capabilities and core rigidities: A paradox in managing new product development. Strategic Management Journal, Vol. 13, pp. 111-125.

[29] VanMaanen, J. (1998). Qualitative studies of organizations. Sage, Thousand Oaks, CA

[30] Yin, R.K. (2003). Case study research: Design and methods. Sage Publications, London/NewDelhi.

[31] Oppenheim, A.V. (2000). Questionnaire design, interviewing and attitude measurement. Pinter, London.

[32] Berelson, B. (1952). Content analysis in communication research. Free Press, Glencoe, IL.

[33] Krippendorff, K. (2003). Content analysis: An introduction to its methodology. Sage Publications, Thousand Oaks, CA.

[34] Kassarjian, H. (1977). Content analysis in consumer research. Journal of Consumer Research, 4: 8- 18.

[35] Tsai, W. and S. Ghoshal (1998). Social capital and value creation: The role of intrafirm networks, Academy of Management Journal, Vol. 41, No. 4, pp. 464-476.

[36] Boschma, R.A. (2004). Competitiveness of regions from an evolutionary perspective. Regional Studies, Vol. 38, pp. 1001-1014.

[37] Rallet, A. & Torre, A. (1999). Is geographical proximity necessary in the innovation networks in the era of global economy? GeoJournal, Vol. 49, pp. 373-380.

[38] Gulati, R. 1998. Alliances and networks. Strategic Management Journal, Vol. 19, No. 4, pp. 293-317.

Chapter 10 - Communication flows in an SME network: the C.I.S.I consortium case

Federica Ceci, Daniela Iubatti, Alberto Simboli

DASTA - Università G. d'Annunzio Chieti - Pescara (Italy)

Abstract - Networks have been hailed as a third organizational form, between markets and hierarchies. One of the main characteristics of networks is the coexistence of personal and professional relationships. This coexistence modifies the development of economic activities; strategic decisions are largely influenced by the presence of trust between network members. This chapter investigates the role played by personal relationships in enabling the diffusion of innovation within networks. We address the following research questions: How do the different types of relationships in a network of SMEs enable the diffusion and adoption of innovations? Furthermore, do personal relationships play a central role in supporting innovative activities? Based on interviews with managers of SMEs in a consortium of Italian firms, we conclude that interaction between personal and professional relationships shapes a unique context that alters the usual dynamics of innovation diffusion.

10.1 Introduction

Theoretical and empirical studies on the coordination of economic activities have focused on the two polar extremes of corporate governance, namely vertical integration and market exchanges. More recently, networks have been hailed as a third organizational form, combining the advantages of these traditional governance mechanisms [1, 2]. Scholars have largely devoted their attention to advancing our understanding of the characteristics of this new organizational form. In particular, studying the factors that enable the creation of networks [3], their inner characteristics [4, 5, 6] and the distinctive features that determine the unique ways in which networks share and transfer knowledge and, as a consequence, the diffusion of innovation [7, 3, 8, 1]. More specifically, networks seem to be able to rapidly evolve and adapt to changing environments, due to the flexibility provided by the smaller organizational units within networks [9, 10, 11]. Empirical research on networks has advanced our understanding of micro-level coordination mechan-

G. Passiante (ed.), *Evolving Towards the Internetworked Enterprise: Technological and Organizational Perspectives*, DOI 10.1007/978-1-4419-7279-8_10,
© Springer Science+Business Media, LLC 2010

isms and has made clear that firms and market exchanges co-evolve to manage changes [12].

Different kinds of relationships coexist within networks: personal and professional, as well as competitive and collaborative relationships. Padgett and Powell [13] focus their attention on the existence of multidimensional links within networks, particularly professional, personal and political ties. These multidimensional links contribute in different ways to the social and economic development of networks. Padgett and Powell hold that the dynamics of economic activities are largely influenced by the multidimensional characteristics of networks. In the present study, we explore the ways in which innovations are diffused within a network. Despite significant attention devoted thus far to the issue of innovation diffusion, we still know very little about the impact that the coexistence of multiple domains has on dynamics. A greater understanding of this issue will shed further light on the role that personal relationships play in economic activities. The research questions that we address in this work are the following: (1) How do the different types of relationships that exist in an SME network enable the diffusion and adoption of innovation? (2) Do personal relationships play a central role in supporting innovative activities?

Answers to these research questions are provided by means of an empirical analysis of data from a consortium of SMEs operating in Abruzzo, Italy. The consortium, CISI, is made up of 15 SMEs operating in the automotive industry and comprises a large variety of horizontal and vertical, as well as formal and informal, relationships. Within this consortium, friendships and business relationships are closely linked. This context represents a unique setting in which we can analyze the role that personal and professional relationships play in promoting the diffusion of innovations, in this case the adoption of new IT technologies.

The remainder of the chapter is organized as follows. In section 2, we review the most relevant contributions investigating the links between innovation and personal relationships within economic networks. We also develop the analytical model that guides the analysis of the empirical evidence. Section 3 describes the empirical context in which the research is grounded, and the last two sections discuss our results, draw conclusions and describe the implications for practitioners and scholars.

10.2 Literature review and model development

10.2.1 Networks and the diffusion of innovation

Many authors have focused on competitive dynamics in an effort to determine the characteristics of, and rationales behind, collaborations between firms [3, 14, 15]. Interfirm collaborations, which include alliances and joint ventures, vary according to the type of underlying contract and in terms of the nature of the reciprocal connections between partners [3]. Networks can be considered a hybrid pattern of economic activity coordination that combines the advantages of the traditional governance mechanisms of vertical integration and market exchanges. This ensures that the network components can develop both as independent elements and as a system [2, 1, 16]. Networks represent the so-called "third way" between markets and hierarchies. They rely on characteristics other than central control and a "stand alone" logic [17]. This third way has been defined by Powell and Smith-Doerr [6] as "a set of nodes linked by a set of relations, such as friendship, kinship, political, etc." In the context of this chapter, network nodes are constituted by firms that relate to each other through various types of relationships.

Networks have been primarily analyzed by economic and management literatures [5, 3, 1, 13, 18]. An industrial district is an example of a network of firms that collaborate to produce innovative outputs [19]. The first conceptualization of a district defined a network as a group of small and medium enterprises (SMEs) that are willing to collaborate with each other to achieve a competitive advantage through personal trust and cooperation, characterized by geographic proximity [20]. In certain contexts, industrial districts are promoted by a large firm believing that a potential competitive advantage is to be gained through the creation of a network of small firms (e.g., subcontractors or suppliers) [21, 14]. Firms organized as a district benefit from what Marshall [20] defines "industrial atmosphere", a specialized environment that enables the generation of innovations. Literature focusing on networks has devoted closer attention to the analysis of the impact of relationships on the generation and diffusion of innovations within networks. Many authors argue that firms belonging to networks are more innovative than isolated firms [22, 23]. This is due to the presence of business networks that enable localized learning and knowledge sharing between firms [24, 18]. Business networks are defined as "a set of relationships established by technical professionals, when they interact with each other on a wide range of business issues" [25]. Examples of such business issues are inputs and service exchanges among members of a consortium.

Consistent with Giuliani and Bell [25], we hold that relationships between firms that belong to a cluster promote knowledge spillovers that enhance the likelihood of solving complex joint problems and, consequently, the generation and diffusion of innovations [7]. This mechanism works under an important condition, specifically a joint purpose. Innovation-related knowledge is therefore "the result of purposeful behavior rather than a random leakage of knowledge" [25]. The diffusion of innovation among firms in a network is the result of their collective effort to gain a competitive advantage. Hence, firms do not innovate alone: they receive continuous stimuli from the environment and from competitors, institutions and clients, as well as from other members of the network. In particular, within networks a flow of knowledge can be observed that facilitates the adoption and diffusion of innovations, increasing the innovativeness of the network as a whole [8]. In fact, according to the resource-based view of the firm, the source of competitive advantage rests on firm resources [26, 27, 28, 29], and from an innovation perspective, differences in resource configurations also determine differences in performance [3, 30].

Furthermore, geographical proximity plays an essential role in generating and facilitating the diffusion of innovative practices [31, 32, 33, 34, 10]. Proximity fosters knowledge flows between network members, which in turn enhances the likelihood of innovation generation; moreover, it represents a powerful tool through which firms can interrelate [35].

10.2.2 Personal relationships and networks

Marsden and Friedkin [36] argue that social networks influence firm actions: the pattern of relationships between network nodes and ties shapes the behavior of other actors in the network. We distinguish between two types of relationships among actors, namely, personal and professional. Following Lincoln [37], we view personal relationships as producing "relations of trust, obligation, and custom among formally independent firms," while professional relationships are identified in terms of the various connections that bring people together to make a business. Personal relationships, such as friendship, kinship, and political and geographic relationships usually rely on informal ties between components [13]. Personal relationships foster the exchange of information that is vital for the growth of a network since they enable partners to trust each other's behavior [3]. This situation favors knowledge creation processes within the system. Trust is also a factor in professional relationships, as is the firm's reputation in its business activities, but we claim that in case of personal relationships firms rely on other network members because they share common values and this enhances their willingness to cooperate and transfer information [3, 13]. The roles of formal and informal relationships jointly allow developing networks and relationships among members. As Powell and Smith-Doerr [38] point out, networks can be considered as formal exchanges between actors willing to create value, and these formal network relationships can lead to "repeated interactions that reduce the need for formal control." Hence, informal relationships follow from repeated formal relationships and enable firms to obtain high levels of performance and, more importantly, the generation of innovation through increased knowledge flows.

10.3 The empirical context: CISI consortium

The empirical context of this study is CISI (Consorzio Italiano Subfornitura Impresa), a consortium of SMEs operating in Abruzzo, Italy. CISI is composed of a number of SMEs operating in the automotive industry. The CISI consortium is located in Val di Sangro, an important industrial district specializing in the mechanical sector, and comprises subsidiaries of Honda Italia, a major automotive player with a production plant located in Val di Sangro. In the late 1970s, Honda Italia's management encouraged the creation of captive suppliers to implement just-in-time procedures with local suppliers. Some of these captive suppliers experienced significant growth, but their relatively small size nevertheless constituted a problem in terms of entering new markets. For these reasons, 13 of these suppliers decided to band together to create a consortium of SMEs, and in 1992, the CISI consortium was founded. In 2007, CISI was composed of 15 SMEs, with over 800 employees and 100 million Euros in annual revenue. The aim of the consortium is to overcome the limitations of the small size of individual members and to leverage their shared vision of the business. (Not surprisingly, Honda's philosophy played a central role in the creation of shared values among consortium members.) The consortium developed common marketing activities, such as participation in expos and specialized events—activities that could not have been undertaken by the firms individually. Honda still plays a central role as the system integrator of these capabilities and as a major client, but CISI continues to increase its client base, which now includes other manufacturers such as BMW, FIAT, Sevel, Rotax, and KGM.

We selected CISI for our case study since the consortium comprises a large variety of relationships, both horizontal and vertical, and formal as well as informal. Moreover, friendship and business relationships are closely linked within CISI. In this context, the analysis of the role that personal and professional relationships play in enabling the diffusion of innovation, for example, in the adoption of new IT technologies, is particularly interesting.

10.4 Method

In this study, we employed a qualitative research approach. Case study methodology is appropriate for explorative analysis because it allows identifying and understanding the different dimensions that characterize a phenomenon [39, 40,

41, 42]. Open-ended interviews constitute our principal source of data. In this type of interview, also called an exploratory interview, researchers ask questions about a specific topic, including the interviewee's particular point of view [43]. The interviews in this study used a semi-structured questionnaire divided into two parts. The first section asked for a description of the workflow in the firm and, for each phase, a description of all the firm's relationships with third parties. Special attention was paid to the description of the content and frequency of formal and informal relationships. The second part of the questionnaire focused on the role of information technologies (ITs) in business activities.

The president of the CISI Consortium was first to be contacted and after hearing about the aim of this research showed great interest in participating. After our initial meeting, he forwarded a letter of introduction to all the members of the consortium describing the research project and strongly encouraging their participation. We then personally contacted all the consortium members and 14 out of 15 agreed to be interviewed. We conducted a total of 25 interviews, 12 with general managers or CEOs and 13 with those responsible for other functions (e.g., sales, purchasing and IT). Interviews of between 30 and 75 minutes each were conducted onsite between February and April 2007. All interviews were digitally recorded and transcribed in their entirety to retain all the details of the conversation.

10.5 Discussion of Results

10.5.1 Strategic activities are mostly enabled by consortium-related associations

.This finding is consistent with the nature of associations in general and with the CISI consortium in particular. CISI was born with the aim of supporting the growth of its members. Its activities focus on actions that cannot be carried out by SMEs in isolation, for example, broad-scale marketing efforts. The small size of individual consortium members does not allow them to participate in big events, but by working together, they can increase their contractual power and exploit economies of scale. As one interviewee pointed out: "If we want to go and participate in an exposition, we have to invest 30,000 Euros. None of us has the power to invest that much money without being sure of the effective returns. If there are ten of us, we spend 3,000 Euros each and we can participate. And this is an incredible opportunity to meet new potential clients." The creation of the consortium also increased the SMEs' power in the local economic system. Another interviewee noted: "Now we are the third [largest] organization in Val di Sangro. We are a consortium with 1,100 employees and revenues of 130 million Euros. After Sevel and Honda, there are no other organizations as large as we are. We, as a company, were born in a church, and now, with the consortium, we can have discussions with multinationals, and we have an important role in the regional economic system."

10.5.2 Strong link between geographic relationships and innovative activities

The relevance of geographic relationships in fostering innovative activities appears to be very strong. This is consistent with the results of prior literature on industrial districts and regional systems of innovation that attribute a fundamental role to geographic proximity in the diffusion of innovation and the facilitation of the adoption of innovative practices [31, 32, 33, 34, 10]. This was also noted by an interviewer, who pointed out, "Many multinational companies are located in our area: Honda, Sevel, Pilkinton (which produce automotive glazing), [and] Honeywell (which produce turbo-compressors). For this reason, there are many successful activities linked with the automotive and motorbike world."

10.5.3 Role of key individuals in strategic activities

As mentioned above, relationships developed within the consortium foster strategic activities. Another important insight arising from the data analysis is the central role that can be played by one key individual who acts as a catalyst for activities. The president of the Consortium is the person who was mentioned most frequently during the interviews. Relationships involving the President of the Consortium appear to encourage the development of strategic activities. Furthermore, the majority of activities connected with these relationships are strategic rather than operational. This was explained in the following way by an interviewee: "...[T]he new president...[is] giving new life to the consortium. The number of companies in the consortium increased, [and] we began to think about starting a service company, about organizing new marketing activities...He's like a volcano. He is full of ideas. Every now and then he has new ideas [such as] the collaboration with the university, the foundation; we have new all-round initiatives."

10.5.4 Role of key clients in the diffusion of organizational innovations

Consistent with Pavitt's taxonomy in his seminal paper [44], the automotive sector, in which the firms we analyzed operate, falls within the specialized supplier category. Moreover, we explored Honda's role as an enabler of economic activities and found that in addition to the large number of operational activities carried out in its relationships with CISI - as the key client of all the firms analyzed - it also played a central role in the diffusion of organizational innovations. In particular, we refer to the just-in-time practices adopted by Honda and diffused among all its contractors. All the SMEs we interviewed implemented this innovation, and Honda's central role is mentioned in many interviews. According to one interviewee, "We follow a just-in-time approach, and the client [Honda] decides the production needs... We have to follow our customer's requirements; this is the game." Another notes, "We do not have warehouses anymore: we ship to Honda up to 3 times per day. This is what Honda requires to lower [their] cost, and we have to follow."

10.5.5 Personal relationships enable the diffusion and adoption of innovation

Relationships with clients are the main enablers of innovative activities; however, the personal aspect of those relationships increases their innovative potential. Relationships with other clients (i.e., not Honda) and with professionals have a stronger impact on facilitating the adoption of innovations. In fact, the presence of trust, shared values and mutual objectives facilitates the start of a difficult and risky path, such as that characterizing the adoption of innovation. Our empirical evidence supports this: if personal relationships exist alongside professional relationships, the likelihood that these relationships enable innovative activities increases. The uncertainty that characterizes the innovation process is decreased by a firm's increased trust in its partners; increased trust reflects a lower risk of opportunistic behaviors that could endanger the success of the business.

10.6 Conclusion

Innovations are diffused and adapted within networks following partially unknown paths. This topic appears to be particularly relevant judging from the large number of scientific studies devoted to deepening our understanding of network dynamics and innovation diffusion [2, 10, 45, 3, 1, 30]. In this present work, our aim has been to contribute to this research stream by analyzing the role played by personal relationships in enabling the diffusion of innovations.

Our work has important implications for scholars. It enlarges existing knowledge on innovation diffusion and adoption and on the significant role played by personal relationships and trust within economic contexts. In fact, we find that personal relationships positively mediate the role of professional relationships in enabling the diffusion and adoption of innovation. Consistent with Granovetter's [5] and Powell's [2] conclusions, our findings contribute to the research stream, documenting the importance of personal relationships in economic contexts. The presence of trust, shared values and mutual objectives facilitates the start of a difficult and risky path, such as that characterizing the adoption of innovation. Our empirical evidence supports this: if personal relationships exist alongside professional relationships, the likelihood that these relationships enable innovative activities increases. The uncertainty that characterizes the innovation process is decreased by a firm's increased trust in its partners; increased trust reflects a lower risk of opportunistic behaviors that could endanger the success of the business. This finding has important implications for managers and policy makers. Organizations may sometimes want to push their clients or suppliers to adopt new technologies or new productive processes, and in these cases, the existence of personal relationships between partners will facilitate the success of the initiative and the diffusion of innovative practices, which in turn will increase the organizations' competitiveness.

However, this study has certain limitations arising from the case study methodology pursued. The research involves a single case study, which limits our ability to generalize our findings. To enhance the generalizability of results, a replication of the case study using the same methodology is suggested. This replication would allow researchers to determine whether the results of our study are due to the specific contingencies of operating contexts or whether they are generalizable in different contexts. To increase the generalizability of the results, it may also be possible to structure the quantitative data collection (e.g., by means of a survey) in such as way as to capture the characteristics of the phenomenon on a larger basis, in different sectors and geographical contexts.

References

[1] Kogut, B (2000), The networks as knowledge: Generative rules and the emergence of structure, Strategic Management Journal, vol. 21, no. 3, pp. 405-425.

[2] Powell, W (1990), Neither market nor hierarchy: Network forms of organization, Research in Organizational Behaviour, vol. 12, pp. 295-336.

[3] Gulati, R (1998), Alliances and networks, Strategic Management Journal, vol. 19, no. 4, pp. 293-317.

[4] Granovetter, MS (1983), The strength of weak ties: A network theory revisited, Sociological Theory, vol. 1, pp. (201-233.

[5] Granovetter, MS (1985), Economic action and social structure: The problem of embeddedness, American Journal of Sociology, vol. 91, pp. 481-510.

[6] Powell, W & Smith-Doerr, L (1994), Network and economic life, in Smelser, N & Swedberg, R (eds), Handbook of economic sociology. Princeton University Press, Princeton, NJ, pp. 368-402.

[7] Knoke, D (1990), Political networks: The structural perspective. Cambridge University Press, New York.

[8] Edquist, C (2000), The systems of innovation approach and innovation policy: An account of the state of the art, DRUID Conference, (2001).

[9] Dosi, G (1988), Sources, procedures and microeconomic effects of innovation, Journal of Economic Literature, vol. 36, pp. 1126-1171.

[10] Cooke, P (1996), Regional innovations systems: An evolutionary approach, in Baraczyk, H, Cooke, P & Heidenriech, R (eds.), Regional innovation systems. London University Press, London.

[11] Cooke, P & Wills, D (1999), Small firms, social capital and enhancement of business performance through innovation programmes, Small Business Economics. vol. 13, no. 3, pp. 219-234.

[12] Lorenzoni, G & Lipparini, A (1999), The leverage of interfirm relationships as a distinct organizational capability, Strategic Management Journal, vol. (20, no. 4, pp. 317-338.

[13] Padgett, J & Powell, W (2003), Market emergence and transformation, MIT Press, Cambridge, MA, forthcoming.

[14] Smith, HL, Dickson, K & Smith, SL (1991), "There are two sides to every story": Innovation and collaboration within networks of large and small firms, Research Policy, vol. (20), pp. 457-468.

[15] Powell, W, Koput, & Smith-Doerr, L (1996), Interorganizational collaboration and the locus of innovation: Networks of learning in biotechnology, Administrative Science Quarterly, vol. 41, no. 1, pp. 116-145.

[16] Giuliani, E & Bell, M (2005), The micro-determinants of meso-level learning and innovation: evidence from a Chilean wine cluster, Research Policy, vol. 34, no. 1, pp. 47-68.

17] Grandori, A (1997), Governance structure, coordination mechanism and cognitive models, Journal of Management and Governance, vol. 1, pp. 29-47.

[18] Giuliani, E (2007), The Selective Nature of knowledge Networks in Clusters: Evidence from the Wine Industry, Journal of Economic Geography, vol. 7, no. 2, pp. 139-168.

[19] Marshall, A (1890), Principles of economics: An introductory volume, McMillan & Co, London.

[20] Storper, M & Walker, R (1989), The capitalist imperative: Territory, technology and industrial growth, Basil Blackwell, Oxford.

[21] Dosi, G, Pavitt, K & Soete, L (1991), The economics of technical change and international trade, New York University Press, New York.

[22] Baptista, R & Swann, P (1998), Do firms in clusters innovate more? Research Policy, vol. 27, 525-540.

[23] Baptista, R (2000), Do innovations diffuse faster within geographical clusters? International Journal of Industrial Organization, vol. 18, pp. 515-535.

[24] Keeble, D & Wilkinson, F (1999), Collective learning and knowledge development in the evolution of regional clusters of high technology SMEs in Europe, Regional Studies, vol. 33, no. 4, pp. 295-303.

[25] Giuliani, E & Bell, M (2007), Catching up in the global wine industry: Innovation systems, cluster knowledge networks and firm-level capabilities in Italy and Chile, International Journal of Technology and Globalisation, vol. 3, pp. 197-223.

[26] Penrose, ET (1959), The theory of the growth of the firm, John Wiley, New York.

[27] Ansoff, HI (1965), Corporate strategy: An analytic approach to business policy for growth and expansion. McGraw-Hill, New York.

[28] Barney, J (1991), Firm resources and sustained competitive advantage, Journal of Management, vol. 17, no. 1, pp. 99-120.

[29] Grant, R.M (1999), The resource-based theory of competitive advantage: Implications for strategy formulation, in Zack, MH (ed), Knowledge and strategy, Butterworth-Heinemann, Oxford/Boston, pp. 3-24.

[30] Ferlie, E, Fitzgerald, L, Wood, M & Hawkins, C (2005), The nonspread of innovations: The mediating role of professionals, Academy of Management Journal, vol. 48 no. 1, pp. 117-134.

[31] Becattini, G (1986), Small firms and industrial districts: The experience of Italy, Economia internazionale, vol. 39, nos. 2-3-4, pp. 98-103.

[32] Becattini, G (1992), The Marshallian industrial district as socio-economic notion, in Pyke, F, Becattini, G & Sengenberger, W (eds.), Industrial district and inter-firm cooperation in Italy, International Institute for Labour Studies, Geneva.

[33] Breschi, S & Malerba, F (1997), Sectoral innovation systems, in Edquist, C (ed.), Systems of innovation: Technologies, institutions and organizations, Pinter, London.

[34] Cantwell, J & Iammarino, S (1998), MNCs, technological innovation and regional systems in the EU: Some evidence in the Italian case, International Journal of the Economics of Business, vol. 5, no. 3, pp. 383-408.

[35] Rallet, A & Torre, A (1999), Is geographical proximity necessary in the innovation networks in the era of global economy? GeoJournal, vol. 49, pp. 373-380.

[36] Marsden, P & Friedkin, N (1993), Network studies of social influence, Sociological Methods & Research, vol. 22, no. 1, pp. 127-151.

[37] Lincoln, JR (1990), Japanese organizations and organizations theory, in Cummings, LL & Staw, B (eds), Research in Organizational Behavior, vol. 12, pp. 255-294.

[38] Powell, W & Smith-Doerr, L (2003), "Networks and economics life".

[39] Eisenhardt, K (1989), Building theories from case study research, Academy of Management Review, vol. 14, no. 4, 532-550.

[40] Leonard-Barton, D (1992), Core capabilities and core rigidities: A paradox in managing new product development, Strategic Management Journal, vol. 13, pp. 111-125.

[41] VanMaanen, J (1998), Qualitative studies of organizations, Sage, Thousand Oaks, CA.

[42] Yin, RK (2003, Case study research: Design and methods, Sage Publications, London/NewDelhi.

[43] Oppenheim, AV (2000), Questionnaire design, interviewing and attitude measurement, Pinter, London.

[44] Pavitt, K (1984), Sectoral patterns of technical change: Towards a taxonomy and a theory, Research Policy, vol. 13, pp. 343-373.

[45] Uzzi, B (1997), Social structure and competition in interfirm networks: The paradox of embeddedness, Administrative Science Quarterly, vol. 42, pp. 35-67.

Chapter 11- Tisettanta case study: the interoperation of furniture production companies

Fabrizio Amarilli, Alberto Spreafico

Fondazione Politecnico di Milano

Abstract - This chapter presents the Tisettanta case study, focusing on the definition of the possible innovations that ICT technologies can bring to the Italian wood-furniture industry. This sector is characterized by industrial clusters composed mainly of a few large companies with international brand reputations and a large base of SMEs that manufacture finished products or are specialized in the production of single components/processes (such as the Brianza cluster, where Tisettanta operates). In this particular business ecosystem, ICT technologies can bring relevant support and improvements to the supply chain process, where collaborations between enterprises are put into action through the exchange of business documents such as orders, order confirmation, bills of lading, invoices, etc. The analysis methodology adopted in the Tisettanta case study refers to the TEKNE Methodology of Change (see Chapter 2), which defines a framework for supporting firms in the adoption of the Internetworked Enterprise organizational paradigm.

11.1 Introduction

Tisettanta S.p.A. is a leading Italian home furniture manufacturer based in the worldwide-known Brianza furniture district. This chapter aims to describe the current company collaboration process (AS-IS process), focusing on the exchange of information with both customers (distribution chain) and suppliers (supply chain). A TO-BE scenario has been developed from the requirements identified, which foresees the introduction of an electronic platform for the exchange of business documents to support collaboration activities with industrial partners (supply chain).

A general overview of the company (section 11.2) is followed by a focus on key activities related to the collaboration process (sections 11.3 to 11.6) and on the current ICT infrastructure (section 11.7). The chapter concludes with the definition of possible improvements that the introduction of a support platform for the exchange of electronic business documents can bring to the company (section 11.8) and modeling the AS-IS collaboration process and its TO-BE candidate evolution (section 11.9).

11.2 Company overview

Tisettanta S.p.A. is an Italian home furniture manufacturer based in Giussano (MI) with production plants located in Giussano (MI) and Mariano Comense (CO). The company is located in the very center of the Brianza furniture district, which covers Monza and Brianza (MB), Como and Milan provinces. The district counts over 4700 furniture-related manufacturers, employing approximately 23000 people [1] [2] [3].

Tisettanta manufactures the following types of products:

- Wall and load bearing cupboards
- Padded furniture (beds, sofas)
- Kitchens
- Décor accessories

The company's turnover is around 30 million Euros and although cupboard sales account for the largest portion of turnover décor accessories also contribute considerably (12%).

Tisettanta's main market is the domestic (Italian) market, accounting for over 60% of the company's turnover. The remaining 40% is generated from sales across European countries, especially France, Spain and Eastern Europe. Tisettanta also operates in the "contract market", furnishing entire structures such as hotels and apartment blocks, especially in the Japanese and British market (through subsidiaries Tisettanta Japan Ltd and Tisettanta Ltd).

The company has developed a set of prestigious brands such as Halifax (a décor accessories line), Mixel (bedroom furniture for young people) and Elam (the kitchen design and manufacturing company acquired in 1999). Tisettanta has 164 employees: the purchasing department employs 2.5 FTEs and the planning department 2 FTEs; the sales department is more structured, with two department managers (one for the domestic market and one for foreign countries), 7 sales representatives (3 for the domestic market and 4 for foreign countries), 5 order management employees, a technical product design expert and an office manager. The ICT department has a department manager and 2 technicians for ICT infrastructure, systems maintenance and CAD/CAM software.

11.3 Supply chain

Suppliers

Tisettanta's main suppliers are:

- Raw materials suppliers
- Finished components and décor accessories suppliers
- Third-party contractors

Raw materials suppliers are generally large companies producing chipboards, the main component of over 80% of Tisettanta's products, thereby rendering this a strategic component.

Tisettanta has business relationships with two types of finished components suppliers:

- "fixed" components suppliers (metal tables and sofa structures)
- décor accessories suppliers. These products are purchased and resold without any further processing

Third-party contractors are involved in applying gloss finishes to sofa manufacturing and carpentry finishing wood panels.

Purchase order management

Tisettanta's list of materials and production plans are processed over a weekly time horizon. This process generates purchase orders sent to suppliers via fax or email.

The use of email does not entail any significant advantages compared to fax, since invoices and other business documents are attached in an "image format" (TIFF-PDF), which is not machine-readable. Fax is the most used communication channel with Italian partners, while email is adopted for foreign companies. An exception is household appliances, directly purchased with extranet transactions over the Rex/Electrolux system.

Concerning raw materials, Tisettanta has signed frame agreements with hinge manufacturers and open orders with chipboard manufacturers. These types of agreements commit Tisettanta to buying a defined quantity of material thus rendering order confirmation unnecessary and reducing the communications required in a purchasing transaction.

11.4 Stock management - outline

Raw materials (chipboard and panels) and glass are completely stock-managed and do not entail any relevant problems.

Space issues have to be considered in the management of some semi-finished and semi-processed components as they burden the warehouse.

Sofa and bed supply management instead has to cope with problems related to the high variety of measures (mattresses and bed bases) and colors (sofa upholstering).

Tisettanta manages standard dimension product stocks with respect to finished products (mainly cupboards).

11.5 Production process - outline

Product manufacturing is almost entirely implemented internally: outsourcing to third-party contractors is limited to specific finishing processes.

Low-level raw materials constitute the main supply quota. Chipboard panels are entirely treated and processed internally: cutting, squaring, rounding, drilling, varnishing and other finishing processes such as lacquering and polishing. The choice to in-source all manufacturing processes derives from the fact that potential contractors are considered unreliable in respecting delivery dates, thus increasing the risk of production and distribution stoppages.

The average production process lead-time is:

- 3 weeks for in stock standard goods that need customization
- 4 weeks for products composed of semi-finished/semi-processed components in stock

Décor accessories are instead purchased and resold without any further processing.

11.6 Distribution chain

The distribution chain is composed of:

- two main single-brand retail outlets directly owned by Tisettanta
- five single-brand retail outlets owned by third parties
- a network of multi-brand retail outlets owned by third parties

Multi-brand retail outlets include:

- resellers (150 shops in Italy and 60 in foreign markets) directly supported by Tisettanta by means of brochures, price lists and free updates
- customers (460 shops in Italy and 600 in foreign markets), who are standard businesses that buy products from the company

Sales representatives and purchase groups complete the sales network.

To support purchase order management, Tisettanta uses the "Metron" graphical product configurator, which converts technical drawings of products into a corresponding list of materials used to plan the production process and the sourcing of materials and components.

The main problem in this management process lies in the distribution outlets' lack of training on the software. Hence, Tisettanta often receives only a paper sketch of the furniture requested by the end customer that needs to be interpreted by the company and then converted with the software, leading to possible mistakes and misinterpretations.

11.7 ICT infrastructure and applications

Software
Tisettanta's operations are supported by ERP software called "SME UP", based on the AS400 platform. This software was adopted in 2001 and integrated with other specific systems such as CAD/CAMs ("Pro-E" and "Solid thinking" 3D design software) and the graphical configurator "Metron". CAD/CAM technical drawings are used to obtain the list of materials and entered into the ERP software system. Single components are then re-entered via CAD software to support the production processes.

Hardware
The hardware infrastructure consists of:

- 1 AS400 server for the ERP system;
- 1 Domain, antivirus and Pro-E DB server (Windows platform);
- 1 Backup server;
- 3 Linux server (production department, domain and WSS);
- 74 personal computers (mainly based on the Windows platform).

All computers are connected through a LAN network. The company is connected to the Internet by a double ADSL line, with an ISDN backup line.

Recently, the company introduced a Wi-Fi network for portable barcode readers used on the shop floor to increase internal and outbound logistics efficiency.

The annual overall ICT expenditure amounts to 300.000 Euros mainly spent on maintenance and updating services.

11.8 Possible improvements enabled by ICT technologies

Supply chain

ICT can bring significant improvements to supply chain operations and processes: business documents are currently sent via traditional communication channels such as fax or unstructured electronic mail messages. Considering the company's prevalently internal sourcing and production strategy, identifying a set of raw materials and basic components suppliers to test new business document electronic exchange support platforms should be possible. Furthermore, this kind of system can also help support document exchanges in relation to décor accessories, which generally require the definition of a large set of product characteristics (dimensions, finishes, colors, etc.). Effective and efficient transactions are therefore a critical factor [4].

Distribution chain

Dealing with the distribution chain is quite a complex activity with respect to relationships with suppliers. First of all, the need for a graphical product configurator ties the company to proprietary and very complex software solutions, hence scarcely standardizable. Moreover, training in the software among the distribution chain's actors is lacking. Furthermore, each furniture manufacturer adopts their own configurator solution, making any standardization attempt that involves multi-brand resellers extremely difficult. Although the need for standardization is clearly important, it is extremely difficult to design and develop a "neutral" software solution capable of managing products of different brands and offering a unique and entire set of specific features.

11.9 Collaboration process models

From the Tisettanta case study and generalizing it to a generic furniture production company, AS-IS and TO-BE collaborative process models have been defined. The AS-IS model represents the actual process used by generic furniture production companies in their collaboration activities, while the TO-BE model shows the candidate process that companies could adopt with the support of an electronic platform for the exchange of business documents.

AS-IS process

The AS-IS model represents an abstraction of the current processes and sets aside the particularities of the specific companies analyzed (customers and suppliers) in order to present a general scheme. The entire process logic related to internal production (specific and different for every company) has thus been encased in a "black box". The process starts with the acceptance of the sales order and its input in the company's information system. The information system processes the entire order and converts each row into corresponding purchase orders. To verify the correctness each purchase order is then analyzed by the purchasing department. If the specific order requires the attachment of technical drawings, the technical department takes part in the activity. On completion of the last correctness checks, the purchase order is sent to the specific supplier, usually by fax (only household appliance manufacturers use a proprietary electronic B2B platform). In parallel to this activity, the company organizes the internal production. When the supplier receives the purchase order, a feasibility check is performed: in case of problems in terms of quantities or the delivery date, the supplier contacts the company by fax or phone and defines the new terms to be confirmed. If the purchase order is feasible, an order confirmation is sent back to the company. The supplier then completes production and arranges the delivery of goods with the issuing of the bill of lading, usually in paper form along with the delivery carrier. Entry of the goods in the company's warehouse and the input of the bill of lading in the company's information system determine the conclusion of the process. The AS-IS process presents some critical elements identified during the analysis phase of the internal and external processes:

- the Just-In-Time production is sensitive to all kinds of changes such as strikes, delivery and production difficulties, etc., thus making the collaboration process extremely dependent on the timeliness of the information exchanged between partners [5] [6]
- email, in the rare cases it is used to send and receive communications on purchase orders, is only read by suppliers periodically, thus countering the advantages connected to the timeliness of this medium [7]
- the poor structural form of the technical documents is unsuitable for electronic information storage
- order cancellation and changes are often managed manually, thus rendering the information system unaware of updates in the supply process
- the order confirmation document is often missing in a purchase transaction, introducing potential problems in the collaboration process
- the supplier is generally an SME with an information system with limited capabilities [8]

The elements listed guided the definition of the TO-BE model for the collaboration process described in the following section.

TO-BE process

The TO-BE model described represents the revision of activities of the AS-IS abstraction and is designed to tackle all the critical elements identified during the analysis performed in the case study. The TO-BE model starts with the acceptance of the selling order and its processing in the company's information system. The main activities are in fact the same as those defined in the AS-IS process, but a broad revision of the communication methods has been introduced. This revision was modeled through the introduction of a new "virtual actor" joining the customer (the company) and supplier. This "virtual actor" represents a B2B support platform, introduced with the purpose of managing all information exchanges between the partners. These exchanges are represented and formalized by business documents such as sales and purchase orders, order confirmation, bill of lading, invoices, etc. By means of structured documents, all these communications can be easily and directly integrated into the partners' information systems, thus rationalizing the media used for the exchange, switching from traditional and unstructured types such as fax or phone to a structured and synchronous type (for example, XML documents) [9] [10]. The adoption of the type of support platform proposed in the TO-BE process can generate a variety of benefits, both quantitative, such as the reduction of hard costs (i.e. paper and traditional communication media - phone and fax - expenses) and qualitative, through improving the reactivity of the supply chain, achievable by means of a reduction of information processing and transmission times [11] [12].

11.10 Conclusions

From the Tisettanta case study and generalizing it to a generic furniture production company, we are able to state that the use of an ICT structure for electronic document exchange allows "to make the same things spending less" and "to make them better".

Currently, the exchange process is based on traditional communication technologies, such as phone and fax. Redesigning the collaboration with the introduction of a B2B electronic platform for the exchange of business documents enables companies to tackle all the critical elements related to traditional communication forms and to leverage all the benefits that new technologies (Internet, XML, etc.) entail, both quantitative (e.g. hard cost reduction) and qualitative (e.g. increase information availability and reduce processing-transmission times).

Providing a business document in a structured and shared standard format leads to a reduction of interpretation and misunderstanding errors of the document itself and simplifies the traceability, automatic control and processing of the contents [13].

The business ecosystem of Italian wood-furniture industrial districts represents an appropriate environment for this kind of innovation: the large base of SMEs offers an extensive network of close and extremely frequent relationships that can be greatly improved by the support of a B2B electronic document exchange platform. This system can lead to improvement in efficiency of the overall district supply network management process, unifying the communication channels between components suppliers and main manufacturers.

In conclusion, this type of support platform could concretely represent an opportunity to upgrade current partnership relations and potentially open new ones, strengthening the district's dynamic nature in the new global context. However, in order to develop such an innovation in concrete terms, the "network of enterprises" concept is crucial: effective collaboration requires a large base of partners willing to share a common goal.

References

[1] AA.VV. (2008) Rapporto di previsione sul settore del mobile in Italia. Fondazione CSIL

[2] Bramanti A (2007) Il distretto del legno-arredo in Brianza. Libri Scheiwiller

[3] Traù F (2003) Tendenze di lungo periodo della filiera legno-arredo. Centro studi Confindustria.

[4] AA.VV. (2005) Report Osservatorio B2B: eProcurement, eSupply Chain: una scelta tattica o strategica? School of Management Politecnico di Milano.

[5] Chopra S, Meindl P (2004) Supply chain management: strategy, planning, and operation. Prentice Hall

[6] Burt D N, Dobler D W, Starling S L (2003) World class supply management: the key to supply chain management. McGraw-Hill Irwin

[7] AA.VV. (2007) Report Osservatorio ICT&PMI: PMI: innovare per sopravvivere. School of Management Politecnico di Milano.

[8] AA.VV. (2010) Report Osservatorio ICT&PMI: ICT as a Service: ennesima moda o reale opportunità per le PMI?. School of Management Politecnico di Milano.

[9] Bracchi G, Francalanci C, Motta G (2010) Sistemi informativi d'impresa. McGraw-Hill

[10] Jelassi T, Enders A (2005) Strategies for e-business: Creating value through electronic and mobile commerce. Prentice Hall

[11] Bartezzaghi E, Amarilli F, Brivio O, Cagliano R, Corso M, et al. (2010) L'organizzazione dell'impresa - Processi, progetti, conoscenza, persone. Etas

[12] Gattorna J L, Walters D W (1996) Managing the supply chain: a strategic perspective. MacMillan Business

[13] Bartezzaghi E, Spina G, Verganti R (1994) Nuovi modelli d'impresa e tecnologie d'integrazione. Franco Angeli

Chapter 12 – An analysis of models and practices in Human Resource Management processes and the relationship between firms and outsourcers: a case study

Stefano Cirella

Department of Management, Economics and Industrial Engineering - Politecnico di Milano

Abstract - The complexity of the networked organizations field is here investigated by proposing an analysis of models and practices on the relationship between companies and outsourcers with regards to Human Resource Management processes, illustrating an HR Outsourcing (HRO) case study. The chapter is organized in five sections. The first section provides a brief introduction to HRO. The second section presents a review of different aspects of the relationship between companies and HR service suppliers. The third section analyses an HRO case study by describing its objectives, outsourced HR activities, HRO process phases and solutions implemented. The fourth section is a brief conclusion based on a reflective analysis of the case in point.

12.1 HR Outsourcing

Outsourcing takes place when an organization contracts other organizations to provide services or products that include key functions or activities. Work that is traditionally implemented internally is shifted to an external provider. Today outsourcing is considered one of the most prevailing trends in Human Resource Management. Rationales for outsourcing HR functions include financial savings, an increased ability to focus on strategic issues, access to technology and specialized expertise, and the ability to demand measurable and improved service levels. However, there are some indications that these benefits are in fact not attained. Furthermore, the implications include a serious effect on employee morale and the risk of transferring expertise and insider knowledge to vendors. Management of the outsourcing arrangement is critical.

G. Passiante (ed.), *Evolving Towards the Internetworked Enterprise: Technological and Organizational Perspectives*, DOI 10.1007/978-1-4419-7279-8_12,
© Springer Science+Business Media, LLC 2010

12.1.1 The reasons a company outsources its HR processes

There are a number of reasons, on both a strategic and operational level, for firms to want to outsource HR activities. Many of these reasons are analogous to those for outsourcing other organizational functions. In particular, demands for increased productivity, profitability and growth have forced organizations to examine their internal HR processes. As Greer, Youngblood and Gray [1] observe, HR outsourcing decisions are frequently a response to an overwhelming demand for reduced HR service costs. Downsizing and tougher competition implicate that the HR function is under increasing pressure to demonstrate value, both in terms of efficiency and effectiveness. Although some elements of the HR function, as noted earlier, may have always been performed by external service providers, Brewster observes that a new dimension "is this finance-driven idea connecting outsourcing to human resource management - the idea that you can save a lot of money by outsourcing" [2]. In addition, outsourcing is seen as a way of freeing HR professionals within the client organization to perform the more strategic role of designing and implementing programs aimed at retaining the workforce and enhancing its performance. This rationale is in line with Ulrich's [3] seminal thesis on the four roles of HR, in which he proposes that HR should be a strategic partner, an administrative expert, an employee champion and a change agent. In a similar vein, Greer et al. [1] argue that HR outsourcing is consistent with the business partner role that the in-house HR department is attempting to assume. These roles are arguably where HR can add the greatest value to the organization, but they are difficult to measure quantitatively. Outsourcing HR is also seen as an effective way to bypass organizational politics and improve efficiency.

12.1.1.1 Cost Reduction

Often, but not always, the primary objective of outsourcing decisions is cost reduction. A supplier specialized in a specific service, aggregating demand from numerous businesses and achieving high supply volumes, is able to achieve economies of scale. Achieving economies of scale is a primary source of competitive advantage and helps reduce unit costs. The core business' focus on a specific service or set of services also allows achieving economies in terms of human resource specialization and technology, developing systems of differential competences with respect to companies where these activities take the form of general service enhancement. Outsourcing naturally transactional activity thus renders cost reduction easier. In fact, these activities enable the supplier to achieve economies of scale, specialization and input utilization at a lower cost. Finally, it should be noted that even when outsourcing of these activities does not lead to effective cost reduction it nevertheless allows customers to vary the structure according to fluctuations of the volume of services used.

12.1.1.2 Improvement of service levels

Relying on highly specialized external suppliers allows accessing skills, methodologies and tools considered best management practices, which would be difficult to develop internally and would be economically unviable especially for small firms. Paradoxically, the use of external suppliers can lead to better cooperation in the definition of services. On one hand, the supplier has the experience and tools that facilitate the analysis and definition of customer needs: on the other, service users are more inclined to devote attention to their own needs rather than those relating to internal structures. A great concern, for example, is the definition of indicators on service level agreements: when the supply is internal, renegotiation can take place almost continuously. Finally, another important improvement factor is related to the possibility of achieving greater uniformity in production and service supply in relation to expanding the organization.

12.1.1.3 Rendering the cost structure of the HR function flexible

People employed in the execution of less strategic tasks can be freed to focus on segments of activities that have a more direct impact on business capacity and that necessarily require internal management. These dynamics also offer a better perspective of skills and the individual development of those who demonstrate having the necessary capabilities; conversely, operators who remain anchored to the system of skills in the medium term, risk a state of professional obsolescence, structures that are intended to be slimmed down transform their mission from direct service production to the governance of their strategic delivery system.

12.1.2 Selecting HR processes to outsource

As with outsourcing of other organizational functions, a key issue in outsourcing HR is deciding which HR activities should be outsourced. In making this decision, organizations need to consider the impact that outsourcing these activities will have on the organization's performance. To this end, they may need to distinguish between "core" and "non-core" activities. Finn [4] suggests that a basic distinction can be made between HR "core" and "noncore" activities. The former include top-level strategies, HR policies and line management responsibilities (e.g., appraisal and discipline), while the latter include specialist activities (e.g., recruitment and outplacement), routine personnel administration (e.g., payroll and pension), and professional HR advice (e.g., legal advice related to employment regulations). Ulrich [3] goes one step further by suggesting that core activities are transformational tasks that create unique value for employees, customers and investors. Noncore activities are transactional tasks that are routine and standard and can be easily duplicated and replicated. While strategic management literature warns of the danger of outsourcing core activities, do firms really follow this advice in making their decisions on which HR activities to source from external service providers? Do any clear patterns arise from HR outsourcing activities? Hall and Torrington [5] find that training and management development, recruitment and selection, outplacement, health and safety, quality initiatives, job evaluation, and reward strategies and systems are the most likely HR activities to be outsourced, either because they are considered non-core or because the organization lacks the expertise to manage them internally. Hall and Torrington's findings are supported by Shaw and Fairhurst [6], who find that training and development, along with facilities management, are the most likely areas to be outsourced, while industrial relations expertise is the least likely. What remains unclear is how firms reach the decision on why these particular HR activities are to be outsourced and whether they truly constitute the non-core activities of the firm. In the following section, a quick overview of each of the three relevant organizational approaches is offered: the Core Competence View, the Resource Based View and Transaction Cost Economics.

12.1.2.1 Core Competence View

The Core Competence View (CCV) is one of the most successful organizational theories in the entire history of management - the most famous reference cited is Prahalad and Hamel's "The Core Competence of the Corporation" published by Harvard Business Review [7]. The idea behind the Core Competence View is that, in the long run, the competitiveness of an enterprise is given by its ability to create and maintain core competences that lead to the implementation of innovative products/services. Core competence is the integration of knowledge and skills applied to business processes through which the company is able to create added value for the end customer and adapt to changes in the context in which it operates. The Core Competence View is widely cited in literature devoted to outsourcing, since it decisively contributes to explaining its origin and supporting its diffusion. A firm should ideally concentrate all its resources on activities directly related to its core business and entrust the management of those activities considered non-core to third parties [8]. Outsourcing non-core activities allows the company to ease its structure and improve its ability to react to the changing external environment while maintaining resources for activities that legitimize its competitive position. From the HR services outsourcing point of view, the decision to wholly or partly outsource a particular HR service depends on the degree to which the service is considered core with respect to the HR characteristics and function. According to the Core Competence View, any HR services (or any of their sub-processes) considered core should be kept in-house, to avoid losing or weakening the distinctive HR characteristics that most directly impact on competitiveness. By contrast, HR services (or sub-processes) considered non-core can be assigned to specialized external suppliers.

12.1.2.2 Resource Based View

The Resource Based View (RBV) aims to demonstrate how a firm can achieve a "sustainable competitive advantage". The RBV approach was developed almost simultaneously alongside the Core Competence View, and shares its basic principles. The formulation of the Resource Based View is traced in its original version to Barney's "Firm Resources and Sustained Competitive Advantage" [9]. Distant from research that privileged the study of exogenous factors to analyze reasons in support of creating competitive advantage, Barney based his study on the premise that "to transform a short-run competitive advantage into a sustained competitive advantage requires that these resources are heterogeneous in nature and not perfectly mobile". By resource, we mean any asset, tangible or intangible, that the firm can use to develop and implement its competitive strategy. However, not all resources are potential sources of sustainable competitive advantage. Barney identifies four parameters that are able to identify the resources that have the highest strategic potential. They must be valuable (to facilitate the exploitation of opportunities and reduce the threats that characterize its competitive environment), rare (not available to direct competitors), in-imitable (not obtainable by a competitor) and non-substitutable (they cannot be replaced by other equivalent resources to implement the same type of strategy). From a strategic point of view, the company bases its competitive advantage on managing all resources that meet these conditions. By definition, in order to maintain these properties, strategic resources must be managed internally to discourage any attempts to replicate the resources and thus devalue them. Outsourcing activities in favor of specialized providers typically involves the assignment, or at least sharing, of multiple types of resources: individuals, skills, information, technology, physical assets. Outsourcing tends to modify the properties that render a resource a source of sustainable competitive advantage, with particular reference to rarity and in-imitability. According to the principles of the Resource Based View, therefore, the choice of activities to be outsourced can be influenced by the type of resources used in each specific activity. In particular, potential outsourcing candidates are those processes or services that do not represent or employ resources considered strategic and therefore fundamental to maintaining firm competitiveness. To the contrary, those processes or services that represent or employ resources capable of generating competitive advantage should not be outsourced. In the case of HR outsourcing, the choice of services (or sub-processes) to be outsourced must therefore start from considerations on the characteristics of associated resources. For those HR services employing valuable, rare, in-imitable and non-substitutable resources, the company must retain their management in-house.

12.1.2.3. Transaction Cost Economics

Transaction Cost Economics (TCE), originally devised by Coase in the 30's and subsequently developed by Williamson in the late 70's, provides a view of firm structure in relation to its level of vertical integration. In particular, according to Williamson [10], a company tends to undertake those activities necessary for its business, implementing them internally or on the market according to supply methods that minimize transaction costs. Transaction costs are defined as those costs that are associated with the transaction of goods or services from a potential supplier in exchange for a corresponding payment from a potential customer, and therefore managing the relation as a whole [8]. These costs include the search and selection of potential suppliers, communication of specific goods or services sought (research and information costs), negotiation of contract terms with suppliers, awarding supplier contracts, drafting of contracts (bargaining costs), supply control and the management of any contentions (policing and enforcement). According to TCE, when the cost of implementing or purchasing the product/service is the same, the company will chose its supply from the source that minimizes transaction costs. When transaction costs for a particular service are low, they are the supply characteristics of a competitive market characterized by standardized products/services, the short duration of relations and the intrinsic nature of these negotiations. When transaction costs are higher, but nevertheless sustainable, the typical supply conditions of collaborative markets emerge. When, instead, transaction costs are high, the conditions for an intermediate market are not created and it thus becomes necessary to develop and manage the activity internally. The level of transaction costs depends on three key factors [11]: descriptive complexity, asset specificity and uncertainty. Briefly, high descriptive complexity, asset specificity and uncertainty increases the associated transaction costs since activities such as seeking and selecting suppliers and the negotiation and management of supply contracts become more complex. It is therefore more likely that collaborative intermediate markets develop for services/goods characterized by the low values of these three parameters. Where these factors determine elevated transaction costs, the service/goods will continue to be implemented in-house. Thus, in outsourcing an HR activity, the decision on which particular service or process should be outsourced must be made consistently to minimize transaction costs and in relation to the existence of competitive intermediate or collaborative markets that can adequately provide the supply.

The information derived from an analysis using three organizational theories allows us to address the choice of outsourcing an HR activity from a solid conceptual base. The most commonly outsourced HR activities are, for example, recruitment, training, payroll, compensation planning, benefits, employee assistance, retirement plan, outplacement services.

12.2 HRO Relationships

The relationship between the client company and suppliers is one of the most important aspects determining the dynamics of HR outsourcing. It concerns the type of relationship established between the customer and supplier. It also concerns downstream definitions of HR activities to be outsourced and the identification of the primary objectives leading to the decision to outsource. It is important to consider the characteristics that the relationship with the chosen supplier should have to adequately support the outsourcing process. At this point four aspects emerge regarding the relationship between the client company and the supplier: the types of relationship, the level of delegation given to the supplier, the governance of the relationship and the organizational interface between customer and supplier.

12.2.1 Types of relationships

The customer/supplier relationship can be classified into two macro categories: contractual and collaborative. In the contractual relationship, the customer and supplier approach the exchange with contrasting objectives, dictated by reasons of convenience referring almost exclusively to economic variables. In the collaborative form instead, they jointly define the objectives of the relationship with a view to sharing the risks and benefits deriving from the establishment of a strategic partnership aimed not so much at the purchase of single tasks but at the integration of the parties' resources. Contractual relationships characterize intermediate competitive markets focused on short to medium term performance and generally relate to the acquisition of high standard services with a view to minimizing the unit purchasing transaction cost such as for example, payroll production in the specific context of HR outsourcing. In partnerships (collaborative relation), the relationship horizon is projected to the medium and long-term, supplier evaluation is based in large measure on the technical and technological skills that are available to supply the service as well as on management and financial skills put in the field to assist clients. The relationship is effective in managing processes that are standard with direct impact on staff productivity but require more complex business planning and management.

12.2.2 The level of supplier delegation

The second element that characterizes the relationship between the client and supplier corresponds to the level of delegation granted to the supplier in managing the outsourced service. Four basic stages regulate the service supply process: definition of needs, service projection, operation planning and execution of operations. The level of delegation could be measured in relation to the phases delegated to the supplier; executive employment when only in charge of the operational phase of the process, while the definition of needs, design service and operation planning are conducted directly by the customer who transfers the results as inputs for the supplier's organizational activities. In the case of intermediate employment, the level of delegation also extends to the planning phase of operations and partially to service design activities. The client predefines his needs and works together with the supplier in the choice of business model and technological tools that best suit the design requirements of the service to be outsourced. In full employment, the supplier has full responsibility for the service, extending his control to the definition of needs phase. In this case, the client is supported in identifying his needs and the gap and inefficiencies in the management of candidate services to be outsourced is highlighted. The supplier's activity does not end with supplying the service and its planning and design, but also includes business planning and control, since the achievement of results and jointly defined customer benefits are the basis of the relationship.

12.2.3 Relationship governance

When outsourcing concerns activities that can be standardized with low levels of customization and executive employment, the supply contract typically focuses on catalog performance. More developed relations involving service provision with higher and more critical strategic and personalization levels are managed via intermediate or full employment. In the supplier selection process, not only is the offer evaluated but it is also tested, thus extending the technical and managerial capabilities pursuant to the specific relationship. From the customer side, the Request For Proposal (RFP) explains the purpose of the outsourcing project and objectives to be achieved. Based on this document, the supplier develops a proposal consistent with the criticalities highlighted by the RFP and demonstrates ownership of all the skills and resources necessary to successfully complete the project. Based on this proposal, the outsourcing process proceeds with supplier selection and with it begins the due diligence process, which translates into a joint assessment of the project's feasibility. The process ends with the definition of the contract and in particular the service level agreement. Contractual tools define service metrics and tools that must be respected by the supplier. Service Level Agreements (SLA) ensure the supply of the service as negotiated and are contractually linked to incentives and penalties.

12.2.4 The organizational interface between customer and supplier

It is particularly important that customers be equipped with the skills needed to manage the supplier relationship and that these skills be widely used by staff with human resource functions at various levels. Indeed, coordination levels, according to which the customer and supplier control the results of their relation, are manifold and can involve all players in the HR function. These levels and their areas of intervention are termed operative, tactical and strategic.

The operative level corresponds to the interaction between customer and supplier in the daily management of resources directly involved in the supply service, both from the supplier and client side. Consider, for example, an outsourced travel expenses reimbursement service. The solution proposed by the supplier includes the use of a software application that can automate 100% of the operation with the support of an operator dedicated to the management of the process for the resolution of particular cases. Clearly, if the application software was poorly designed, does not work correctly, is not user friendly and has not been sufficiently supported by end-users, employees tend to bypass it to communicate directly with the operator. Thus, all the benefits of the automation service are lost, leading to a further overload of upstream resources (dedicated operator). In this case, capabilities are limited, largely unable to respond and would require additional resources to extend response times, with a subsequent deterioration of the service level.

The tactical level consists in the management of the relationship and contract involving the supplier and the head of the processes outsourced by the customer. It is crucial that communication be effective to allow appropriate corrective action of the underlying bad functionality in the supply process. At the same time, collaboration between actors operating at this level makes it possible to plan interventions to continuously improve performance.

The strategic level is the highest level of collaboration between the customer and supplier. The players involved at this level are typically the head of the organization, outsourcer and the director of the customer's HR function. It is here that performance is monitored regularly and decisions are made on the extension or renewal of the relationship. A solid relationship on a strategic level allows securing adequate sponsorship to overcome the difficulties in the outsourcing start-up process and re-launch the relationship in times of difficulty.

12.3 The Complexity of HRO Projects: a case study

This section analyses an HRO case study by describing its objectives, outsourced HR activities, HRO process phases, solutions implemented in HR activities, essential competences for managing HRO and the role of the HR Department. The data sources are interviews with company managers together with secondary data sources. The name used (Bank Italy) is fictional for privacy reasons.

12.3.1 The case

Bank is a large financial services provider operating in Europe, North America, Middle East, Latin America, Australia, Asia and Africa. The Group's strategy aims to ensure long-term growth through a diversified business portfolio and its presence in markets with high growth rates.

Bank consists of two main business units differentiated by business segments (each one consists of other business units at a lower level). The third business area is represented by the Group Center consisting in different functions responsible for providing support services to the organization.

Bank has strengthened its presence in the Italian territory with the creation of a highly integrated multi-channel bank (Bank Italy) that has a network of branches, financial professionals and a web-based home banking system. The success factors of Bank Italy are a competitive offer, a high level of assistance and qualified financial consulting.

12.3.2 Objectives of HRO and outsourced activities

The main reason that drove the company (Bank Italy) to use HR Outsourcing was the search for flexibility in specific activities related to HRM. For example, the use of an external specialized provider allowed acquiring temporary resources in order to cope with workload peaks. HR Outsourcing is configured as a useful "tool" to help the organization in heavy workload periods but at the same time is not binding when the need for additional resources decreases. This has been extremely useful, for example, in the recruitment process that has at times been very intensive (400-500 people per year).

Moreover, HR outsourcing has also provided senior staff with specialist skills and experience, willing to work within the organization for a defined period who have also provided internal staff with personal growth opportunities in the form of "role-models" whilst not representing a "threat" to employees, since they come from a specialized company (the provider) with no intention of being employed by Bank.

A further HR outsourcing relationship came about when the company had to introduce the HR SAP system: the company has benefited from technical and specific skills necessary for the implementation and adaptation of the system according to the HR processes and training on practices for delivering HR services. In this case, HR Outsourcing provided the opportunity to outsource activities that required very specialized skills (especially technological skills).

Another objective was to achieve cost reductions associated with training activities and with HR operational and administrative activities that do not require sophisticated skills, such as payroll.

The outsourced activities were thus human resources selection, training, payroll and other administrative activities.

12.3.3 Phases in the process towards HR Outsourcing

The phases in the process towards HR Outsourcing (HRO process) in the Bank case were Analysis, Strategy Development, Supplier Selection, Implementation, and Monitoring. We describe each phase with these variables: what, who, how and when relevant, problems and solutions.

ANALYSIS. Analysis is the identification of objectives, potential HR processes to be outsourced and potential suppliers.

What: modeling the potential HR process to be outsourced and defining the objectives.

Who: HR Manager.

How: process modeling tools (workflow, activity diagram, SCOR, ...).

STRATEGY DEVELOPMENT. Strategy development is the analysis of risks and benefits and the definition of the implementation strategy.

What: setting priorities among the objectives identified in the Analysis phase and verifying the consistency of the proposed HR Outsourcing project with the corporate strategy.

Who: HR Manager and line management

SUPPLIER SELECTION. Selection of the most appropriate suppliers and the definition of the types of relationship.

What: organization of procedures aimed at selecting the supplier and defining the Request For Proposal (RFP). Particularly, the choice of supplier takes into account not only technical, professional and economic issues, but also the trust that characterizes the relationship between the parties.

Who: HR, Purchasing and Legal Departments. Given the complexity of the services, the Purchasing Department intervenes in the supplier selection process in order to better define the RFP and in the contract renewal process. The Legal Department formalizes the contract.

How: definition of specifications, procedures and Service Level Agreement (SLA).

Problems: risk of selecting suppliers that behave opportunistically.

Solutions: identification of the provider's "core business" in order to understand whether he is specialized in providing the required HR services. Moreover, the company implements continuous analyses of potential vendors to improve the quality of the relationship with the actual provider, identifying new ideas and stimuli.

IMPLEMENTATION. This phase includes the implementation of the proposed HR Outsourcing project, communication of organizational changes within the company, definition of the governance structure both internally and between the company and the supplier.

What: in-depth analysis of the chosen HR activities, definition of responsibilities between the company and suppliers, definition of the governance system of relationships, definition of interfaces between the company's and supplier's information and technological systems.

Who: HR Department, IT Department, Suppliers.

How: Key indicators on chosen HR activities (number of transactions, schedules, etc.) to facilitate understanding of the outsourced activities and definition of a Responsibility Assignment Matrix (RAM) to attribute the responsibilities both internally and between the company and the suppliers.

Problems: inefficiency and ineffectiveness of information exchanges between the company and suppliers.

Solutions: specific technological solutions.

MONITORING. The "day to day" management of the relationship with suppliers, monitoring the benefits and identifying new potential requirements.

What: monitoring supplier performances, quantifying gaps in expected results and identifying areas for improvement.

Who: a performance evaluation team, composed of company and provider representatives.

How: analysis of problems and risks (risk management system), performance indicator dashboard.

Problems: risk of excessive dependence on external suppliers; risk of performance level reduction.

Solutions: identification of possible alternatives to be implemented in case of "failure" of the relationship with the supplier; implementation of planned and regular monitoring by someone not involved in the outsourcing relationship in order to ensure objectivity.

12.3.4 Mapping the flow of outsourced HR processes

The HR processes here considered are recruitment, training and payroll.

12.3.4.1. Recruitment

The company relies on a supplier for the recruitment process. For low-level profiles, Bank Italy's HR Department is accountable for the final selection. For high-level profiles, the candidate undergoes a further interview with the HR manager at Bank's headquarters.

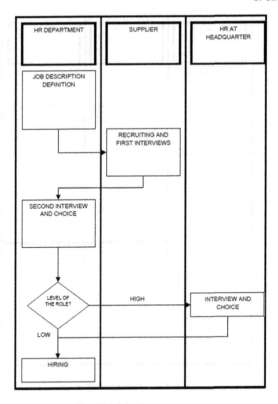

Fig. 12.1 Selection process

12.3.4.2 Training

Another outsourced HR process is training. The activities are managed in collaboration with HR within the company (Bank Italy), the supplier and at Bank's headquarters.

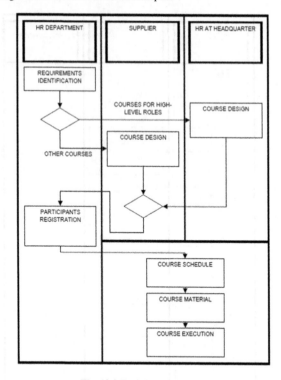

Fig. 12.2 Training process

12.3.4.3 Payroll

The company provides the inputs (through an information system), evaluates the accounting issues and manages the fiscal aspects. Information is passed onto the supplier who is responsible for payroll implementation.

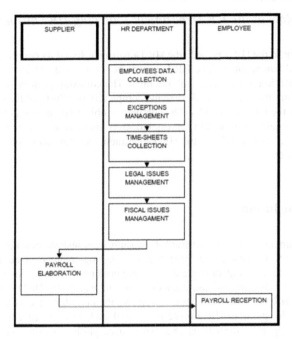

Fig. 12.3 Payroll process

12.3.5 Competencies required by the HR Outsourcing process

Bank Italy maintains in-house staff with the skills needed to perform all HR activities. In this way, the organization has the ability to actively support the provider in managing and executing the HR services. For example, the company encountered numerous problems caused by the lack of internal payroll expertise: it was necessary to hire an experienced person to monitor supplier performance and act as their point of reference.

The company also considers the HR Department's negotiation ability as fundamental, since it was necessary to define the terms of the supply contract more specifically, including for example SLA, clauses and costs. Particularly, the HR Department is supported by the IT, Legal and Purchasing Departments. Finally, managerial skills are considered very important, for example those related to the analyses of processes and technologies.

12.3.6 Role of the HR Department following HR Outsourcing

Subsequent to the HRO project, the HR Department found its equilibrium in terms of size and competences. The HR Department is now characterized by very high-quality staff, in close contact with the lines. The company positively evaluates the HR Outsourcing experience, despite the complexity of HRO and the time required to achieve the intended results. The company's objective, in fact, is to refocus the HR Department's role within the organization: more repetitive and standardized tasks can be outsourced and the HR Department can thus focus on higher value-added services.

12.4 Conclusion

The theoretical issues and the Bank case study demonstrate that outsourcing Human Resources Management processes can be implemented in numerous ways, depending on differing strategic choices and contingent factors. In the Bank case, the strategic dimensions and choices analyzed were: the HRO objectives, the choice of HR processes to be outsourced and the complex process towards HRO. For example, possible HRO objectives could include cost reduction, improving services, acquiring specialized and experienced skills, focusing the HR Department's attention more on strategic activities, and improving the technological level of HR services. Thus, in every specific HRO case, the importance of each objective is different and this should determine the different ways of developing the HRO process and HRO implementation.

According to the Bank case, HRO success seems to be related to coherence between all the strategic dimensions, choices and factors that concern the HRO process. Unfortunately, many companies have negative HRO experiences, without achieving the projected benefits (for example, higher than expected costs to manage the outsourced activities or lower than expected service levels). The reasons can be various. These companies are possibly too focused on the short-term view, do not have the required competencies (listed above in the Bank case), or are unable to structure relationships with other functions and departments (IT Department, for example) or with suppliers.

Thus, HRO and its management are critical. An important lever that could support these complex processes is technology. In the Bank case, solutions to problems reported in the implementation phase (inefficiency and ineffectiveness in information exchanges between the company and suppliers) were specific technological solutions. In this sense, suppliers of HR services can provide technologies to integrate the client's technological instruments (for example ERP and administrative applications) with their own. Finally, a company could obtain HR outsourcing services from different service providers, providing an opportunity to integrate information between providers but this requires careful cost-benefit analyses.

References

[1] Greer C R, Youngblood S A, Gray D A (1998). Human resource management outsourcing: The make or buy decision. Academy of Management Executive, 13, 3

[2] Turnbull J (2002). Inside outsourcing. People Management: Connected HR, 10-11

[3] Ulrich D (1998). A new mandate for human resources. Harvard Business Review, Jan-Feb, 124-134

[4] Finn W (1999). The ins and outs of human resources. Director, 53, 66-67

[5] Hall L, Torrington D (1998). The human resource function: The dynamics of change and development. London: Financial Times-Pitman Publishing

[6] Shaw S, Fairhurst D (1997). Outsourcing the HR function-personnel threat or valuable opportunity. Strategic Change, 6, 459-468

[7] Prahalad C. K. & Hamel G. (1990). The core competence of the corporation. Harvard Business Review, 68, 79-91

[8] Spina G (2008). La gestione d'impresa. Organizzazione, processi decisionali, marketing, acquisti e supply chain. ETAS

[9] Barney J (1991). Firm resources and sustained competitive advantage. Journal of Management, 17, 1, 99-120

[10] Williamson O E (1975). Markets and Hierarchies: Analysis and Antitrust Implications. Free Press

[11] Ellram L, Billington C (2001). Purchasing leverage considerations in the outsourcing decision. European Journal of Purchasing and Supply Management, 7, 1, 15-27